Shaping Work-Life Higher Education

Shaping Work-Life Culture in Higher Education provides strategies to implement beneficial work-life policies in colleges and universities. As compared with the corporate sector, higher education institutions have been slow to implement policies aimed at fostering diversity and a healthy work-life balance, which can result in lower morale, job satisfaction, and productivity, and causes poor recruitment and retention. Based on extensive research, this book argues that an effective organizational culture is one in which managers and supervisors recognize that professional and personal lives are not mutually exclusive.

With concrete guidelines, recommendations, techniques, and additional resources throughout, this book outlines best practices for creating a beneficial work-life culture on campus and documents cases of supportive department chairs and administrators. A necessary guide for higher education leaders, this book will inform administrators about how they can foster positive work-life cultures in their departments and institutions.

Laura Koppes Bryan is Dean of the Yale Gordon College of Arts and Sciences and Professor of Psychology at the University of Baltimore. She is a U.S. Fulbright Scholar and a Fellow of the American Psychological Association, the Association for Psychological Science, and the Society for Industrial and Organizational Psychology.

Shaping Work-Life Culture in Higher Education

A Guide for Academic Leaders

Laura Koppes Bryan

with Cheryl A. Wilson

Routledge
Taylor & Francis Group

NEW YORK AND LONDON

First published 2015
by Routledge
711 Third Avenue, New York, NY 10017

and by Routledge
2 Park Square, Milton Park, Abingdon, Oxon, OX14 4RN

Routledge is an imprint of the Taylor & Francis Group, an informa business

© 2015 Taylor & Francis

Library of Congress Cataloging-in-Publication Data

Bryan, Laura L. Koppes.
  Shaping work-life culture in higher education : a guide for academic
leaders / Laura Koppes Bryan, Cheryl A. Wilson.
      pages cm
  Includes bibliographical references and index.
  1. Universities and colleges—United States—
Administration.   2. Education, Higher—United States—
Administration.   3. College teachers—Professional
relationships—United States.   4. College teachers—Workload—
United States.   5. College teachers—Family relationships—
United States.   6. College teachers—Job satisfaction—United
States.   I. Wilson, Cheryl A.   II. Title.
  LB2341.B713 2014
  378.1′01—dc23
  2014001768

ISBN: 978-0-415-52738-5 (hbk)
ISBN: 978-0-415-52740-8 (pbk)
ISBN: 978-0-203-11888-7 (ebk)

Typeset in Perpetua and Bell Gothic
by Apex CoVantage, LLC

Printed and bound in the United States of America by Publishers Graphics,
LLC on sustainably sourced paper.

Contents

Tables and Figure

Tables

Figure

Foreword

It is a somewhat perplexing reality that higher education lags behind other sectors when it comes to adequately addressing work-life issues. Major corporations long ago recognized the need to adjust personnel policies to attract and retain men and women seeking to better "balance" career and family, ushering in flextime, telecommuting, job sharing, and other "family friendly" innovations. The United States armed forces understood that diversity was an imperative in order to create the most effective, cohesive, capable military force, adopting policies that put a premium on outreach and inclusion. But colleges and universities have been slow to embrace change in this arena.

While colleges and universities are perceived as being highly progressive, the fact of the matter is that higher education is an extremely conservative enterprise when it comes to change. In a way, this is a source of strength, allowing academe to sustain rock-solid values and avoid chasing superficial fads. There are, however, issues that cry out for change and require higher education leaders to step forward to insure the long-term well being of their institutions.

Fortunately, the reality of work-life circumstances in America today is becoming ever more evident to higher education leaders. Career flexibility and "family-friendly" policies are increasingly seen not as a "nicety" but rather as a necessity. And, there are organizations and institutions that are providing leadership in making changes based on research, best practices, and examples from the private sector.

In the summer of 2013, the American Council on Education (ACE) announced a challenge to presidents of higher education institutions to become involved with a national campaign promoting faculty career flexibility. College and university leaders were invited to sign a statement of support for expanding workplace flexibility. As a member of the Board of the ACE Women's Network, I was pleased to share the ACE challenge with University System of Maryland Presidents, and all have signed on. Fortunately, this ACE effort has brought significant visibility and momentum to the importance of work-life balance to colleges and universities across America.

With this new book, *Shaping Work-Life Culture in Higher Education: A Guide for Academic Leaders,* Drs. Laura Koppes Bryan and Cheryl A. Wilson of the University of

Baltimore have provided all of academia with a valuable service: a literal "guide"—written specifically for administrators by administrators—to share empirical research findings, outline organizational level policies and programs, and highlight best practices. The text will help higher education leaders better understand their role in responding to the work-life challenges impacting faculty and staff and their responsibility to facilitate a campus culture that is work-life friendly.

The nature of workplaces in general has changed dramatically in the past several decades, moving from a society where most families had one wage earner to a society where the vast majority of families have two working adults in the household; moreover, the whole nature of what constitutes a "family" is changing.

As Bryan and Wilson demonstrate, higher education has not been immune to these changes, which have created an entirely new dynamic on our campuses in terms of how faculty and staff consider their responsibilities to the job and their roles at home. The authors provide in-depth analysis of why—and real-world examples of how—universities are modifying and revising policies and practices to more effectively address the needs of faculty and staff. The impact of increased flexibility, more accommodating leave policies, options for full-/part-time roles, and services on campuses to support faculty and staff in meeting their needs and responsibilities both at work and with their families are all explored in detail. In addition, the importance of implementing updated recruiting policies, educating administrators, and securing presidential leadership are all discussed.

Institutions cannot be successful today unless they have enlightened policies on work-life issues; it is that important for the morale and capacity of faculty and staff to meet their responsibilities. Leaders need to get well informed on these matters, for this is an area where leadership is not just important, it is essential. The question of top-down or bottom-up initiatives is always a challenge in higher education, but this is an area that requires a strong measure of top-down leadership. Any significant policy or practice must, of course, be vetted and embraced by faculty/staff. But, in this day and age, leaders cannot afford to sit back, wait, and hope that the important and complex changes needed in this area will percolate up through the organization. This is an instance where leaders must put ideas and concepts on the table and facilitate their incorporation into faculty policies and practices.

The productivity of a university's workforce is obviously dependent upon individuals' ability to dedicate their time and energy to meeting the responsibilities of the organization. The more support/assistance/help universities can provide so that the burdens of external responsibilities can be alleviated and accommodated, the better the morale, focus, and attention of faculty and staff. The pages of this timely and important book provide a road map that can help institutional leaders align the policies and practices of their colleges and universities with the realities of work-life circumstances in the 21st century.

William E. "Brit" Kirwan
Chancellor, University System of Maryland (USM)

Preface

WORK-LIFE CULTURE, AN INSIDE VIEW: LAURA KOPPES BRYAN

While working as the Director of Work-Life for a large and complex research-intensive university, I was immersed in identifying and implementing strategies to facilitate the success of faculty and staff members. These strategies focused on enhancing satisfaction with juggling work-life-family responsibilities and resulted from a grassroots effort of surveying faculty and staff (over 50% response rate). Relying on the data analyses, we collaboratively, with the institution's leadership, developed a work-life strategic agenda that included priorities and initiatives. Although I had studied organizational and individual effectiveness, including leadership and work-life satisfaction, for many years as an industrial and organizational psychologist, in this position I gained firsthand experience with the influence that leaders can have on shaping the organization's work-life culture. I directly observed how an individual life was positively impacted because an elder care specialist referred her to legal and adult care experts that facilitated her caregiving responsibilities. I witnessed how a male professor's morale improved because he could modify his duties rather than taking unpaid leave when his fifth child was born. The widespread impact of attention to work-life needs cannot be understated, yet working with chairs and deans across campus, it became apparent that academic leaders without specific work-life expertise did not have readily available information to help them shape work-life cultures.

The importance of leadership became increasingly salient as I assumed administrator roles. As the department chair then director at a master's comprehensive university, I worked directly with faculty and staff to enhance their work-life satisfaction. Flexibility in scheduling was provided, and department meetings were held over the noon hour with lunch provided. We held social events that included family members and provided various teaching options for faculty members who had children during the semester. In one instance, a candidate interviewed with us shortly after giving birth; to help her with the rigorous interview schedule, we provided frequent breaks and private space in my office for breastfeeding. I also advocated for improving the institution's work-life culture as the principal investigator for a National Science Foundation (NSF) ADVANCE PAID grant that included several work-life initiatives. In my current role as dean, enhancing the Yale Gordon College of Arts and Sciences work-life culture is a goal in the college's strategic plan. I have appointed a work-life committee and piloted modified duties guidelines for individuals with life-changing events. We also implemented a tenure clock extension policy and provide flexible work arrangements for staff. Although many of these activities are institution-wide, I have been committed to finding ways to improve work-life satisfaction within my college.

When I served as the president of the College and University Work-Life-Family Association (CUWFA) national professional organization, we frequently discussed the importance of leaders in supporting the effective management of work and life obligations. For example, at the 2009 and 2010 national CUWFA conferences, recent recipients of the Alfred P. Sloan Foundation (SLOAN)/ American Council on Education (ACE) grants and the NSF ADVANCE grants discussed their universities' progress in improving faculty careers. Flexible work schedules and the role that department chairs as well as other administrators play were identified as key aspects in improving the quality of faculty work-life. If senior leadership does not support flexibility in academic careers, faculty and staff may be reticent to use any policies adopted to help them, resulting in lower morale, job satisfaction, and productivity, and poor recruitment and retention. In a recent survey of CUWFA members, some of the greatest barriers to accomplishing work-life initiatives on campus included a lack of funding, a decentralized structure, a lack of staff resources, a lack of information on faculty/staff needs, a *lack of support from senior administration and deans/department chairs, and a lack of understanding by senior leadership.*

University work-life efforts address both the needs for daily flexibility, as well as the need for career flexibility, for faculty and staff. Despite recent growth in work-life supports, many campuses are not effectively communicating the availability of these supports to their faculty, staff, or students, or to the key administrators to whom campus members turn for help with work-life needs. Moreover, administrators and managers are not trained properly about how their behaviors can specifically foster a work-life friendly culture in their departments and colleges. Most faculty and many staff on campus report directly to academic department chairs; without easy access to clear and consistent information and appropriate training, chairs are not able to stay current in their knowledge of available resources, advocate for policy use by their faculty or staff, or implement campus work-life policies consistently. No academic text exists for campus administrators seeking information about best practices in shaping a work-life culture, written specifically for administrators by an administrator. Therefore, I proposed this guide to inform academic leaders of ways they can be proactive and supportive, which in turn, will help faculty and staff to flourish and be their best.

In order to ensure that I created a guide that would be helpful for those who don't have the scholarly and practical understanding of work-life satisfaction and effectiveness, I invited a full-time English faculty member, Cheryl Wilson, to assist me with this project. I knew it would be important to include a faculty perspective as well as the views of someone with limited administrative experience. This collaboration was also particularly suited to the subject of the book, as one work-life strategy I implement is mentoring faculty for leadership positions. Reflections of Cheryl's experience with this project are in the section titled **Work-Life Culture, an Outside View**.

PURPOSE

This guide considers the implications of effectively managing work and life responsibilities in higher education institutions, discusses research-based strategies and best practices, and communicates specific experiences and practices of leaders who are responsive to faculty and staff with regard to their work, family, and life needs. From reading this guide, academic leaders will gain in-depth understanding of how they can shape flexible and inclusive work-life cultures or climates in their units. A university culture that embraces the values of effectively managing work and life has recruiting procedures that are fair, policies and benefits that promote flexibility in work-life arrangements, and programs that educate leaders on how to embody these values in their management decisions. Institutions with a work-life culture tend to hire leaders who are responsive to employees' needs when juggling multiple work, life, and family obligations. These leaders encourage faculty and staff to use family-supportive benefits and are creative with strategies and solutions to support employee success. We demonstrate throughout this guide that leaders are essential for shaping a climate that is supportive of work-life satisfaction and effectiveness, resulting in enhanced recruitment, retention, and performance of employees. As universities have been slow to institute work-life friendly-oriented policies (as compared with the corporate sector), supportive leaders are especially important in maintaining the quality and global competitiveness of U.S. universities.

WORK-LIFE CULTURE, AN OUTSIDE VIEW: CHERYL A. WILSON

Approaching the study of work-life as a faculty member and a newly elected department chair, rather than as a disciplinary specialist, has allowed me to focus on the needs and interests of the audience for this guide. In doing so, and considering the applications of work-life research to higher education, I have become acutely aware of the myths and misconceptions surrounding work-life as well as its relevance for academia.

Work-Life Isn't Compatible With Higher Education: College and university faculty and, to a lesser extent, staff, have frequently encountered misperceptions about the nature of their work from those outside the academy: "You teach *only* three classes?" "You don't go to campus until noon?" "You get summers off?" Such incredulous questions, of course, reflect the invisible nature of much faculty work, which is often highly individualized and self-directed. Indeed, the ability to have considerable control over one's schedule, make independent decisions about teaching and research, and operate outside the confines of the 9-to-5 workday, is certainly an appealing aspect of academic life for many faculty. At the same time, however, such flexibility may create stress with regard to work-life and professional obligations. The pervasive nature of faculty work, much of which can be done away from the classroom or the office, often makes it difficult to maintain a sense of separation between work time and family time, as one can easily encroach upon the other. Even more damaging is the idea that given the academic schedule, it is not appropriate or wise—particularly for tenure-track faculty—to seek accommodations for work-life needs because such needs are always already met by the very nature of working in higher education. Developed within the corporate world, work-life policies may seem out of sync with academia and even damaging to the careers of those who wish to use them. In reality, of course, higher education *needs* work-life, and policies and procedures can be developed and implemented in ways that complement, rather than compete with, the academic enterprise. It is the responsibility of academic leaders, then, to recognize that need and find creative, responsible ways to create a work-life culture.

Work-Life Policies Are Just for Parents: Or, to put it even more narrowly, just for mothers. Although such matters as maternity leave, breastfeeding, and child care are staples of many work-life policies, as we demonstrate throughout, an effective work-life culture addresses needs that arise over the course of an individual's career, including elder care, social and community responsibilities, and transitions to retirement. Understanding work-life more broadly helps to integrate work-life throughout the culture of the institution and eliminates bias against those faculty and staff who use such policies. Even actions as simple as scheduling meeting times that do not conflict with after-school pickups or inviting retired faculty to department events can contribute to the well-being and productivity of all members of a department and make a tremendous difference in the culture.

Work-Life Is Code for "Special Treatment": Academia rewards individualism. At the same time, however, parity and equity are also important to the successful functioning of a campus. How can it be "fair" for a faculty member who has been teaching eight courses per year for six years to be evaluated for tenure alongside someone who has been away from campus for a year caring for an elderly parent, stopped the tenure clock, and thereby gained an "extra" year to complete her book manuscript? Why should a department chair have to change the way he has been scheduling courses to accommodate the family responsibilities of multiple faculty? Such questions might constitute an initial response to discussions about work-life, yet they are somewhat shortsighted and do not reflect the bigger cultural implications of such discussions. While a particular work-life policy may not affect a faculty member or academic leader at a given moment in her or his career, or, indeed, *ever* be relevant for that individual, the very existence of such policies creates a culture where individual needs and situations can be met in productive and mutually beneficial ways. Life will interface and even interfere with work. As the stories of academic leaders appearing in Chapter 5, and excerpted throughout the text, demonstrate, having work-life friendly academic leadership ensures that when faculty and staff needs arise, accommodations can be made. Thus, regardless of the particular policy or practice, integrating work-life into higher education creates a culture that benefits everyone and can have positive, dramatic results.

INTENDED AUDIENCE AND CONTENT

The intended audiences for this text are administrators and managers in non-profit higher education institutions. Strategies for and experiences of department chairs, deans, and other key leaders are provided throughout. It is also likely that scholars who research work-life effectiveness and administrators in similar contexts (K–12 education, health care) may be interested in this guide. As work-life effectiveness is currently an extremely relevant mainstream topic nationwide, this text could also serve as a supplemental text for coursework in higher education leadership, administration, student affairs, and other related disciplines.

Most research on this topic has been conducted in environments other than higher education, with the exception of work conducted by grant-funded institutions and recent studies noted in the reference list. Best practices are gleaned from empirical studies, NSF ADVANCE funded institutions, SLOAN/ACE funded institutions, and other relevant sources. Additionally, interviews were conducted with effective leaders.

We begin by using Chapter 1 to "make the case" for a work-life culture. We provide several findings and activities that serve as justifications for the premise of this text; that is, the importance of leaders in shaping the culture.

In Chapter 2, we discuss prevalent work-life issues in higher education settings. Traditionally, work-life efforts focused on child care, but more recently campuses have begun to respond to work-life needs that have grown beyond support for new parents; many faculty and staff are challenged by elder-care demands and various "late career" aspects such as preparing for their own transition to retirement. We review the empirical research to gain a deeper understanding of work-life issues for faculty and staff.

Chapter 3 presents descriptions of programs, policies, and benefits that support work-life in higher education institutions. Here, we attempt to identify and describe the most comprehensive and best-known efforts currently underway at universities across the United States.

In Chapter 4, we examine more closely the concept of culture, specifically a work-life culture. We provide an overview of culture change models, and then describe four specific examples of how to accomplish such change.

Chapter 5 includes the reflections of academic leaders, such as department chairs, deans, and presidents, who were identified as being supportive of work-life effectiveness. These leaders discussed their experiences with various work and life situations concerning faculty and/or staff and offer strategies for others.

In Chapter 6, we provide recommendations for academic leaders, which were identified from the reflections as well as other empirical research and emerging practices. Although changing a culture can be daunting, there are numerous ways that a leader can demonstrate care, concern, and support for faculty and staff.

Finally, in the Appendix we offer work-life resources, as well as a bibliography that includes additional resources.

While other texts on work-life or work-family exist, those authors focus on either empirical research findings without strategies or focus on organizational level policies and programs. Although not an exhaustive literature review, we include scholarly findings as well as practical strategies and suggestions throughout the guide. At the end of each chapter, we provide discussion questions to facilitate creative thinking and emphasis on work-life issues.

We admit that not all types of institutions (e.g., community colleges) or constituents are directly included here, but given the busy schedules of academic leaders, we decided to prepare a succinct guide, rather than a lengthy and complicated review. We believe this approach is well suited to the aims of this text—the first for campus leaders seeking information about best practices in shaping a work-life culture, written specifically for leaders by leaders. We hope you enjoy reading this guide as much as we enjoyed preparing it!

Laura Koppes Bryan
Cheryl A. Wilson
Baltimore, Maryland

Chapter 1

The Importance of a Positive Work-Life Culture

In the summer of 2013, the American Council on Education (ACE) announced a challenge to presidents of higher education institutions to become involved with a national campaign promoting faculty career flexibility. College and university leaders were invited to sign a statement of support for expanding workplace flexibility that includes the following conviction: "We believe that supporting flexibility must become a core leadership competency to enable our faculty to meet the increasing demands of twenty-first century workplaces and to meet their personal and family responsibilities."[1] We commend ACE for issuing this challenge; it is somewhat surprising that academic leaders must be convinced in 2014 given that corporations have been responding to employees trying to balance work and family responsibilities (i.e., work-life) for more than 40 years.[2] Corporate leaders have recognized that demographic changes over the past four decades, such as an increase in the number of women working full time, rise of dual-career and single-parent families, and the expansion of an aging population, have resulted in an increasingly diverse workforce and a greater potential for individuals to face work-life conflict and stress.[3]

Numerous empirical studies have demonstrated that conflict and stress resulting from work-life demands negatively affects individuals, families, and organizations.[4] Thus, organizations have realized the necessity and value of implementing strategies, benefits, programs, and policies to promote work-life effectiveness and satisfaction among their employees.[5] Family-friendly policies include "any benefit, working condition, or personnel policy that has been shown empirically to decrease job-family conflicts among employed parents."[6] More recently, "work-life policies include any organizational programs or officially sanctioned practices designed to assist employees with the integration of paid work with other important life roles such as family, education or leisure."[7] Flexible work environments, alternative work schedules (flextime, telecommuting), and dependent care (child and elder care) are common examples of

Table 1.1 Importance of Work-Life in Higher Education[8]

A recent survey of 511 full-time faculty members conducted by Horizons Workforce Consulting revealed the following:

- Nearly 80% of all faculty members surveyed would consider leaving their current work situation for a more supportive work environment.
- 65% of Full Professor survey respondents indicated they had considered leaving their institutions in the last year.
- 45% of Assistant Professor respondents reported they considered leaving the academy in the past year.
- 60% of the respondents stated they would consider leaving their current institution to spend more time with their families.
- 35% indicated they would think about leaving to help with elder care.
- 25% reported that they would consider leaving because of child-care conflicts.

organizational strategies that have been implemented to help employees manage their work and life obligations.

Colleges and universities are not immune to demographic and societal changes; thus, one of the most critical issues facing higher education today is the changing workforce in the academy. Giving birth, adopting a child, and caring for children are the primary reasons that women faculty, in particular, leave academe or do not achieve tenure and/or promotion. As men become more engaged with child caregiving, they, too, have reported increased conflicts from managing faculty and family responsibilities. In addition, elder care is rapidly becoming a significant concern for both men and women (Table 1.1).

As effective academic leaders, we are expected to see the big picture and anticipate forthcoming issues and challenges facing our institutions. Although it is beyond the scope of this guide to review all of the literature on effective leadership (e.g., characteristics, behaviors, skills) in academic settings,[9] most academic leaders agree that "Creating and sustaining a culture of support and excellence . . . at all levels of the institution involves the president, provosts, deans, department chairs, and senior faculty."[10] In contemporary higher education institutions, academic leaders must also facilitate an institutional culture that is responsive to work-life needs (i.e., work-life culture) in order to support the success and excellence of faculty, staff, and students (Table 1.2). Supervisors and leaders are the gatekeepers for employee participation in policies; thus, it is critical to understand the importance of the academic leader's role in responding to work-life issues.[11] An effective academic leader is one who understands the prevalence of work and life obligations and is proactive, open, and creative about helping faculty and staff to succeed at work while also managing life responsibilities.[12] This guide provides strategies for achieving excellence in the role of an academic leader by facilitating a work-life culture that is supportive of faculty, staff, and students.

Table 1.2 Work-Life Scenarios in Higher Education

Scenario 1

A department chair maintained an open-door policy so that faculty, staff, and students could feel welcome to discuss various matters. One day, a tenure-earning faculty member stopped by while the chair was working on an upcoming semester class schedule and asked to speak about the schedule. She closed the door as she walked into the office, which immediately raised a red flag in the chair's mind; the chair thought, "Oh no, we have a problem. Is she leaving?" The assistant professor informed the chair that she was 8 weeks pregnant and was concerned about her ability to fulfill her professional responsibilities, given the timing of the expected birth.

How would you react to a faculty member who tells you she is pregnant and will give birth during the semester?

As a chair who understands work-life obligations, what strategies would you suggest to help her fulfill professional responsibilities?

Scenario 2

A director noticed that one of the division's professional staff members was missing work regularly and seemed distracted on the job, both unusual behaviors for him. These behaviors were problematic, not only from the perspective of performance expectations but also because his primary responsibilities included providing support for all technology in the department. When the director acknowledged the pattern of change in performance, the staff member asked to talk with him about a personal situation. He informed the director that his elderly mother had become very ill and that the children (he and his siblings) had decided to move her to an assisted living facility. He and his sister agreed that one of them would check on their mother every day. The visiting schedule would require the staff member to leave early on some days.

How would you react to a staff member who has these elder-care responsibilities?

As a director who is responsive to work and life obligations, what strategies would you offer to help this staff member assist with elder care and fulfill his job responsibilities?

A NATIONAL CONVERSATION ABOUT WORK-LIFE

The importance of addressing employee work-life satisfaction and effectiveness through flexible workplaces is a topic of national conversation. In 2003, the U.S. Congress designated October as National Work and Family Month to celebrate healthier and flexible work environments. In 2013, U.S. President Barack Obama proclaimed the month of November as National Family Caregivers Month, explaining,

> Across our country, more than 60 million Americans take up the selfless and unheralded work of delivering care to seniors or people with disabilities or illnesses. The role they play in our healthcare system is one we must recognize and support. During National Family Caregivers Month, we thank these tireless heroes for the long, challenging work they perform behind closed doors and without fanfare every day, and we recommit to ensuring the well-being of their loved ones and of the caregivers themselves.[13]

3

In March 2010, the U.S. President's Executive Office of the President, Council of Economic Advisers issued a report titled "Work-Life Balance and the Economics of Workplace Flexibility" following from The White House Workplace Flexibility Forum. Upon a review of changes in the U.S. workforce, an examination of current flexible work arrangements, and a discussion of the economic benefits of workplace flexibility, the report concludes that "especially at this time as the U.S. rebuilds after the Great Recession, it is critical for the 21st century U.S. workplace [including higher education] to be organized for the 21st century workforce."[14]

During 2010 and 2011, the Women's Bureau of the U.S. Department of Labor led a National Dialogue on Workplace Flexibility [15] consisting of a series of forums that brought together stakeholders from various communities across the United States. The

> "The best available evidence suggests that encouraging more firms to consider adopting flexible practices can potentially boost productivity, improve morale, and benefit the U.S. economy."[16]

discussions focused on meeting the challenges of improving workplace flexibility while also achieving organizational goals.[17] Additionally, throughout 2013, numerous relevant articles about the role of women in the workplace, in particular, were published in The New York Times, Atlantic Monthly, Huffington Post, The Chronicle of Higher Education, Women in Higher Education, Dean and Provost, and The Washington Post.

Although the work-life conversation is newer to academe compared to the corporate world, a few private and public research intensive universities recognized the value of promoting work-life balance for faculty as a recruitment and retention strategy as early as the 1990s when work-life professionals and researchers formed a national professional organization called the College and University Work/ Family Association (CUWFA) (now known as the College and University Work-Life-Family Association) to provide a venue and network to discuss best practices and research. In 2001, the American Association of University Professors (AAUP) issued a statement of principles for family responsibilities and work, followed by an entire issue of Academe in 2004 focused on balancing faculty careers and family work.[18] In 2005, the ACE issued a groundbreaking report titled An Agenda for Excellence: Creating Flexibility in Tenure-Track Faculty Careers that addressed critical work-life dilemmas in the academy.[19] A national panel of presidents and chancellors from major research universities across the country endorsed this report, and it was the first national call for institutional leaders to implement flexible career policies and practices to help faculty manage work and life demands more effectively. The Alfred P. Sloan Foundation in partnership with ACE has funded many relevant initiatives, including the Alfred P. Sloan Awards for Faculty Career Flexibility. Additionally, the National Science Foundation ADVANCE grant program has promoted best practices and strategies for programs and policies specifically geared toward faculty members (e.g., tenure-clock extension, modified duties, reduced or part-time appointments).[20] In 2013, The Chronicle of Higher Education Annual Survey of the Great Colleges to Work

For revealed work-life balance to be a dimension of a "great" college or university.[21] The next section reviews some strategic reasons that justify a more serious attention to work-life satisfaction and its connection to the effectiveness of faculty and staff.[22]

STRATEGIC REASONS FOR A WORK-LIFE CULTURE

Researchers found that an "increased demand for work/life balance was among the demographic and social trends most likely to have a major strategic impact on the workplace in the coming years."[23] In another survey, 9 of every 10 human resources professionals responded that the implementation of formal flexible work arrangements had a positive impact on employee morale (job satisfaction and engagement).[24] Fostering a culture that is supportive of work-life satisfaction promotes employee effectiveness and provides organizations with a competitive advantage, while also alleviating stress within employees' lives.[25] Research studies consistently demonstrate the strategic value to organizations that comes from responding to the work and life needs of employees, and various organizations have now implemented work-life programs and policies, such as flextime, telecommuting, leave arrangements, and dependent care assistance.[26] These strategies are viewed by employees as enabling them to manage their work and non-work commitments and are discussed in more detail in Chapter 3.[27]

Researchers empirically demonstrated that organizations offer family-friendly benefits for the following reasons: internal economic pressures (high performance expectations; turnover), external economic pressures (recruitment and retention of employees), and external institutional pressures (legal mandate and equal opportunity).[28] Similarly, others have identified several correlates of work-life satisfaction and effectiveness (Table 1.3):[29]

- Improved retention, recruitment, advancement
- Enhanced productivity
- Cost savings
- Quality of employee well-being
- Risk management.

A work-life friendly culture can attract and retain talent and promote advancement and progression through a career.[30] For example, 41% of human resources professionals perceived balancing work and life obligations as a moderate or large threat to employee retention. These professionals (89%) also reported that retention of employees was affected positively by the implementation of flexible work arrangements.[31]

Scholars and practitioners have also demonstrated that workers in flexible work-life organizations are more likely to be involved with facilitating their organizations' successes, experience job satisfaction, and be both physically and mentally healthy.[32] A work-life culture can increase diversity, loyalty, social responsibility, and

Table 1.3 Correlates of Work-Life: Research Findings

Improved Recruitment, Retention, Advancement	• The Hudson and Highland Group, Inc. (2008) found that "a study of more than 1,500 U.S. workers reported that nearly a third considered work-life balance and flexibility to be the most important factor in considering job offers."[i]
	• Williams (2001) reported "in a survey of two hundred human resource managers, two-thirds cited family-supportive policies and flexible hours as the single most important factor in attracting and retaining employees."[ii]
	• "When employees are satisfied with stress levels and work-life balance, they are more inclined to stay with their companies (86% versus 64%) and more likely to recommend them as places to work (88% versus 55%)."[iii]
	• According to Ransom and Burud (1988) "a child care program can reduce turnover by 37% to 60%."[iv]
Enhanced Productivity	• Pruchno et al. (2000) reported "a study on the impact of workplace flexibility conducted by the Center for Work & Family in 2000 found that 70% of managers and 87% of employees reported that working a flexible work arrangement had a positive or very positive impact on productivity."[v]
	• Corporate Voices (2005) reported "Ernst & Young found that individuals' perceptions of their own flexibility are highly predictive of level of commitment, which in turn is highly predictive of revenue per person."[vi]
Cost Savings	• "An emergency back-up child-care program at KPMG had a 125% ROI [return on investment] within six months of implementation and a 521% ROI by the fourth year."[vii]
	• "Flexible scheduling at Chubb reduced unscheduled time off by 50% each month and overtime by 40% per employee."[viii]
	• Shellenbeck (2004) claims "child care breakdowns leading to employee absences cost businesses $3 billion annually in the United States."[ix]
	• Friedman (1986) reported "fifty-four percent of employers report that child care services had a positive impact on employee absenteeism, reducing missed workdays by as much as 20% to 30%."[x]
	• Corporate Voices for Working Families (2006) reported "one study estimated that employee stress due to concerns about balancing obligations with children and work lead to higher rates of absenteeism, with absenteeism costs to businesses ranging from $496 to $1,984 per employee per year."[xi]

Quality of Employee Well-Being	• Galinsky et al. (2004) claims "67% of employees report high levels of job satisfaction in organizations with high levels of workplace flexibility, versus 23% in organizations with low levels of flexibility."[xii]
	• Corporate Voices (2005) reported that "employees at Bristol-Myers Squibb who use flexible work arrangements are 30% less likely to report feeling stressed and burned out. IBM employees who have flexibility report less work-life stress than employees who do not have flexibility."[xiii]
Risk Management	• In an analysis of over 2,100 caregiver discrimination lawsuits collected through 2009, the Center for Worklife Law (2011) reported that despite "limited income, FRD [family responsibilities discrimination] lawsuits brought by low-wage workers have resulted in hefty verdicts. [For] example, a hand finisher of aerospace parts received $761,279 in a settlement and attorneys' fees and costs when his absences to care for his son with AIDS were held against him and he was fired in violation of the FMLA and state equivalent."[xiv]
	• Calvert (2010) found "verdicts and settlements in family responsibilities discrimination cases average over $500,000."[xv]

[i] as cited in Council of Economic Advisors (2010), p. 16, see endnote 14.
[ii] as cited in Council of Economic Advisors (2010), p. 16, see endnote 14.
[iii] as cited in Van Deusen et al. (2008), p. 4, see endnote 35.
[iv] as cited in Shellenback, K. (2004). *Child care & parent productivity: Making the business case.* Ithaca, NY: Cornell University Press, p. 1.
[v] as cited in Van Deusen et al. (2008), p. 4, see endnote 35.
[vi] as cited in Van Deusen et al. (2008), p. 4, see endnote 35.
[vii] as cited in Van Deusen et al. (2008), p. 4, see endnote 35.
[viii] as cited in Van Deusen et al. (2008), p. 4, see endnote 35.
[ix] as cited in Shellenback (2004), p. 1.
[x] as cited in Shellenback (2004), p. 1.
[xi] as cited in Council of Economic Advisors (2010), p. 7, see endnote 14.
[xii] as cited in Van Deusen et al. (2008), p. 5, see endnote 35.
[xiii] as cited in Van Deusen et al. (2008), p. 5, see endnote 35.
[xiv] as cited in Bornstein, S. (2011). *Poor, pregnant, and fired: Caregiver discrimination against low-wage workers.* Retrieved from http://worklifelaw.org/pubs/PoorPregnantAndFired.pdf, p.10.
[xv] as cited in Sloan Work and Family Research Network. (2010). *Questions and answers about family responsibilities discrimination (FRD): A Sloan work and family research network fact sheet.* Retrieved from https://workfamily.sas.upenn.edu/sites/workfamily.sas.upenn.edu/files/imported/pdfs/FactSheet_FRD.pdf, p.3.

productivity while reducing absenteeism.[33] As noted earlier, research studies have linked work-life balance with stress and the quality of employee well-being,[34] and

> According to information provided in 2002 by Chrysalis Performance Strategies, stress is responsible for 19% of absenteeism, 40% of turnover, 55% of EAP costs, 30% of short-term and long-term disability costs, and 60% of workplace accidents, and costs U.S. industry over $300 billion per year.[35]

Work-life programs can reduce the financial risks posed by rising health-related costs as well as the legal risks associated with certain employment practices, such as caregiver bias. As discussed later, "Family responsibilities discrimination (FRD), also called caregiver discrimination, is employment discrimination against workers based on their family caregiving responsibilities."[36] Work-life policies and programs can help protect an organization from the legal risks associated with these illegal employment practices. Other costs associated with programs and policies include heightened insurance premiums or self-insured expenses related to the use of medical, prescription, and mental health services in company-sponsored health benefit plans as well as the costs surrounding faculty turnover. For example, Iowa State University measured the impact of new flexibility policies on recruitment and retention through an examination of start-up costs for faculty and search costs when faculty leave the institution.[37]

It is clear that most of these findings were discovered in other settings than universities and colleges. However, as we discuss throughout, recent studies have revealed similar results with regard to faculty and staff at higher education institutions. For the ACE's 2013 national challenge to university and college presidents, the following strategic reasons for supporting work-life balance were provided:[38]

- Revitalizing and retaining faculty
- Promoting inclusion and diversity
- Remaining competitive internationally
- Keeping up with the private sector
- Recruiting and retaining future generations
- Saving the institution money.

Within a highly competitive job environment, there are specific economics to retaining women faculty members;[39] however, institutional attention to work-life can help in the recruitment and retention of all scholars—both men and women—who are reporting increasing levels of work-life conflict.[40] Moreover, a work-life culture will not only help to revitalize and retain junior faculty, but it can also revitalize senior faculty: "The contributions of senior faculty can be immense, as these individuals are often the principal investigators on grants, usually hold senior administrative positions, and provide mentoring to junior colleagues on teaching philosophies and techniques."[41] A work-life culture can facilitate retirement transitions through the implementation of policies and practices that continue to engage retired faculty while also providing the flexibility to manage family responsibilities during the culminating stages of one's career. In the next section, the evolving workplace, we consider the more compelling reasons for the national attention to work-life in order to more fully understand the rising need to effectively manage work, life, and family responsibilities.

> "We need to develop a more holistic approach to work life that sees the responsibilities of care and caregiving as an integral part of adult human life and not as an exceptional scenario requiring specific adjustment and strategies.... It is crucial to signal that family and personal life are not separate entities which have no place in the work environment but on the contrary to acknowledge the reality of care responsibilities." (Dr. Monika Shafi, Department Chair, University of Delaware)

THE EVOLVING WORKPLACE

It has been well documented that the American workforce has undergone major transitions throughout history. For example, the 9-to-5 traditional work schedule is outdated, and dramatic changes in the nature of work, employees, and work settings have emerged.[42] Changes include, but are not limited to, the following: technological advances (e.g., PDAs/smartphones, VPN access, virtual desktops); growth in economic pressures and global competition; increased workplace opportunities for women, resulting in dual-career households; a rise in single-parent families; an increase in the number of employees with caring responsibilities (e.g., child care, elder care); the diversification of values among workers because of generational gaps in the workplace; and an emphasis on organizational sustainability (e.g., "an organization's ability to balance financial performance with contributions to the quality of life of its employees, the local community, and society at large").[43] It is beyond the scope of this guide to capture all of the changes and trends in the domestic and global workforce;[44] instead, we consider how colleges and universities, specifically, have been affected by changes to the workforce, as represented by three major trends: workforce demographics, shifts in households, and the nature of work.

Workforce Demographics

The American workforce has become increasingly diverse with regard to the race, gender, and age of workers.[45] African Americans compose 11.3%, Hispanic Americans compose 13.1%, and Asian Americans compose 4.3% of the U.S. labor force.[46] The largest change has been the increase in women workers, and some authors speculate that the recent recession has caused more women to enter the workplace.[47] In 1950, 34% of women age 16 and older participated in the labor force. By 2010, this figure rose to 59% for women overall. Particularly notable is that mothers with young children compose the fastest growing group of working women.[48] In 1975, 47% of mothers with children under 18 years of age were members of the U.S. workforce. By 2007, 32 years later, that proportion had risen to 71%. Women now represent 49% of the wage and salaried workforce. Interestingly, a slight reverse in this trend was observed for men. Men's participation in the national labor force decreased from 88.5% in 2008 to 87.9% in 2009.[49]

There have been small, yet significant, increases in the numbers of women and people of color who compose both the student body and the faculty/administrative body at colleges and universities. Although white men held most of the tenured faculty positions in 2007, their total percentage had decreased by 12% since 1997. The proportion of tenured white women increased by 18% during this same time period. For women of color, the increase was 67%, whereas for men of color, the increase was 25%.[50]

In recent years, women represented 45% of doctoral students, and more women than men have earned bachelor's degrees and master's degrees since 1982.[51] Overall, women represent a lower percentage of the tenure-track (44%) and tenured faculty (30%)[52] and constitute 39% of all full-time faculty nationwide.[53] Although the number of women representing full-time and part-time faculty has increased over the past two decades, the increases are less promising when viewing the numbers by discipline, institutional type, position, and rank.[54] For example, we would expect that the rise of women into assistant professor positions would lead to increasing numbers of women in associate, senior, and administrative ranks, yet this is not the case. Additional analyses reveal that although women have progressed in many disciplines at entry levels, they are less likely to advance to the associate and senior ranks, creating a succession problem for the future academy.[55] The representation of women is lower for higher ranks, especially in prestigious institutions. Women are most frequently hired at community colleges and institutions granting bachelor's and master's degrees rather than research-oriented and PhD-granting institutions.[56] They are also underrepresented in certain fields, including science, technology, engineering, and mathematics (STEM),[57] despite an increase in doctorates awarded to women in these disciplines.[58]

Another demographic shift is the aging of the population, which has resulted in significant generational differences in the workplace as well as more caregiving responsibilities for workers.[59] An increasing number of younger workers are entering the workforce, and many older individuals are postponing their retirements, primarily because of financial instability. One in five workers ages 50 and older has a retirement job today; 75% of workers ages 50 and older expect to have retirement jobs in the future.[60] A similar phenomenon is observed in higher education as a large percentage of the tenured faculty approaches retirement.[61] "According to an ACE Issue Brief, using the National Study of Postsecondary Faculty data from 2003–2004, only 3% of faculty members at four-year institutions in tenured or tenure-track positions were individuals ages 34 or younger"; the percentage increases to 15% when considering tenured or tenure-track faculty ages 35 to 44.[62] The Center for WorkLife Law notes that slightly over half

(50.5%) of tenured faculty are 55 years of age or older.[63] Given the number of retirements expected in the coming years, then, the question arises: will future hiring practices correct the disproportionate representation of women and people of color in tenure-track positions?[64]

Shifts in Households

The rise of working women has had implications for the structure of households. For example, in the middle of the 20th century, the traditional home included a father who worked full time and a mother who was not employed outside the home.[65] Today, this traditional household is less common, and we now live in a dual-earner/career society. In 1977, 66% of couples were composed of two people working outside the home, whereas that percentage rose to 80% in 2008.[66]

The dual-earner/career society has implications for children in the household. In 1968, 48% of children were raised in a traditional household; forty years later, in 2008, only 20% of children lived in such households. More recently (2010), 97% of dual-career couples reported having a child under 18 years of age in the home.[67] The dual-earner/career phenomenon is pervasive in higher education. In the United States, 35% of male faculty and 40% of female faculty partner with another academic,[68] and a number of recent studies have addressed this issue.[69] The implications of child care as well as the dual-earner/career couple are discussed later in this guide.

Nature of Work

The nature of work has evolved and will continue to evolve. Some authors noted that there are four national shifts affecting work: a decline in job security, a decrease in autonomy, an increase in demands for access to workers, and employer expectations that workers will enhance their commitment and dedication to their work.[70] Additionally, other authors[71] reported increased workloads and longer work hours, resulting from the outsourcing or elimination of jobs, as well as globalization. These authors also note the impact of technological advances, such as personal digital assistants, cell phones, tablets, and the Internet. Technological advances certainly enhance work opportunities for employees; however, these same advances are shaping the boundaries between work and life by blurring the parameters. Along with these changes, 44% of Americans indicated that they were overworked.[72] The survey respondents self-reported that they were making more mistakes, feeling heightened levels of resentment and stress, and experiencing poorer health.

Within higher education, the nature of faculty work has undergone numerous changes. These changes can vary by institution type (e.g., Carnegie classifications); however, there are several overarching trends.[73] Factors influencing faculty work include "new methods, technologies and venues for knowledge production and dissemination; cuts in funding; competition for grants and other funding; expectations for accountability and transparency as well as higher expectations for research, teaching and service" and the changing demographics and learning capabilities of students.[74] It has become the norm that faculty members are expected to be available 24/7 for their work and constantly accessible to students. Recently, researchers contend that the challenges with managing work and life responsibilities are due, in part, to a significant work overload.[75]

Another noteworthy shift affecting the nature of work in academia is an increase in part-time and non-tenure track faculty positions, resulting in a greater reliance on a contingent faculty workforce.[76] "A 13% increase in part-time faculty and a 6% decrease in full-time faculty were observed in U.S. institutions (excluding faculty at two-year colleges, private liberal arts colleges, and medical schools) between 1997 and 2007":[77]

> There were fewer tenured faculty as a percentage of the total in 2007, a decrease of 14 percent; only slightly more tenure-track faculty, an increase of nearly 5 percent, and a much higher percentage of non-tenure track faculty, an increase of 26 percent.[78]

Women are much more likely than men to be employed outside of the tenure system, holding neither tenured nor tenure-track posts.[79] Across all racial/ethnic groups, a decline in tenured faculty and increase in non-tenure track faculty has been observed. As a result of this growing reliance on part-time faculty, the work of regular full-time faculty has increased, particularly with regard to services obligations, student supervision, and advising.

OVERVIEW OF WORK-LIFE ISSUES

Changes in workers, households, and the nature of work are inextricably linked to work-life satisfaction and the effectiveness of employees because these changes have caused many workers to face conflicts between their work and their personal lives.[81] High demands and expectations

> In a recent survey, The Families and Work Institute found that "41 percent of workers reported that job and family life interfered with each other 'a lot' or 'somewhat.'"[80]

for job performance that result in more time at work increase negative stress in family life.[82] Although women are now more involved in the workforce, they have not substantially reduced their engagement at home. For example, mothers spent the same number of weekday hours with their children in 2008 as they did in 1977, and the majority of married/partnered women indicate they do most of the cooking (70%) and cleaning (73%) in their households.[83]

Effectively managing work and life is a challenge for both men and women. Participants in the changing workforce (women, members of ethnic and racial minorities, partners in dual-earner / career couples, single parents) are challenging the traditional expectations and roles of the ideal worker[84] and the relationship between work and life: "For the first time in 2008, men's and women's views about appropriate work and family roles have converged to a point where they are virtually identical and not significantly different."[85] The high level of work-life conflict described by women has not changed significantly over the past three decades, yet men, too, report that their levels of work-life conflict have greatly increased.[86] A 2010 Boston College study on fatherhood found that working fathers are reprioritizing family over work; consequently, men reported spending more time with their children at the expense of professional advancement.[87] In 2000, over 50% of men surveyed stated that they would cut their salaries by one fourth if they could have more family or personal time.[88] According to a 2013 Pew Research Study, fathers with children younger than 18 years of age reported that they felt pressed for time and had challenges in managing family and work responsibilities that were similar to those long experienced by mothers. Forty-six percent of the survey respondents indicated that they are not spending enough time with their children. The fathers also reported that they were less likely than mothers to believe that they are doing a good job as a parent.[89] Additional research findings about fathers are in Table 1.4.

The generation gap has also contributed to the changing nature of the workplace—younger workers have values that are different from those of the baby boomers who have dominated the workforce. Thus, employers are challenged to implement strategies that respond to the needs of workers at different life stages and also help different "generations work together more productively and overcome differences in values and work styles."[90] Younger workers expect

Table 1.4 Research Findings About Working Fathers

"There are approximately 68 million fathers in America, a 4 million increase since 2008, with approximately 26 million having children under 18."[i]

"Men are taking more overall responsibility for the care of their children in 2008 than in 1992, according to themselves and their wives/partners."[ii]

"Men are taking more responsibility for other family work as well, according to themselves and their wives/partners."[iii]

"From 1977 to 2008, the average workday time fathers spent with their children increased significantly from 2 to 3.1 hours and their time doing household chores also increased significantly from 1.3 to 2.3 hours a day."[iv]

[i] U.S. Census Bureau. (2010). *Facts for features: Father's day centennial: June 20, 2010.* Retrieved from www.census.gov/newsroom/releases/archives/facts_for_features_special_editions/cb10-ff11.html
[ii] Galinsky et al. (2011), p. 16, see endnote 48.
[iii] Galinsky et al. (2011), p. 17, see endnote 48.
[iv] Matos & Galinsky (2012), p. 1, see endnote 17.

more flexibility in the workplace so they may pursue interests outside of work; thus, some organizations have begun to provide concierge-type services (e.g., meal preparation, dry-cleaning, pet sitting).

The aging society also has an impact on caregiving responsibilities. As noted in the report prepared by the U.S. President's Executive Office of the President Council of Economic Advisers, individuals born around 1940 have a life expectancy that is 10 years longer than that of the previous generation (born in 1910), resulting in additional responsibilities for workers to care for older family members. According to a recent study by the Families and Work Institute, 42% of employed Americans (almost 1 in 2 workers) had provided elder care in the previous five years (Table 1.4). [91]

The impact of a changing workforce in higher education and the need for work-life-friendly policies is documented in the literature. Faculty and staff often have spillover of work into family life, as a result of long work hours and/or needing to take work material home, which may interrupt or interfere with family life.[92] Tenure-track faculty, especially, have great responsibilities to their institutions in order to fulfill expectations to conduct research, publish articles, obtain grant funding, teach students, and perform service. Some current work-life trends and issues in higher education are faculty retirements, wellness, dual-career couples, and child and elder care.[93] Faculty in academic dual-earner/career relationships are particularly affected by the need for caregiving and home responsibilities. A recent survey of CUWFA members revealed that the most serious issues facing universities and colleges are workload, morale, stress and burnout, dependent care, wellness and resilience, and

Table 1.5 Research Findings About Caregivers for Elders

- "Among those who have provided elder care in the past 5 years, almost half (44%) have cared for more than one person.

- 17% of workers in the workforce are currently providing elder care.

- Among the entire workforce, women (20%) and men (22%) are equally likely to have provided family care in the past 5 years and equally likely to provide care at the current time (9% versus 8%).

- Many of these caregivers are in the sandwich generation—46% of women who are caregivers and 40% of men also have children under the age of 18 at home.

- Just under half of the workforce (49%) expect to be providing elder care for a family member in the coming 5 years."[i]

- "According to one national study, approximately 43.5 million Americans—the majority of them women—served as unpaid caregivers to a family member over the age of 50 in 2008."[ii]

[i] Aumann et al. (2008), p. 2, see endnote 91.
[ii] National Alliance for Caregiving (NAC) & AARP. (2004). *Caregiving in the U.S.* Retrieved from www.caregiving.org/data/04execsumm.pdf

flexible work arrangements.[94] Although there is less research about staff and students, they will also require accommodations because of children and aging parents.

> "Providing faculty these flexible policies and programs allows them to be less stressed and reduces burnout, which in turn improves the quality of instruction for students. Flexible work arrangements allow for faculty to be more productive regarding the number of grants that they bring in, thus benefiting the institution. Flexible work arrangements also improve morale and employee relations."[95]

Doctoral students note the constant pressure and stress in their teachers' and advisors' work, leaving some to wonder whether a balanced life is possible or whether they should rethink their career goals.[96] Research universities are at risk of losing some of their best talent because many doctoral students are looking for careers that allow them to have well-balanced lives:[97] authors have noted it is important to respond to the needs of not only faculty members but also doctoral students. Both female and male scholars who are beginning their academic careers prefer to work for institutions that support the effective management of personal life and work responsibilities.[98] Moreover,

> Colleges and universities need to establish policies and practices and a culture that encourages all faculty members to be productive, successful, and happy institutional citizens. This is necessary in order to recruit and retain the most qualified, generative, diverse, and productive faculty.[99]

Early university adopters of work-life began with issues related to parenting.[101] In recent years, however, campuses have responded to work-life needs that have grown beyond support for new parents; many faculty and staff are also challenged

> "74 percent of the next generation of male scholars are concerned about how family-friendly their potential institution is."[100]

by elder-care demands and various "late career" concerns, such as preparing for their own transition to retirement.[102] Thus, higher education institutions have begun to address both the daily needs for workplace flexibility and the broader needs for career flexibility. Work-life issues specific to faculty, staff, and students are discussed in more detail in Chapter 2.

A STRATEGIC IMPERATIVE

As noted earlier in this chapter, ACE's report *An Agenda for Excellence: Creating Flexibility in Tenure-Track Faculty Careers* was the first national call for higher education leaders to implement flexibility practices and policies to ensure diversity

Table 1.6 How to Calculate the Business Case for Your Organization[103]

"Based on the recommendations and approaches from CWF corporate partners, we have developed a list of suggestions for calculating cost savings and other business impacts. Since every organization has its own unique goals and cost measures, we provide only general suggestions that can help pave the way for making the most appropriate business case."

1. Employer Impact	a. Calculate turnover costs in your industry, organization, and business unit
	b. Calculate sick leave, absenteeism, mental and physical health care costs
	c. Calculate space savings for telecommuters and others
	d. Measure return-on-investment for child care, fitness, and other programs
2. Employee Impact	a. Measure the degree of employee satisfaction, engagement, and stress
	b. Measure current usage and need/desire for various types of programs
3. Environmental Impact	a. Measure energy and emission savings for telecommuters
Useful references for calculating some of these impacts:	• Sample calculations for absenteeism, turnover, and ROI are provided by Karen Shellenback in her 2004 article on *Child Care and Parent Productivity: Making the Business Case.*
	• Explanations for calculating turnover costs and the employee breakeven point are included in the 2005 Catalyst study *Beyond a Reasonable Doubt: Building the Business Case for Flexibility.*
	• *The Metrics Manual* published by the BC Center for Work & Family in 1999 describes a wide variety of approaches for measuring work-life efforts:
	– Benchmarking
	– Standards of Excellence approach
	– Needs assessments
	– Analyzing availability and utilization
	– Establishing the link with business strategies
	– Measuring impact on the bottom line
	– Evaluation using a participatory approach
	– Examining impact on supervisors and co-workers
	– Measuring impact on external stakeholder relationships
	– Assessing unintended consequences

and equity in the professoriate, enhance the excellence of the academic profession and higher education, and improve the quality and global competitiveness of U.S. higher education. If this call or the more recent ACE National Challenge are not convincing about the importance and prevalence of work-life issues, then it might be helpful to review your institution's strategic priorities and goals. Most institutions have strategic goals related to faculty and staff recruitment, retention, and advancement as well as workforce diversity. Related to these goals are high performance and productivity, satisfaction, engagement, organizational commitment, and employee well-being. In recent years, institutions have placed greater emphasis on efficiency and effectiveness, including such areas as cost savings, time savings, quality improvement, risk management, establishing an equitable and fair workplace, and sustainability and social responsibility. A work-life culture will help higher education institutions meet one or more of these strategic objectives and goals. Additionally, examining costs associated with work and life responsibilities (e.g. absenteeism, sick leave) will contribute to the business case for a supportive culture (Table 1.6). It is imperative to take action and improve the quality of academic work-life because it is not just a personal issue but also an institutional concern.

EFFECTIVE ACADEMIC LEADERS AND A WORK-LIFE CULTURE

Despite the acknowledgement of a changing workforce and the implications for managing work-life responsibilities, workers frequently avoid using flexible and work-life supports and continue to be unsatisfied. How can we account for this? Practitioners note that the breakdown in effectively managing work and life can be due to leaders who are often gatekeepers of policies, programs, and services: "An unsupportive supervisor may actively discourage employees from using family-supportive benefits."[104] Moreover, supervisor bias against those who use work-life policies and procedures discourages employees from using them.[105] For example, if senior leadership does not support flexibility in academic careers, faculty may be reluctant to use any policies adopted to help them, and this reluctance can result in poor performance and negative career consequences:

> Many faculty and staff fear retaliation for taking time off and the perception among their peers that they had more time to produce more work. The fear of not being taken seriously about their work also plays in a part of low utilization of some family-friendly policies related to parental leave.[106]

Beyond the implementation of programs, benefits, and policies, many organizations have come to realize that it is important to create a culture that promotes and facilitates work-life effectiveness and satisfaction (see Chapter 2 for further discussion of these terms).[107] Definitions of work-life culture are presented in Chapter 4, but it is important to note here that leaders play an important role in influencing that culture. Because leaders create and change cultures, they are instrumental in shaping the work-life culture in organizations.[108] Recent research studies suggest that leaders' behaviors play a significant role in fostering a culture that is supportive of work-life satisfaction effectiveness[109] and have documented that the presence of leaders who understand work and life responsibilities is related to positive outcomes such as employee retention, satisfaction, performance, and commitment.[110]

In both higher education and corporate settings, organizations that foster a flexible and inclusive work-life culture hire leaders who understand employees' needs to effectively manage multiple work and family responsibilities.[111] These leaders encourage employees to take advantage of formal family-friendly policies to better juggle diverse work-life obligations, resulting in a supportive climate or culture for using these benefits.[112] Flexible work environments and supportive department chairs, deans, and provosts have been identified as key factors in improving the quality of faculty work, family balance, and overall life and job satisfaction.[113]

> "Faculty are the single most important resource of an academic institution, and they are seeking flexible approaches for integrating personal and professional demands more than ever before—men and women, minority and majority, and faculty of all ages. This means that policies and practices must evolve if institutions are to recruit, retain, and advance the best and most diverse faculty community possible." (Dr. Mary Dankoski, Associate Dean for Faculty Affairs and Professional Development, Indiana University School of Medicine)

CONCLUSION

Although scholars[114] consistently acknowledge the importance of the leadership and administration in influencing a work-life culture in academe, no text specifically addresses strategies that can be implemented by leaders in higher education. This guide, then, aims to fill that gap by outlining approaches for leaders to facilitate a work-life culture in universities and colleges. According to CUWFA, it is important for leaders to start with a knowledge base of work-life issues and then draw on their institutional knowledge to consider how best to implement such a culture. In ACE's *An Agenda for Excellence: Creating Flexibility in Tenure-Track Faculty Careers*, institutional leaders must do the following:

- "Create hospitable environments that welcome and support a diverse faculty in meeting changing needs throughout their careers."
- "Develop policies and programs that encourage flexible career paths to help faculty members balance work-life issues, avoid stagnation and burnout, and remain productive in various facets of scholarship

throughout the course of their career lifetime so that faculty can contribute to maintaining excellence in teaching, innovative research, and U.S. competitiveness in the global marketplace."[115]

Academic leaders set the tone for their departments, and small shifts in perception and practice can contribute to the institutionalization of a work-life culture that can have tremendous benefits for everyone. This guide provides the foundation to help academic leaders shape a work-life culture and become more effective and supportive champions of work-life satisfaction and effectiveness. If we can normalize work-life issues, then we will have fostered a flexible and inclusive work-life culture—a win-win outcome for everyone.

Questions for Discussion and Reflection

1. How have the demographics of your department changed? How has your department evolved to accommodate those changing demographics?

2. Are you aware of the caregiving responsibilities of faculty and staff in your department? How might you help faculty and staff adjust their work to better balance those responsibilities?

3. Are faculty and staff in your department aware of work-life policies? How can you help them to take advantage of those policies?

4. What outcomes (e.g., increased effectiveness, efficiency, cost savings) are you hoping to achieve in your department? How can becoming a work-life–friendly leader help you to achieve those outcomes?

5. Identify a work-life–friendly leader on your campus. How can you encourage other academic leaders to follow his or her example?

NOTES

1. American Council on Education. (2013a). *National challenge for higher education: Retaining a 21st century workforce.* Retrieved from www.acenet.edu/leadership/programs/Pages/National -Challenge.aspx
2. Alliance for Work-Life Progress. (2011). *Work-life history and timeline.* Session at the National Work-Life Summit, New Orleans, LA.
3. Brough, P., & Kelling, A. (2002). Women, work & well being: The influence of work-family and family-work conflict. *New Zealand Journal of Psychology, 31*(1), 29–38; Bogese, C., Schneider, S. K., & Koppes, L. L. (2010, March). *Preferences for supervisor behaviors: The influence of gender and parenthood.* Poster presented at the 56th annual meeting of the Southeastern Psychological Association, Chattanooga, TN; Hobson, C. J., Delunas, L., & Kesic, D. (2001). Compelling evidence of the need for corporate work/life balance initiatives: Results from a national survey of stressful life-events. *Journal of Employment Counseling, 38*(1), 38–44.
4. Davis, A. E., & Kalleberg, A. L. (2006). Family-friendly organizations? Work and family programs in the 1990s. *Work and Occupations, 33*(2), 191–223; Glass, J. L., & Estes, S. B. (1997).

The family responsive workplace. *Annual Review of Sociology, 23,* 289–313; Higgins, C., Duxbury, L., & Lee, C. (1994). Impact of life-cycle stage and gender on the ability to balance work and family responsibilities. *Family Relations, 43*(2), 144–150; Wallen, J. (2002). *Balancing work and family: The role of the workplace.* Boston, MA: Allyn & Bacon.

5. Beauregard, T. A., & Henry, L. C. (2009). Making the link between work-life balance practices and organizational performance. *Human Resource Management Review, 19,* 9–22.

6. Glass, J., & Fujimoto, T. (1995). Employer characteristics and the provision of family responsive policies. *Work and Occupations, 22*(4), 380–411, p. 382.

7. Ryan, A. M., & Kossek, E. E. (2008). Work-life policy implementation: Breaking down or creating barriers to inclusiveness? *Human Resource Management, 47*(2), 295–310, p. 295.

8. Philipsen, M. I., & Bostic, T. B. (2010). *Helping faculty find work-life balance: The path toward family-friendly institutions.* San Francisco, CA: Jossey-Bass, p. 27.

9. Chu, D. (2006). *The department chair primer: Leading and managing academic departments.* Bolton, MA: Anker Publishing Company, Inc.; Higgerson, M. L., & Joyce, T. A. (2007). *Effective leadership communication: A guide for department chairs and deans for managing difficult situations and people.* Bolton, MA: Anker Publishing Company, Inc.

10. Trower, C. A. (2012). *Success on the tenure track: Five keys to faculty job satisfaction.* Baltimore, MD: The Johns Hopkins University Press, p. 3.

11. Hammer, L. B., Kossek, E. E., Zimmerman, K., & Daniels, R. (2007). Clarifying the construct of family supportive supervisory behaviors (FSSB): A multilevel perspective. In P. L. Perrewé & D. C. Ganster (Eds.), *Research in occupational stress and well-being* (Vol. 6; pp. 165–204). Amsterdam, Netherlands: Elsevier Ltd.

12. Ward, K., & Wolf-Wendel, L. (2012). *Academic motherhood: How faculty manage work and family.* New Brunswick, NJ: Rutgers University Press.

13. Office of the Press Secretary. (2013). *Presidential Proclamation—National Family Caregivers Month, 2013.* Retrieved from www.whitehouse.gov/the-press-office/2013/10/31/presidential-proclamation-national-family-caregivers-month-2013

14. Council of Economic Advisors. (2010). *Work-life balance and the economics of workplace flexibility.* Executive Office of the President, Council of Economic Advisors. Retrieved from www.whitehouse.gov/files/documents/100331-cea-economics-workplace-flexibility.pdf, pp. 25–26.

15. United States Department of Labor. (2010–2011). *National dialogue on workplace flexibility.* Retrieved from www.dol.gov/wb/media/natldialogue3.htm

16. Council of Economic Advisors (2010).

17. Matos, K., & Galinsky, E. (2012). *Workplace flexibility in the United States: A status report.* New York, NY: Families and Work Institute. Retrieved from http://familiesandwork.org/downloads/WorkplaceFlexibilityinUS.pdf, p. 1.

18. American Association of University Professors. (2001). *Statement of principles on family responsibilities and academic work.* Retrieved from www.aaup.org/file/family-responsibilities-academic-work.pdf; Curtis, J. W. (Guest Ed.). (2004, Nov.–Dec.). Balancing faculty careers and family work. *Academe, 90*(6).

19. American Council on Education. (2005). *An agenda for excellence: Creating flexibility in tenure-track faculty careers.* Washington, DC: Author.

20. National Science Foundation. (2012). *Balancing the scales: NSF's career-life balance initiative.* Retrieved from www.nsf.gov/career-life-balance/brochure.pdf

21. The Chronicle of Higher Education. (2013). *Great colleges to work for.* Retrieved from http://chronicle.com/article/Great-Colleges-To-Work-For/140857

22. Gappa, J. M., Austin, A. E., & Trice, A. G. (2007). *Rethinking faculty work: Higher education's strategic imperative.* San Francisco, CA: Jossey-Bass; Lester, J., & Sallee, M. (Eds.). (2009). *Establishing the family-friendly campus: Models for effective practice.* Sterling, VA: Stylus Publishing, Inc.; Philipsen & Bostic (2010); Trower (2012); Ward & Wolf-Wendel (2012).

23. Society for Human Resource Management. (2008). *Workplace flexibility in the 21st century: Meeting the needs of the changing workforce.* Retrieved from www.shrm.org/Research/Survey

Findings/Articles/Pages/WorkplaceFlexibilityinthe21stCenturyMeetingtheNeedsofthe ChangingWorkforce.aspx, p. 2.

24. Society for Human Resource Management. (2008).
25. Allen, T. D. (2001). Family-supportive work environments: The role of organizational perceptions. *Journal of Vocational Behavior, 58,* 414–435.
26. Konrad, A. M., & Mangel, R. (2000). The impact of work-life programs on firm productivity. *Strategic Management Journal, 21*(12), 1225–1237.
27. Smith, J., & Gardner, D. (2007). Factors affecting employee use of work-life balance initiatives. *New Zealand Journal of Psychology, 36*(1), 3–12.
28. Davis & Kalleberg (2006).
29. Sullivan, E., Duckett, S., & Nuter, J. (2012). *Making the business case for work-life policies and programs at colleges and universities.* Retrieved from www.cuwfa.org/assets/documents/making. the.business.case.jun.2012.pdf
30. Galinsky, E., Bond, J.T. & Hill, E.J. (2004) *When work works: A status report on workplace flexibility: Who has it? Who wants it? What difference does it make?* Retrieved from http://familiesandwork. org/3w/research/donwloads/staus.pdf
31. Society for Human Resource Management (2008).
32. Gappa et al. (2007).
33. Casper, W. J., & Buffardi, L. C. (2004). Work-life benefits and job pursuit intentions: The role of anticipated organizational support. *Journal of Vocational Behavior, 65,* 391–410; Lobel, S.A., Googins, B.K., & Bankert, E. (1999). The future of work and family: Critical trends for policy, practice, and research. *Human Resource Management, 38*(3), 243–254.
34. Galinsky, E., Bond, J., Kim, S., Backon, L., Brownfield, E., & Sakai, K. (2004). *Overwork in America: When the way we work becomes too much.* New York, NY: Families and Work Institute.
35. Van Deusen, F., Ladge, J., James, J., & Harrington, B. (2008). *Building the business case for work-life programs.* Boston College Center for Work-Life & Family. Retrieved from www.bc.edu/content/dam/files/centers/cwf/research/pdf/BCCWF_Business_Case_EBS.pdf
36. The Center for WorkLife Law. (2013). *Family responsibilities discrimination: About FRD.* Retrieved from http://worklifelaw.org/frd/, p. 1.
37. Gahn, S., & Carlson, S. (n.d.). *Breaking the norms: Measuring the impact of new policies.* Retrieved from www-provost.sws.iastate.edu/sites/default/files/uploads/advance/2008_10-11gahn carlson_ppt.pdf
38. American Council on Education (2013a).
39. The Center for WorkLife Law. (2012). *The economics of retaining women.* Retrieved from http://worklifelaw.org/womens-leadership/gender-bias-academia/retaining-women/
40. Harrington, B., van Deusen, F., & Humberd, B. (2011). *The new dad: Caring, committed and conflicted.* Chestnut Hill, MA: Boston College Center for Work & Family.
41. American Council on Education. (2013b). *Making the business case: The imperative for supporting and promoting workplace flexibility in higher education.* Retrieved from http://www.acenet.edu/www. acenet.edu/news-room/Pages/Making-the-Business-Case-for-Workplace-Flexibility.aspx, p. 1; Bataille, G. M., & Brown, B. (2006). *Faculty career paths: Multiple routes to academic success and satisfaction.* American Council on Education/Oryx Press Series on Higher Education.
42. Society for Human Resource Management (2008).
43. Matos & Galinsky (2012), p. 1.
44. Society for Human Resource Management. (2008); Matos & Galinsky (2012).
45. Gappa et al. (2007).
46. U.S. Bureau of Labor Statistics. (2005). *Employment projections.* Retrieved from www.bls.gov/ emp/#tables
47. Trower (2012), pp. 6–8; Matos & Galinsky (2012), p. 1.
48. Galinsky, E., Aumann, K., & Bond, J.T. (2011). *Times are changing: Gender and generation at work and at home.* New York, NY: Families and Work Institute. Retrieved from http:// familiesandwork.org/downloads/TimesAreChanging.pdf

21

49. U.S. Bureau of Labor Statistics. (2009). *Issues in labor statistics, April 2009.* Retrieved from www.bls.gov/opub/ils/pdf/opbils74.pdf

50. Trower (2012).

51. Galinsky et al. (2011).

52. Mason, M.A., Goulden, M., & Frasch, K. (2009). *Why graduate students reject the fast track.* Retrieved from www.aaup.org/article/why-graduate-students-reject-fast-track#.UnIO_hCzLpc

53. West, M.S., & Curtis, J.W. (2006). *AAUP faculty gender equity indicators 2006.* Retrieved from www.aaup.org/AAUP/pubsres/research/geneq2006.htm

54. Ward & Wolf-Wendel (2012).

55. National Center for Education Statistics. (2010). *The condition of education 2010* (NCES 2010–028). Washington, DC: U.S. Department of Education.

56. West & Curtis (2006).

57. National Research Council. (2007). *Beyond bias and barriers: Fulfilling the potential of women in academic science and engineering.* Washington, DC: The National Academies Press; Mayer A.L., & Tikka, P.M. (2008). Family friendly policies and gender bias in academia. *Journal of Higher Education Policy and Management, 30*(4), 363–374.

58. Kulis, S., Sicotte, D., & Collins, S. (2002). More than a pipeline problem: Labor supply constraints and gender stratification across academic science disciplines. *Research in Higher Education, 43*(6), 657–690; Mason, M.A., & Goulden, M. (2004). Marriage and baby blues: Redefining gender equity in the academy. *The Annals of the American Academy of Political and Social Science, 596,* 86–103; Trower, C.A. (2002, January 25). *Women without tenure, Part 2: The gender sieve.* Retrieved from http://sciencecareers.sciencemag.org/career_magazine/previous_issues/articles/2002_01_25/nodoi.7900867231599505905

59. Harrington, B., & Ladge, J.J. (2009). The evolution of work-life: Present dynamics and future directions for organizations. *Organizational Dynamics, 38*(2), 131–147.

60. Galinsky et al. (2011).

61. Trower (2002).

62. Trower (2012), p. 22.

63. The Center for WorkLife Law, UC Hastings College of the Law. (2013). *Effective policies and programs for retention and advancement of women in academia.* Retrieved from http://worklifelaw.org/wp-content/uploads/2013/01/Effective-Policies-and-Programs-for-Retention-and-Advancement-of-Women-in-Academia.pdf

64. The Center for WorkLife Law (2012).

65. Council of Economic Advisors (2010).

66. Matos & Galinsky (2012).

67. U.S. Department of Labor Statistics. (2011). *Employment characteristics of families summary.* Retrieved from www.bls.gov/news.release/famee.nr0.htm

68. Astin, H.S., & Milem, J.F. (1997). The status of academic couples in U.S. institutions. In M.A. Ferber & J.W. Loeb (Eds.), *Academic couples: Problems and promises* (pp. 128–155). Urbana: University of Illinois Press; Philipsen & Bostic (2010).

69. Philipsen & Bostic (2010); Gappa et al. (2007); Wolf-Wendel, L., Twombly, S.B., & Rice, S. (2003). *The two-body problem: Dual-career-couple hiring practices in higher education.* Baltimore, MD: The Johns Hopkins University Press.

70. Gappa et al. (2007).

71. Harrington & Ladge (2009).

72. Galinsky et al. (2004).

73. Trower (2012).

74. Trower (2012), p. 23.

75. Duxbury, L. (2013). *Adding new work-life data to the research vault: The 2012 national study.* Keynote presentation for the Annual Conference of the College and University Work-Life-Family Association, Toronto, Canada.

76. Trower (2012).
77. Trower (2012), pp. 4–5.
78. Trower (2012), p. 13.
79. Trower (2012).
80. Galinsky, E., Aumann, K., & Bond, J.T. (2011). *Times are changing: Gender and generation at work and at home.* 2008 National Study of the Changing Workforce. Retrieved from http://familiesandwork.org/downloads/TimesAreChanging.pdf
81. Council of Economic Advisors (2010).
82. Voydanoff, P. (2005). Toward a conceptualization of perceived work-family fit and balance: A demands and resources approach. *Journal of Marriage and Family, 67*(4), 822–836; Edwards, J.A., Van Laar, D., Easton, S., & Kinman, G. (2009). The work-related quality of life scale for higher education employees. *Quality in Higher Education, 15*(3), 207–219.
83. Gornick, J. & Meyer[s], M. (2005). Supporting a dual earner/dual career society. In Heyman, J. & Beem, C. (Eds). *Unfinished work: Building equality and democracy in an era of working families.* New York: The New Press.
84. The notion of an ideal worker was introduced by Arlie Hochschild (1995) to describe an employee who is completely dedicated and committed to work without outside responsibilities or distractions.
85. Galinsky et al. (2011), p. 9.
86. Galinsky et al. (2011).
87. Harrington, B., Van Deusen, F., & Ladge, J. J. (2010). *The new dad: Exploring fatherhood within a career context.* Chestnut Hill, MA: Boston College Center for Work & Family.
88. Drago, R., & Williams, J. (2000). A half-time tenure track proposal. *Change: The Magazine of Higher Learning, 32*(6), 46–51.
89. Parker, K., & Wang, W. (2013). *Modern parenthood: Roles of moms and dads converge as they balance work and family.* Retrieved from www.pewsocialtrends.org/2013/03/14/modern-parenthood-roles-of-moms-and-dads-converge-as-they-balance-work-and-family
90. Harrington & Ladge (2009), p. 4.
91. Aumann, K., Galinsky, E., Sakai, K., Brown, M., & Bond, J.T. (2008). *The elder care study: Everyday realities and wishes for change.* New York, NY: Families and Work Institute.
92. Gallie, D., & Russell, H. (2009). Work-family conflict and working conditions in Western Europe. *Social Indicators Research, 93*(3), 445–467.
93. Hoffman, C., Sullivan, S., & Nuter, J. (2012). *How to make the business case for work-life balance.* Retrieved from http://worklife.columbia.edu/files_worklife/public/n_in_Higher_Ed_Hoffman_Article_Sept_2012__2_.pdf#
94. Koppes, L. L., & Civian, J. (2010, May). *CUWFA findings: State of work-life survey.* Presentation for the Annual Conference of the College and University Work Family Association, Harvard University, Boston, MA.
95. American Council on Education. (2013b). *Making the business case: The imperative for supporting and promoting workplace flexibility in higher education.* Retrieved from www.acenet.edu/news-room/Pages/Making-the-Business-Case-for-Workplace-Flexibility.aspx
96. Austin, A. E. (2002). Preparing the next generation of faculty: Graduate education as socialization to the academic career. *The Journal of Higher Education, 73*(1), 94–122.
97. Mason et al. (2009).
98. Rice, R. E., Sorcinelli, M. D., & Austin, A. E. (2000). Heeding new voices: Academic careers for a new generation. *New Pathways Inquiry #7.* Washington, DC: American Association for Higher Education.
99. Ward & Wolf-Wendel (2012), p. 12.
100. Philipsen & Bostic (2010), p. 27.
101. Connelly, R., & Ghodsee, K. (2011). *Professor mommy: Finding work-family balance in academia.* Lanham, MD: Rowman & Littlefield; Evans, E., & Grant, C. (2009). *Mama PhD: Women write about motherhood and academic life.* New Brunswick, NJ: Rutgers University Press; Mason,

M.A., & Ekman, E. M. (2007). *Mothers on the fast track: How a new generation can balance family and careers.* New York, NY: Oxford University Press; Monosson, E. (Ed.). (2008). *Motherhood, the elephant in the laboratory: Women scientists speak out.* Ithaca, NY: Cornell University Press.

102. Lester & Sallee (2009); Nuter, J. L. (2011). *Work life practitioners: A force for change in the academic setting.* (Unpublished doctoral dissertation). Benedictine University, Lisle, IL; Philipsen, M. (2008). *Challenges of the faculty career for women: Success and sacrifice.* San Francisco, CA: Jossey-Bass; Philipsen & Bostic (2010).

103. Van Deusen et al. (2008).

104. Dickson, C. E. (2008). Antecedents and consequences of perceived family responsibilities discrimination in the workplace. *The Psychologist-Manager Journal, 11*(1), 113–140, p. 120.

105. Drago, R. (2007). *Striking a balance: work, family, life.* Boston, MA: Dollars & Sense.

106. Wolf-Wendel, L., & Ward, K. (2006). Academic life and motherhood: Variations by institutional type. *Higher Education, 52*(3), 487–521, p. 495.

107. Galinsky, E., Bond, J.T., & Friedman, D.E. (1996). The role of employers in addressing the needs of employed parents. *Journal of Social Issues, 52*(3), 111–136; Koppes, L. L. (2008). Facilitating an organization to embrace a work-life effectiveness culture: A practical approach. *The Psychologist-Manager Journal, 11*(1), 163–184; Kossek, E. E., & Lambert, S. J. (Eds.). (2005). *Work and life integration: Organizational, cultural, and individual perspectives.* Mahwah, NJ: Lawrence Erlbaum Associates; Pitt-Catsouphes, M., Kossek, E. E., & Sweet, S.A. (2006). *The work and family handbook: Multi-disciplinary perspectives, methods, and approaches.* Mahwah, NJ: Lawrence Erlbaum Associates.

108. Schein, E. (1990). Organizational culture. *American Psychologist, 45*(2), 109–119; Harrington, B. (2008, March). *The evolution of the work-life field.* Presentation at the Annual CUWFA Conference, University of North Carolina, Chapel Hill.

109. Hammer, L., Kossek, E., Yragui, N., Bodner, T., & Hanson, G. (2009). Development and validation of a multidimensional measure of family supportive supervisor behaviors (FSSB). *Journal of Management, 35*(4), 837–856; Koppes, L. L., & Schneider, S. (2009, June). *What leadership behaviors do employees find helpful for their work-life effectiveness?* Seminar conducted at the meeting of the College and University Work/Family Association, Seattle, WA; Koppes, L. L., Schneider, S. K., & Linnabery, E. (2009, April). What managers' behaviors support employees and their work-life effectiveness? In L. L. Koppes (Chair), *Multiple paths in driving engagement through work-life flexibility.* Symposium conducted at the annual meeting of the Society for Industrial and Organizational Psychology, New Orleans, LA; Koppes, L. L., Schneider, S., Linnabery, E., Dollwet, M., & Bogese, C. (2010, April). Leader behaviors that support work-life of university staff. In L. L. Koppes (Chair), *Leadership and work-life effectiveness in universities.* Symposium conducted at the Annual Conference of the Society for Industrial and Organizational Psychology, Atlanta, GA.

110. Allen, (2001); Erdogan, B., & Enders, J. (2007). Support from the top: Supervisors' perceived organizational support as a moderator of leader-member exchange to satisfaction and performance relationships. *Journal of Applied Psychology, 92*(2), 321–330; Koppes, L. L., & Swanberg, J. (Eds.). (2008). Work-life effectiveness: Implications for organizations [Special issue]. *The Psychologist-Manager Journal;* Thompson, C.A., Beauvais, L.L., & Lyness, K. S. (1999). When work-family benefits are not enough: The influence of work-family culture on benefit utilization, organizational attachment, and work-family conflict. *Journal of Vocational Behavior, 54*(3), 392–415.

111. Hammer et al. (2007); Hammer et al. (2009); Koppes & Civian (2010); Koppes & Swanberg (2008); Yen, J.W., Lange, S. E., Riskin, E.A., & Denton, D. D. (2004). *Leadership development workshops for department chairs,* WEPAN 2004 Conference Proceedings, Albuquerque, NM.

112. Ryan & Kossek (2008); Thompson et al. (1999); Allen (2001); LaPierre, L. M., Spector, P. E., Allen, T. D., Poelmans, S., Cooper, C. L., O'Driscoll, M. P., . . . Kinnunen, U. (2008). Family-supportive organization perceptions, multiple dimensions of work-family conflict, and employee satisfaction: A test of model across five samples. *Journal of Vocational Behavior,*

73(1), 92–106; Smith & Gardner (2007); O'Neill, J.W., Harrison, M.W., Cleveland, J., Almeida, D., Stawski, R., & Crouter, A. C. (2009). Work-family climate, organizational commitment, and turnover: Multilevel contagion effects of leaders. *Journal of Vocational Behavior, 74*(1), 18–29.

113. American Council on Education (2005); Smith, G. C., & Waltman, J.A. (2006). *Designing and implementing family-friendly policies in higher education.* Retrieved from www.cew.umich.edu/sites/default/files/designing06.pdf; Yen et al. (2004).
114. Philipsen & Bostic (2010).
115. American Council on Education (2005).

Chapter 2

Understanding Work-Life Challenges

Research on work-life challenges in higher education began as early as the 1980s and it remains an emerging area of scholarship; studies have proliferated in the past 15 years.[1] These studies examine work-life in the context of understanding the job satisfaction of faculty and staff and offering specific recommendations for best family-friendly practices.[2] Most attention in both practice and research has been given to full-time faculty at research-intensive universities rather than those at other types of universities such as master's comprehensive, liberal arts colleges, historically black colleges and universities (HCBUs), or community colleges.[3] The focus on faculty is because institutions recognized early on that work-life support would enhance recruitment and retention of the most talented faculty. Two studies, the women's study and the men's study, describe the challenges that both female and male faculty face when managing their professional and personal lives. Throughout the text *Helping Faculty Find Work-Life Balance,* the authors integrate stories of faculty members with institutional efforts. Staff, students, and adjunct faculty have specific work-life needs, too, yet attention to their needs appears primarily in discussions of strategies rather than in empirical research findings.[4] Although these authors and other researchers consistently acknowledge the importance of the leadership and administration, there is currently no text that specifically addresses the stories of leaders in higher education—such stories appear here in Chapter 5. The purpose of this chapter is to provide an overview of activities in higher education institutions by providing work-life definitions, followed by a look at recent scholarly efforts, and a description of higher education initiatives.

WORK-LIFE SATISFACTION AND EFFECTIVENESS

As we have noted, since the 1980s, academic scholars and practitioners have examined the linkages between work and family issues because of concerns about real and potential conflicts between work and family caregiving responsibilities.[5] Initially, work and family "balance" was emphasized; to be balanced was to approach each role (i.e., work and personal/family) with approximately equal levels of time and/or commitment.[6] Additionally, the idea of balance refers to a maintained equilibrium between one's work obligations and one's role outside of work with related family responsibilities.[7] Balance also implies an equal level of attention, time, involvement, or commitment to these multiple roles and responsibilities.[8] The assumption is that individuals who achieve a greater balance between their dual roles as employees and family members are more effective in their role-specific contexts than individuals with less balance between these roles.[9] The term "work-family conflict," then, has been widely used to indicate when such balance is not achieved, resulting in stress both at home and at work.

In recent years, the word "balance" has been replaced by other terms to better reflect the management of multiple obligations. Scholars and practitioners have realized that it is possible to manage these various responsibilities without achieving a specific, equal balance. Other concepts in the literature that refer to these situations include work-family interference, work-family facilitation, and work-family enrichment.[10] Moreover, because of the changing demographics of the workforce over the past decade, practitioners have formally recognized that workers are whole human beings with multiple aspects to their personal lives in addition to caregiving responsibilities; thus, the trend has been to move away from work-family to "work-life" because the latter reflects connections between work experiences and myriad life issues.[11] Increased attention, now, is given to achieving work-life enrichment, work-life integration, work-life interaction, work-life effectiveness, and work-life satisfaction. These concepts highlight a mutually beneficial relationship between work and life because workers are effectively managing multiple roles and responsibilities.[12] Indeed, one recent author advocated for "work-life energy."[13]

In some contexts, "career-life initiative" or "career flexibility" are terms that are used in lieu of work-life balance because these terms emphasize *flexibility*. For example, ACE's recent national challenge to support workplace flexibility includes the following statement of support:

> "Move from work life balance to work life energy ... Stop trying to balance and start thinking about ways we can be fully energized and creative for all of our life."[14]

Based on extensive research in the private sector and ACE's own experience in assisting institutions in working toward workplace *flexibility* in the last 10 years, we believe that well-implemented supports for workplace *flexibility* lead to improved recruiting, increased faculty commitment and engagement, greater productivity, reduced turnover, and reduced stress. These factors help to increase institutional capacity to advance the mission and to meet strategic goals of diversity and inclusion by supporting a harmonic workplace culture that fosters academic excellence.[15]

27

Definition of Work-Life Satisfaction/Effectiveness

For the purposes of this text, the concepts of work-life satisfaction and work-life effectiveness are used most broadly. Work-life satisfaction is the "positive feeling that individuals develop when they feel they are suc-

> "When work is effective, life benefits; and when life is working, work benefits."[16]

cessfully meeting the demands of work and personal life."[17] Work-life effectiveness is achieved when a mutually beneficial relationship exists between work and life.

For example, Emory University defines work-life effectiveness on its Work Life Resource Center website as follows:

- Finding meaningful achievement of the things you enjoy most on a daily basis. This might include factors such as your family, friends, self, spirituality, and work.
- A work-life balance does not mean an equal balance of all factors.
- What works for one person does not work for all people.
- What works for you now may not work for you in the future. You must continually reassess your situation and make changes as necessary.[18]

Research Findings of Faculty and Staff Work-Life Satisfaction

The Collaborative on Academic Careers in Higher Education (COACHE) survey measures job satisfaction and success of faculty from various universities.[19] Trower's recent text, *Success on the Tenure Track: Five Keys to Faculty Job Satisfaction*, highlights the findings from exemplary public research institutions, including questions about satisfaction with work-life balance.[20] One particular item asked the survey respondents to indicate their satisfaction or dissatisfaction with "the balance you are able to strike between professional time and your personal or family time."[21] The average rating was 2.81 on a 5-point scale with 1 being "very dissatisfied" and 5 being "very satisfied." This rating, along with ratings reflecting other specific work-life issues (i.e., having and raising children in the academy), is among the lowest of the survey.[22] In another study, university employees were found to be significantly more negative about the work-family climate at their workplaces than employees in industry.[23] Additional research studies have been conducted to assess work-life satisfaction of faculty in academia, by examining variations by institutional type, community colleges, and non-tenure track faculty.[24]

As described in Chapter 1, effectively managing one's work and personal life increases job and family satisfaction, well-being, and organizational commitment.[25] A greater level of work-life satisfaction also results in increased individual work performance as well as increased organization profitability.[26] Conflicts between work and life responsibilities, on the other hand, have been found to be directly related to negative job-related outcomes such as job dissatisfaction and turnover[27] as well as psychological and physiological indicators of stress.[28] Data clearly show that the majority of academic employees experience challenges in effectively managing work and personal/family life,[29] and a landmark study revealed the effects of family responsibilities on academic success.[30]

Institutions leading the way to support work-life satisfaction of faculty and staff regularly conduct surveys to gain an understanding of the work-life needs of their specific cultures. As will be discussed in Chapter 3, in order to shape a culture that is supportive of work-life satisfaction and effectiveness, it is first important to identify the needs of employees. These institutions striving for a work-life friendly culture or climate have gathered data about their members' satisfaction as well as issues about the climate and culture. The University of California system, The Ohio State University, University of Kentucky, and Oregon State University, to name a few, have collected such data about their faculty and staff.

WORK-LIFE CHALLENGES

Studies seeking to understand work-life satisfaction and effectiveness have shifted from focusing on women in their child-bearing years to encompass a broader life cycle perspective. Employees experience work-life challenges throughout their careers because of the needs of school-aged children, elderly parents, advancement in rank, retirement, and so forth. During April 2014, academic practitioners shared their perceptions of top work-life issues on the CUWFA listserve such as, flexibility, workload, diversity, well-being, cultural change, stress management, childcare, lactation support, retirement, and boundary management. Leading work-life institutions acknowledge and respond to these work-life issues across the life span. Thus, the umbrella of work-life can range from specific family concerns, such as caregiving, to a broader definition of quality of work and life at the university. The Families and Work Institute identified the following six criteria of effective workplaces: job challenge and learning, autonomy, supervisor task support, climate of respect and trust, economic security, and work-life fit.[31] The University of Kentucky conducted two Work-Life surveys in which they identified a wide range of specific issues of concern to their faculty and staff: trust, value, communication, career development, inclusivity, burnout, child care, and elder care.[32] It is beyond the scope of this text to provide a review of all dimensions of an effective workplace and all work-life issues; however, in the following sections we present some of the most pervasive work-life challenges and consider their implications for academic leadership.

A Gender Gap

An increased attention to work-life in academia can be linked to the observation of a gender gap between women and men faculty with regard to advancement in the professoriate. As explained in Chapter 1, overall, women represent a lower percent of the tenure-track (44%) and tenured faculty (30%),[33] and constitute 39% of all full-time faculty nationwide.[34] Seventy to eighty percent of the tenure-track jobs at research institutions are held by men.[35] This representation of women is surprising given that the number of doctorates awarded to women has been increasing consistently across all disciplines, with women earning 45% of all doctorates in 2008, and more women than men have earned bachelor's degrees and master's degrees since 1982.[36] When starting doctoral programs, 45% of men and 39% of women wanted to pursue a professorship with a research focus. However, at follow-up (1 to 7 years later) only 36% of men and 27% of women maintained this career goal.[37]

In the disciplines of science and engineering, although women earn 40% of the doctorate degrees, they constitute only 28% of tenured or tenure-track faculty; this figure declines to 19% for full professor positions.[38] In 2005–2006, women held 24% of the full professor positions at all institutions nationwide, while men held 76% of those positions.[39] The lowest percentages of women full professors were in highly prestigious paid positions.[40] As recently as 2010, 43% of full professors were women across all campuses in the United States.[41]

Why the gap? The most robust explanation is the gendered nature of faculty work and the resulting gender biases. Early work-life research focused on the perspective of gender inequity in the academy and the implications for tenure.[42] Faculty positions have traditionally been designed for the male professor as the predominant worker within a family structure where the husbands and fathers were the professors and the wives and mothers stayed at home. In this scenario, the male professor was the ideal worker because he could devote all of his time to work. This male-centered approach does not take into consideration that the beginning of the tenure track usually occurs during the time a woman wants to begin a family[43] and the biological cycle during which most women have children.

Consequently, female faculty face much greater odds[44] because the nature of faculty work is designed to accommodate a male career trajectory.[45] Most tenure-track positions do not offer the flexibility for women to manage families and children while also maintaining their professional productivity; thus, many women abandon their tenure pursuits in favor of job opportunities that allow for improved work flexibility.[46] Some women leave the academy altogether, while others pursue faculty positions in different types of institutions, such as community colleges, comprehensive institutions, or liberal arts colleges, where the scholarship expectations are different from those of research-intensive institutions. Research has shown that marriage and having young children have strong negative effects on the probability of women entering tenure-track positions.[47]

The uncertainty of being able to become tenured following the probationary period results in many faculty postponing a family until they achieve tenure. Female faculty also report pressures to relinquish childbearing or to hide their pregnancies.[48] In cases where children are already members of the family, the strain of work responsibilities often overshadows family duties, creating conflict and stress. For women faculty who do stay the course and earn tenure, personal sacrifices may be made. Women in tenure-track positions are more likely to be single and childless or single parents than are men or women in non-tenure track jobs.[49] Women who achieve tenure are more than twice as likely as tenured male faculty to be single 12 years after earning the doctorate and more likely to be single and childless in general than male academics.[50] Almost half of female faculty members remain childless, regardless of marital status, while the majority of their male counterparts marry and have children.[51] Clearly, there is a disparate impact on men and women having children, resulting in a significant equity issue in the academy.

Research studies have consistently revealed a chilly climate upon examining the reasons that women leave the academy, especially as they progress through the pipeline.[52] Yet, as several studies have noted, "attempts to mitigate that chilly climate have failed to address fundamental issues of unexamined bias and gender stereotyping that continue to drive women out of the academy."[53] For example, academic leaders find it difficult to compete for the best candidates when biased remarks by search committee members may reflect an unsupportive climate to candidates.

Gender bias can take many different forms, some that are directly observable and others that are more subtle. The Center for WorkLife Law has identified four basic patterns of gender bias:

- The Maternal Wall: Bias experienced by women when they have children;
- Prove-It-Again: Bias experienced by women whey they have to work hard to establish competence;
- Double Bind: Bias experienced by women when assertive women are seen as difficult or aggressive even though the job requires a proactive or assertive approach;
- Gender Wars: When gender bias pits women against each other.

In addition to these patterns, results from focus groups revealed numerous other biases experienced in the academy, such as ambivalent sexism in teaching and service demands (heavier loads for women); social isolation or not fitting in; senior women taking on traditionally patriarchal roles and snubbing junior faculty; students' ambivalent sexism and challenges to women's authority; and caregiving bias avoidance.[54]

Bias Against Using Work-Life Friendly Policies

As noted in Chapter 1, employees will minimize or hide family commitments as a response to biases against caregivers. Female faculty, in particular, believe taking short-term parental leave will be detrimental to their tenure decisions.[55] In a study of more than 1,300 faculty, 33% of women faculty opted not to take their designated maternity leaves because of concerns about tenure and only 30% opted to take the full leave for childbirth as provided by the university.[56] Recently, an entire special issue of *Journal of Social Issues* was devoted to the stigma linked with workplace flexibility.[57]

"A 2002 national survey of over 4,000 faculty members revealed that 33% of faculty who were parents—mothers and fathers—did not ask for parental leave, and just less than 20% did not ask to stop the tenure clock, even though they thought they would have benefited from doing so."[58]

A survey of 4,188 faculty found a substantial engagement in bias avoidance (BA) behaviors. The empirical research demonstrated two types of bias avoidance behaviors: productive BA behaviors and unproductive BA behaviors. A productive

"Forty-two percent of tenure-track females report returning to work sooner after childbirth than they would have liked."[59]

BA occurs when a faculty member minimizes family commitments to facilitate career success by improving work performance. An unproductive BA occurs when a faculty member disguises family commitments to give the appearance of career commitment.[60] One important finding is that these behaviors are gendered, meaning that women engage more frequently in both unproductive and productive behaviors then men.

Biases in the workplace can result in caregiver discrimination, introduced in Chapter 1 as family responsibilities discrimination (FRD), which includes discrimination against workers because of their caregiving responsibilities (Table 2.1). Unfortunately, employers do often base personnel-related decisions on the biases and stereotypes about the ways in which caregivers will perform, given their family responsibilities.[61]

Table 2.1 Examples of Family Responsibilities Discrimination (FRD)

- firing or demoting employees when they become pregnant;
- passing over highly qualified mothers for hire or promotion in favor of less qualified fathers or women without children;
- firing employees without valid business reasons when they return from maternity or paternity leave;
- denying flexibility to employees who want it for child care reasons, while allowing flexibility to employees for non-family reasons (e.g., to participate on a sports team);
- firing employees whose spouses or elderly parents become disabled for fear of increased absenteeism or higher health insurance premiums; and
- fabricating work infractions or performance deficiencies to justify dismissal of employees with family responsibilities.[i]

---

[i] The Center for WorkLife Law (2013), see endnote 36 in Chapter 1.

Researchers have revealed that a "family-responsive organizational climate" is related to reduced levels of bias avoidance and FRD. We will discuss supportive institutional and departmental cultures in Chapter 4.

Although women's issues have been at the forefront of work-family research and practice, the challenges men face in integrating work and the rest of their lives have often been overlooked. It had been generally assumed that family-friendly benefits and supportive leader behaviors were more attractive to and relevant for women than for men. Yet, as more fathers take more active roles in raising their children, these family-friendly benefits are equally attractive to parents of both genders.[62]

Caregiving

Child Care: Motherhood and Fatherhood

There is a parenting divide in contemporary society, in which parents experience greater time pressures than non-parents because of their added roles.[63] For example, employed parents in comparison with employed non-parents frequently reported feelings of increased time pressure, a perceived lack of work-life balance, and a decreased sense of emotional well-being.[64] An increasing number of dual-earning couples with children prefer a more supportive work-life environment.[65]

Researchers consistently reveal the challenges of academic motherhood. In fact, there are entire books devoted to these challenges, including *Academic Motherhood: How Faculty Manage Work and Family* [66] and *Do Babies Matter? Gender and Family in the Ivory Tower,*[67] which clearly reflect the challenges faced by women in taking on multiple roles and responsibilities as well as the biases often exhibited toward mothers. From a survey of women faculty,

> 16 percent stayed single because they believed they did not have time for a family and a successful academic career, 25.5 percent had fewer children than they wanted in order to achieve academic success, and nearly 13 percent delayed having a second child until after receiving tenure.[68]

Indeed, "Women with children leave the academy at a disproportionately higher rate than men, experience conflicts between academic work and motherhood, and report difficulties in reentering academe after leaving the professoriate."[69] In a study of 800 postdoctoral fellows at University of California-Berkeley (UC-Berkeley), "59 percent of married women with children considering leaving academe."[70] As discussed previously, the simultaneous ticking of tenure and biological clocks is a challenge for women. Although women graduate students are advised not to get pregnant during graduate school and to wait until they are tenured to have children, waiting poses many risks associated with being outside the prime years for childbearing.[71]

In addition to the timing of pregnancy, the significant workload associated with caregiving can be challenging, including the need for lactation support. Female faculty with children reported an average total of 101 hours per week engaged in professional, housework, and caregiving activities, whereas male faculty with children reported an average of 88 hours per week engaged in these activities. Men and women faculty without children reported working an average of 78 hours per week.[72] Research has also shown that female faculty with dependent children exhibit a lower level of research productivity than their counterparts without dependent children; however, among men, having dependent children is associated with more research productivity.[73]

In addition to facing the pressures associated with the desire to start a family and assumption of caregiving responsibilities, women assistant professors find that senior women colleagues are not always supportive of young untenured professors becoming mothers. The senior women inform their young counterparts that (a) their career progression will be harmed by taking time off from work for child care, (b) not all their needs will be covered by benefits such as maternity leave, child care, and tenure clock extension, and (c) the likelihood of achieving tenure is reduced by having children before tenure.[74] Other research findings on women faculty as mothers are in Table 2.2. In one study,

> about 30% of women respondents who had no children before taking a tenure-track faculty position ever became mothers, and those who did have children were twice as likely as male faculty to convey that they had fewer children than they originally wanted.[75]

Other research finds that women are held to higher performance and time commitment standards when they are mothers as compared with non-mothers, while fathers are held to lower performance and time commitment standards than their non-father peers, and they are also held to lower standards compared with mothers.[76]

"Leaving a faculty position mid-semester in order to take a six-week maternity leave is not at all comparable to leaving any other job for maternity leave, since the faculty member still has to plan the entire course, has to leave instructions for the people covering her classes, usually has to respond to e-mail questions from both the faculty and students during her maternity leave, and possibly has to come back to submit grades." (Dr. Therese Bennett, Department Chair, Southern Connecticut State University)

More recently, academic men are also reporting greater stress and conflict from parenting.[77] Although gender inequity still exists, there is growing dissatisfaction among men faculty, especially the younger generation. Men of younger generations are more involved as parents than those from older generations, and this involvement has created changing roles and engagement with caregiving and

Table 2.2 Research Findings on Women Faculty as Mothers

- "Over all disciplines in the U.S., 52 per cent of women in tenure-track jobs have children, whereas 75 per cent of men have children."[i]

- "Broken down further by rank among female academic staff, 31 per cent of junior staff have children, and 49 per cent of tenured staff have children, illustrating the practice of delaying children (through either childbirth or adoption) until after tenure."[ii]

- "Of women in non-tenure track faculty positions, 66 per cent have children."[iii]

- Analyses from the Survey of Doctorate Recipients (SDR) indicate that for each year after the PhD, married men with children under 6 are 50% more likely to enter a tenure-track position than are married women with children under 6.[iv]

- Many women with early babies (within five years of the PhD) leave academia before obtaining their first tenure-track job.[v]

- Women with late babies (more than five years after the PhD) do as well as women without children.[vi]

- "While the likelihood of obtaining tenure drastically declines for women who have children within their first five years on the tenure track, a male academic's likelihood of obtaining tenure increases by 38 percent should he become a father during this period."[vii]

[i] Mayer & Tikka (2008), p. 367, see endnote 57 in Chapter 1.
[ii] Mayer & Tikka (2008), pp. 367, 370, see endnote 57 in Chapter 1.
[iii] Mayer & Tikka (2008), p. 370, see endnote 57 in Chapter 1.
[iv] Mason & Goulden (2004), see endnote 58 in Chapter 1.
[v] Mason & Goulden (2004), see endnote 58 in Chapter 1.
[vi] Mason & Goulden (2004), see endnote 58 in Chapter 1.
[vii] Trower (2012), p. 70, see endnote 10 in Chapter 1.

domestic work. Junior faculty fathers demonstrating a commitment to their children heavily emphasize the importance of being an engaged parent, and scholarly interest in the male perspective is increasing accordingly.[78]

A recent study in which in-depth interviews were conducted with junior male tenure-track faculty with children, researchers found that respondents identified pervasive conflict and strain associated with family responsibilities. Additionally, the research participants noted that the stress from pressures for work productivity impacted their family obligations. They also perceived a bias against active fathering. The respondents noted that their comfort level with discussing family and work responsibilities depended upon the department's culture.[79] Comparing the 2002–2003 data from The National Study of the Changing Workforce with the same study from 1977, researchers learned that men were spending about an hour more per weekday performing housework than they had been performing 25 years earlier.[80]

Focus group participants "agree that their male colleagues seem to get a 'pass' for their family status," yet some research suggests that men are penalized for transgressing the normative expectation of the ideal worker if they take time off from work for family needs. Workplace cultures present barriers to men's family caregiving, such as when an employee's superiors are not supportive of fathering and when the organizational culture fosters a norm of long working hours,[81] which is often the case in academia. Even when workplace and federal policies provide for job-protected family leave, men are far less likely than women to take family leave, for fear of employer reprisal.[82]

For both professional mothers and fathers, a lack of accommodations for faculty parents can be problematic. Although some institutions may provide child-care centers, these centers may not offer emergency back-up care or care during professional travel. Expenses associated with child care can be a significant financial issue for tenure-track parents.[83] Furthermore, having a child during the academic year can be challenging, especially if parental leave is not available. In some institutions, extending the tenure clock has been offered, but unfortunately, promotion and tenure committees may heighten expectations because of the perception that the candidate has had "more time" to be productive:[84] "A study of assistant professors at Ohio State finds that despite an expressed interest in reducing working hours and the provision of policies for part-time work, only 23% of faculty members have ever used the policy."[85] Between 1992 and 1999, 500 faculty members at one institution became new parents, yet only 7 parental leaves were taken, and none of these were taken by men.[86] This low participation suggests a pervasive cultural expectation in academia not to participate in reduced or part-time work.[87]

Elder Care

Caring for dependent adults or elders is on the rise as the U.S. population ages, providing challenges for both men and women faced with these caregiving responsibilities. When caring for elders, individuals may experience considerable anxiety because of the unknown and unpredictable circumstances, primarily involving medical, physical, emotional, and financial concerns. The care involves a wide range of activities, including preparing meals, providing transportation, assisting with shopping, offering financial assistance, performing household chores, lending emotional support, and providing sick/medical care.[88] Difficult decisions must be made about such issues as finances, living arrangements, and a parent's ability to safely operate a vehicle (Table 2.3). Academic leaders can offer working caregivers flexibility to schedule caregiving activities, access to relevant and current information, financial assistance to support or provide care, and a caring and supportive emotional network.[89] These efforts are also helpful when caregiving for partners, spouses, siblings or other dependent adults (e.g. those with disabilities).

- Almost 1 in 2 individuals in the workforce (42% or nearly 54.6 million employees) has provided elder care over the past five years.
- Among those who provided care in the past five years, almost half (44%) care for more than one person.[90]

Table 2.3 The MetLife Study of Working Caregivers and Employer Health Care Costs: Key Findings[91]

- "Using the average additional cost of a series of major health conditions (such as depression, hypertension, and diabetes) reported by employees with eldercare responsibilities and non-caregiving employees, the estimated average additional health cost to employers is 8% more for those with eldercare responsibilities. Excess medical costs reached almost 11% for blue-collar caregivers and over 18% for male caregivers."

- "When extrapolated to the business sector generally, this 8% differential in health care for caregiving employees is estimated conservatively as costing U.S. employers $13.4 billion per year."

- "Employees providing eldercare were more likely to report fair or poor health in general."

- "Employees providing eldercare were significantly more likely to report depression, diabetes, hypertension, or pulmonary disease regardless of age, gender, and work type."

- "Female employees with eldercare responsibilities reported more stress at home than non-caregivers in every age group. Stress at home appears to affect younger female caregivers most frequently. Caregivers were more likely to report negative influences of personal life on their work."

- "Eldercare demands were associated with greater health risk behaviors."

- "Employed caregivers find it more difficult than non-caregivers to take care of their own health or participate in preventive health screenings."

- "Employees with eldercare responsibilities were more likely to report missed days of work."

- "Excess employee medical care costs associated with eldercare were highest among younger employees, males, and blue-collar workers."

- "Younger caregivers (ages 18 to 39) demonstrated significantly higher rates of cholesterol, hypertension, chronic obstructive pulmonary disease (COPD), depression, kidney disease, and heart disease in comparison to non-caregivers of the same age."

Sandwiched Generation

With both child and elder care, many individuals, especially those in mid-career, are faced with dual responsibilities. These individuals are referred to as the "sandwiched generation" because they are "sandwiched between the needs of their children and their parents, and often, but not always, their jobs."[93] In

> "Many of the elder caregivers are in the sandwich generation—46% of women who are caregivers and 40% of men also have children under the age of 18 at home."[92]

one study, 42% of 9,573 employees in 33 companies were caring for elders and also caring for children.[94] In another study conducted by the National Alliance for Caregiving and AARP, approximately 37% of caregivers of individuals over 18 years of age also had children under the age of 18 living with them:[95] "Researchers have found that those dealing with multigenerational caregiving and work roles tend to experience the highest levels of stress compared to those who engage in fewer role combinations."[96]

In a 10-year national study of dual-career couples in the sandwiched generation, child-care responsibilities decreased while parent-care obligations increased over time, and husbands and wives had higher levels of depression than the general population.[97]

Marriage

The challenges associated with marriage can be traced to the gender stereotypes regarding the roles of the wife and husband in the relationship. Women have traditionally been responsible for household chores and assume the role of caregiving, whereas the husband has been the breadwinner. These general role expectations have been prominent in academia. For example, one study revealed that 89% of female academics were married to full-time working professionals compared with only 56% of men.[98] Because of the gender stereotypes and expectations, married women's tenure outcomes can be adversely affected. In fact, a single female has greater odds of earning tenure than a male, but the opposite is true for married women.[99]

Within science and engineering disciplines, more than 83% of male scientists and engineers in academic positions are married, but less than 67% of their female peers are married. More than 14% of female science and engineering faculty have never married, whereas only 7% of male science and engineering faculty have never been married. Additionally, while only 42% of female science and engineering faculty have children in the household, over half of all male science and engineering faculty have children in the household:[100] "These statistics strongly suggest that in the academy, men are at greater leisure to pursue personal lives than women are."[101] Interestingly, publication rates increased by 40% for those individuals who marry academic professionals within their disciplines.[102] These intradisciplinary marital relationships may provide opportunities for collaboration and provide female academics access to male-dominated academic networks.[103]

Dual Career Marriages and Spouses

The number of dual-career couples including same-sex partners, is on the rise, especially in the academy, with 72% of faculty in dual-career relationships, of which 36% have academic partners.[104] According to a 2013 article in *The Chronicle of Higher Education*, "More than a third of research-university faculty have academics as partners, and of those, nearly 40 percent are coupled with someone who works in the very same department."[105] A study of over 9,000 research university professors, found that 40% of female faculty members are in academic couples, compared with 34% of males.[106]

Belonging to a dual academic career couple can positively affect productivity, yet at the same time, dual-career marriages can create a "two-body problem," which occurs when the husband or wife is offered an opportunity that requires relocating.[107] Additionally, an "accompanying-spouse gap" often occurs because women are more likely than men to follow their spouses, especially when children are involved.[108] This gap results in a substantial difference in salaries as well as career trajectories. For example, it is not unusual for accompanying spouses to be considered for part-time positions, but even when a full-time position is available, a stigma may surface about that spouse with regard to her or his commitment to her or his career.

> There are three key reasons for taking a new look at couple hiring: excellence, diversity, quality of life.[109]

Two-thirds of research institutions use dual-career assistance as a means of competing with other institutions to recruit top scholars.[110] Other institutions provide job assistance or dual-career accommodations, although many of these policies are unwritten. Despite these efforts, these accommodations often have a negative stigma attached to them. Some negative correlates may include questions or concerns about the source(s) of funding, the perception of double dipping, the indirect route of securing a position, the poor qualifications of the spouse, the potential for divorce, and so forth (Table 2.4).[111]

Table 2.4 Dual-Career Academic Couples: What Universities Need to Know: Key Findings[112]

- "Partners matter: Faculty members' career decisions are strongly influenced by partner employment status."

- "As a strategy to enhance competitive excellence, couple hiring (or dual hiring) is on the rise. Dual hires comprise an increasing proportion of all faculty hires over the last four decades (from 3% in the 1970s to 13% in the 2000s), whereas the proportion of academic couples has remained relatively constant."

- "Couple hiring can help build a more diverse, equitable, and competitive workforce, especially with regard to gender.
  - Women are more likely than men to have an academic partner.
  - Women in academic couples report that their partner's employment status and opportunities are important to their own career decisions.
  - Couple hiring is important to attract more female faculty to fields where women are underrepresented, such as the natural sciences and engineering.
  - Historically, men more than women have used their market power to bargain for positions for their partners.
  - An important finding is that recruiting women as first hires breaks the stereotype of senior academics seeking to negotiate jobs for junior partners."

- "Couple hiring may help to advance not only gender equity but also racial/ethnic diversity, which enhances competitive excellence."

- "Universities are in danger of losing prized candidates if suitable employment cannot be found for a partner."

- "Universities need to understand how policies and practices affect faculty attitudes toward dual hires on their campuses."

- "One problem with couple hiring is that a stigma of 'less good' often attaches to a second hire. Study data suggest, however, that second hires, when full-time faculty members, are not less productive than are their disciplinary peers."

Other Life Challenges

On one occasion, a human resources director commented that the institution's work-life initiatives were directed toward parents and caregiving, and was concerned about giving attention to faculty and staff who are not caregivers. This led to the question: what are other challenges associated with life? These challenges may include relocating to a new area for a job or buying a new house within the same location, social pursuits/obligations, increased family/home responsibilities during the holidays, or recreational activities. One of the most important responsibilities is enhancing and sustaining health and wellness. Eating nutritious foods can be expensive and challenging with campus events. Finding the time for fitness and exercise can also be difficult. Responding to illnesses and sickness can be problematic, especially during tenure-earning years or in the middle of the semester. Other obligations may include volunteer commitments to community organizations, religious and spiritual activities, and other hobbies that provide joy and happiness to one's life.

Over 70 million households in the United States have at least one pet or companion animal.[113] For many individuals, these pets are treated as best friends or family members, and research studies consistently demonstrate the benefits of companion animals on health and wellness, attitudes, and life satisfaction. Given the importance of pets in individuals' lives, these household members can pose work-life challenges, including daily care, health and wellness, sick care, and other expenses.

Research suggests that all employees (both parents and non-parents) appear to be looking for ways to be active in their work and also have meaningful involvement in their personal lives.[114] A 2006 survey showed that a majority of men surveyed agreed with women that life apart from work was equally important, or more important, than their jobs.[115] Thus, both men and women increasingly require flexibility at work to effectively manage their personal and professional responsibilities.[116] Ultimately, academic leaders are responsible for dispelling the stereotype that work-life only applies to parents; establishing a work-life culture and an environment that fosters an individual's overall well-being benefits everyone and increases productivity and job satisfaction.

Work Challenges

Much of the work-life literature focuses primarily on life needs and responsibilities. The other side of the equation, however, concerns those challenges associated with fulfilling work responsibilities (e.g. overwork, external research funding, stress management and burnout). Numerous texts provide advice on managing faculty work at all stages of one's career, especially with regard to teaching and scholarship; however, we mention a few work needs here that are important for faculty and staff to succeed and advance in their careers.

Service Obligations

Service obligations are one of the paradoxes of higher education, particularly for faculty at smaller institutions. That is, service nominally comprises the smallest percentage of faculty workload and is given the least consideration in performance reviews (i.e., promotion and tenure dossiers), yet many faculty members attest that they spend as much, if not more, time on their service obligations than on their teaching or research. Service receives an obligatory nod in many guides for tenure-track faculty where the necessity of performing service is noted, yet the attitude toward such work is often dismissive. As Steven M. Cahn writes in *From Student to Scholar: A Candid Guide to Becoming a Professor,* "The work itself is not especially challenging. It mostly involves listening to others talk and occasionally interjecting your own ideas. Helpful, too, is a taste for the ever-present cookies, chips, and cheese."[117] While Cahn advocates being a team player with regard to service, it is also presented as a distraction from the more important tasks of research and teaching. Similarly, James M. Lang opens his chapter on "Serving" in *Life on the Tenure Track: Lessons From the First Year* with the declaration "I hate meetings."[118] While Lang justifies his statement with a plea to make meetings both less frequent and more efficient (although he, too, appreciates the cookies), he shares with Cahn the general idea that service is less valued and more demanding, in terms of time and attention, than other aspects of a faculty member's obligations.

Eliminating, or even reducing, service obligations is not a reality for most faculty. Indeed, even attempts to "protect" tenure-track faculty from becoming mired in service and therefore unable to meet teaching and research expectations are becoming more problematic as the academy evolves and faculty responsibilities change. Nonetheless, there are ways to make service obligations more compatible with the work-life ideals of a department, college, or university. As noted earlier, flexible scheduling can have tremendous impact on a faculty member's ability to manage work and life obligations, and this flexibility should extend to meeting times as well as teaching schedules. For instance, a faculty member may prefer to contribute to new student orientation by participating in evening events rather than weekend activities. Helping faculty find service obligations that are meaningful can also contribute to overall job satisfaction and reduce the sense of service as meaningless work that detracts from time spent taking care of other job or family obligations. Governance, curriculum development, advising, and personnel (hiring, promotion, and tenure) are some of the major strands of service work available to faculty at most institutions, and each of these requires a particular skill set and enables the participants to make a unique contribution. An introverted, non-confrontational faculty member may not be the best choice for a representative to the University Senate, while a quantitatively-minded, detail-oriented person might be the perfect choice to spearhead curriculum review and assessment. Moreover, faculty with complicated family schedules may prefer

41

service work that is more independent while those looking to make connections across the university or community might pursue collaborative projects. Matching faculty with appropriate service responsibilities, rather than just assigning work, is one way that academic leaders can accommodate work-life needs and also improve overall commitment and job satisfaction.

Professional Development

A theme of professional development emerged prominently in response to a work-life survey by faculty at Oregon State University. Particularly important was the need for professional mentoring and support as well as removing barriers to professional development that might be caused by inexperienced department heads and chairs.[119] Mentoring, in particular, is an essential component of the success of junior faculty and the long-term effectiveness of the institution.[120]

> "The use of professional development as a means of supporting and valuing faculty has grown over the years. The percentage of tenure-track and tenured faculty who reported the availability of training to improve research or teaching skills grew from 51.2 in 1992 to 74.4 in 1998."[121]

Faculty professional development is

the process of nurturing the continuous learning, growth, and vitality of the faculty person (in all his or her roles) as a key member in meeting the aims/ goals of the organization, including long-lasting student learning and institutional agility in responding to internal and external forces.[122]

Professional development should promote learning and also empower faculty members to be vital contributors to the university's mission.[123] Faculty on the tenure track can be supported through professional development programs ranging from workshops on grant writing and starting a lab to best pedagogical strategies. Targeted development specifically designed to address the needs of minority and women faculty should also be offered.[124]

> ■ "Establishing effective mentoring programs can help universities improve retention rates, thereby decreasing the costs of start-up packages and retaining accomplished tenure-track faculty.
> ■ Having successful mentors can help new faculty understand the unspoken rules in academia, increase their workplace satisfaction and ultimately result in increased productivity.
> ■ Effective programs such as automatic mentor assignments and networking groups for women can dramatically improve the careers of faculty and strengthen the university as a whole."[125]

Retirement Transitions

As noted in Chapter 1, 50.5% of tenured faculty members are at least 55 years old.[126] Such a large number of impending faculty retirements poses challenges for both the institution and individual faculty members. What are the implications for institutions in managing the faculty composition? What are the challenges facing individual faculty as they approach the culminating stages of their careers? This section focuses on individual challenges, and for more information about the institutional perspective, we suggest reading the review of faculty retirement literature prepared by the ACE.[127]

According to the ACE review, the literature on faculty retirement before and after the elimination of mandatory retirement (1984–2004) focuses on trends in retirement rates, the implications of retirement trends, how faculty plan financially for retirement, and considerations affecting faculty members' decisions to retire. Since 2004, most research has continued to examine transactional issues (e.g., finances, phasing, benefits), but little research has investigated the experience of transitioning to retirements.[128]

From a work-life perspective, we are especially interested in the faculty member's experience while approaching and transitioning into retirement. As noted in the ACE report about retiring from a career, "because career roles are associated with status, identity, power, and money, this transition could be seen as a potential period of crisis" that could be as "devastating to the older individual as job loss at any time in life."[129] Faculty are not immune from experiencing this significant life adjustment. A three-phase framework can be used to describe faculty retirement transitions. First is *preretirement,* which is the "preparation and planning stage," occurring within five years of retirement. Second is *retirement,* which is the "action stage" occurring within six months of retirement to six months after retirement. Third is *postretirement,* which is the "maintenance stage."[130] Faculty face various challenges as they transition through these phases.

What do faculty members experience as they approach retirement, and what factors influence their retirement decisions? Many faculty approaching retirement are concerned with emeriti status, library privileges, office space, teaching opportunities after retirement, and maintaining their health

> "Many senior faculty members . . . want to adjust the level of their involvement in work while continuing some level of professional affiliation."[131]

insurance.[132] Studies have found that some faculty are choosing not to retire in order to keep medical insurance or to finish a particular project. When exploring the retirement decision, the role of the spouse and state of the individual's health are also considered, as is the relationship to the university:

The idea of a culminating legacy is important to many faculty members and institutions that support faculty in fulfilling these legacies will be the most effective in satisfying senior faculty who are dedicated to fulfilling the institution's mission both before *and after* they retire.[133]

There has been interest in examining the satisfaction, dissatisfaction, vitality, and productivity of faculty who stay in their positions beyond the traditional retirement age.[134] Women and minority faculty ages 50 or older revealed elevated levels of job-related stress and also reported feeling more under-appreciated and under-used by their institutions than their white male counterparts.[135]

What do retiring faculty members want from their institutions? Preretirement planning was found to be crucial to faculty satisfaction in retirement.[136] According to the ACE review, "Studies indicate that access to planning tools and information facilitates the retirement planning process, but many faculty do not feel their institutions provided them adequate access to such planning resources."[137] Those faculty late in their careers want institutional support to wrap up projects before they retire, and they also want alternatives to full retirement.[138] For example, many faculty want to phase into retirement rather than retiring fully at the outset[139] in order to continue to contribute to the university and discipline while also attending to life pursuits, such as spending time with grandchildren.

One faculty member stated,

> The best thing the university could do is treat us differently. Reduce our teaching loads and say, "Write guys." It would be nice to see some kind of program for senior faculty who have active research plans to reduce their teaching loads and service and let them write.[140]

Additionally, almost one third of the faculty in one study were energized by their involvement with the campus and were concerned that they "would not be able to continue some of their interests if they left."[141] Phased retirement can re-energize faculty involvement in research or service, which can benefit the institution. In Chapter 3, various approaches to retirement policies and programs, including phased retirement programs, are discussed.

For faculty in postretirement, "the days may be long and empty" if there are not ways to remain involved with institution.[142] Retired faculty who are active with social connections and engaged with their institutions indicated the most satisfaction.[143] Strategies for involving retired faculty might involve building partnerships between the university and the community as well.[144] Results from numerous studies reveal that in addition to an institution helping faculty feel assured about their financial status and health insurance, assisting faculty to maintain their contributions and accomplishments can be positive and beneficial to universities and colleges.[145] One study revealed that over two thirds of retired faculty were involved with professional activities.[146]

"Aside from financial security and health concerns, the greatest needs of retired faculty are 'acceptance and recognition and the opportunity to exercise skills, intellect, and social commitments for positive accomplishments.'"[147]

Although engaged retired faculty may report positive experiences, some retired faculty report that they experience negativity when on campus. Retired faculty revealed that they "are made to feel like guests—nice to have you around, but don't stay too long."[148] The following excerpt is taken from the ACE literature review:

> Chase et al. [132] explored the emotional reactions of faculty to retirement, surveying all faculty retirees at Indiana University from 1995–1999 (87 of 153 responded) and interviewing a subset of 33 retired faculty. They found that almost 40% of retirees indicated feeling some "detachment from their previous world" [132], adding that a smooth transition into retirement contributes to faculty satisfaction postretirement. They also found that retired faculty who continued to be active with their institutions, at least part-time, experienced fewer life changes and therefore less stress than faculty who did not remain active at all with their institutions [132]. Despite finding that many faculty looked forward to retirement, they concluded that "a significant subset of retirees indeed wrestled with emotional reactions to the change of life events."[149]

Studies have examined the demographic variables associated with retirement. For example, researchers "found that faculty who retired from public institutions tended to do so at younger ages than faculty at private institutions and faculty tended to work for longer periods of time before retirement at private institutions than public institutions."[150] For additional resources, we suggest that you consult the comprehensive ACE website, which is capturing the trends, practices, and programs at 15 institutions.[151] Most recently, the ACE has prepared a rubric for institutions to evaluate their retirement policies, practices, and programs, and a monograph including detailed information on institutions that received the ACE/Sloan award is forthcoming.

GENERAL WORK-LIFE LITERATURE

For a larger look at work-life scholarship, numerous texts and studies are available for review. The research on work-life in organizations is quite extensive, and the following tables include contents of two popular, comprehensive texts to demonstrate the breadth of issues addressed in work-life studies. These contents display a wide range of topics and methodology for empirically examining the interface of work, family, and life (Tables 2.5 and 2.6).

Table 2.5 Work and Life Integration: Organizational, Cultural, and Individual Perspectives (2005), Kossek & Lambert (Editors), see endnote 107 in Chapter 1

I. Introductory Chapters	1. "Work-Family Scholarship": Voice and Context
	2. (Re)Considering Conflict Between Work and Family
II. Organizational Perspectives	3. The Changing Demands of Managerial and Professional Work: Implications for Managing the Work-Life Boundary
	4. Technology, Organizations, and Work-Life Integration
	5. Organizational Reliability, Flexibility and Security
	6. Organizational Stratification: Distributing Opportunities for Balancing Work and Personal Life
	7. When Firms Restructure: Understanding Work-Life Outcomes
	8. Family-Friendly Programs and Work-Life Integration: More Myth Than Magic?
	9. The Equity Imperative: Redesigning Work for Work-Family Integration
III. Individual Perspectives	10. The Importance of the Individual: How Self-Evaluations Influence the Work-Family Interface
	11. Work and Family Stress and Well-Being: An Integrative Model of Person-Environment Fit Within and Between the Work and Family Domains
	12. Flexibility Enactment Theory: Implications of Flexibility Type, Control, and Boundary Management for Work-Family Effectiveness
	13. The Decision Process Theory of Work and Family
	14. Professionals Becoming Parents: Socialization, Adaptation, and Identity Transformation
	15. What Is Success? Who Defines It? Perspectives on the Criterion Problem as It Relates to Work and Family
IV. Cultural and Social Perspectives	16. Work-Life Integration and Social Policy: A Social Justice Theory and Gender Equity Approach to Work and Family
	17. Three Reasons for a Transnational Approach to Work-Life Policy
	18. The Role of Speaking Up in Work-Life Balancing
	19. The Development of Psychosocial Capital in Organizations: Implications for Work and Family Life
	20. Supervisor Support and Work-Life Integration: A Social Identity Perspective
	21. Recasting the Work-Family Agenda as a Corporate Social Responsibility
V. Summary Chapters: Future Directions	22. Connecting Theory and Practice
	23. Future Frontiers: Enduring Challenges and Established Assumptions in the Work-Life Field

Table 2.6 Work and Family Handbook (2006); Pitt-Catsouphes, Kossek, & Sweet (Editors), see endnote 107 in Chapter 1

I. Family and Jobs in the 21st Century	1. Charting New Territory: Advancing Multi-Disciplinary Perspectives, Methods, and Approaches in the Study of Work and Family 2. Understanding Diversity of Work in the 21st Century and Its Impact on the Work-Family Area of Study 3. Understanding Diversity of Families in the 21st Century and Its Impact on the Work-Family Area of Study
II. Disciplinary Approaches and Theoretical Perspectives	4. Caregiving and Wage-Earning: A Historical Perspective on Work and Family 5. Work-Family Policies: The United States in International Perspective 6. Demographic Implications for Work-Family Research 7. Family Studies: Situating Everyday Family Life at Work, in Time, and Across Contexts 8. The Anthropology of the Workplace and the Family 9. Advancing a Career Focus on Work and the Family: Insights From the Life Course Perspective 10. Role Theory Perspectives on Work and Family 11. Experimental Social Psychology and the Study of Work and Family 12. Sociological Perspectives on Families and Work: The Import of Gender, Class, and Race 13. The Role of Economics in Work-Family Research 14. Work and Family From an Industrial/Organizational Psychology Perspective 15. A Legal Perspective on Family Issues at Work 16. Connecting Social Work Perspectives to Work-Family Research and Practice
III. Methodological Approaches	17. Ethnography and Working Families 18. Video Ethnography and Ethnoarchaeological Tracking 19. Using Survey Research to Address Work-Life Issues 20. Using Focus Groups to Study Work and Family 21. Longitudinal Research on Work and Family Issues 22. In the Moment: The Benefits of the Experience Sampling Method 23. Case Studies in Work-Family Research 24. Both Art and Science: Employing Organizational Documentation in Workplace-Based Research 25. A Multiple Stakeholder Perspective: Implications for Measuring Work-Family Outcomes 26. Hierarchical Models for Work-Family and Life Course Research 27. The Work-Family Conflict Construct: Methodological Implications 28. Using Mixed Methods in Research Related to Work and Family
IV. Advancing Policy and Organizational Change	29. The Business Case: Managerial Perspectives on Work and the Family 30. Legislatures, Agencies, Courts, and Advocates: How Laws Are Made, Interpreted, and Modified 31. Work-Family Interventions and Experiments: Workplaces, Communities, and Society 32. The Standards of Excellence in Work-Life Integration: From Changing Policies to Changing Organizations 33. The Arbitration of Work and Family Conflicts 34. Leadership in Action: A Work and Family Agenda for the Future

WORK-LIFE INITIATIVES IN HIGHER EDUCATION

Although, as noted earlier, academe has lagged behind other organizations in the recognition of work-life needs and institutionalization of work-life culture, recent strides have been made in these areas. Moreover, resources for the study and implementation of work-life policies have become available through organizations such as the Alfred P. Sloan Foundation and the ACE. This section provides an overview of ongoing initiatives in higher education institutions, and additional resources are available in the Appendix. Becoming involved with one of these efforts may be useful for many academic leaders.

A serious consideration of work-life issues in higher education began in the 1990s when a few private and public research-intensive universities recognized the value of promoting work-life balance for faculty as a recruitment and retention strategy. As briefly mentioned in Chapter 1, a group of professional work-life staff and researchers gathered together at the University of Michigan to discuss best practices and strategies for helping faculty balance work and family obligations. They formed a national professional organization called the College and University Work/Family Association, which is now known as the **College and University Work-Life-Family Association (CUWFA),** to provide a venue and network to discuss best practices and research.

"The mission of the College and University Work-Life-Family Association is to provide leadership in facilitating the integration of work and study with family/personal life at institutions of higher learning. Our mission supports the broader goals of creating a healthy and productive environment throughout the lifespan and enhancing the work-life effectiveness of employees."[152]

To accomplish its mission, CUWFA offers professional support, gathers information regarding emerging issues relevant to campus programs, and contributes to the understanding and development of the work-life field. Recently, CUWFA developed a toolkit for building great work-life websites—a project funded by the Alfred P. Sloan Foundation. CUWFA also issued a report that outlines an approach to making the business case for work-life policies and programs in colleges and universities as a result of high demand from member institutions for guidance on these matters.[153] A different university or college hosts an annual conference every year (e.g., Harvard University, Johns Hopkins University, University of Baltimore, University of Michigan, University of North Carolina-Chapel Hill, University of Toronto, University of Washington), at which staff, faculty, and leaders convene to discuss the latest trends and strategies on their campuses.

The **Work and Family Researchers Network (WFRN)** evolved from the Sloan Work and Family Research Network that was established in 1997 at Boston

College. In 2010, the Sloan Network changed to WFRN and is now based at the University of Pennsylvania. The WFRN is a membership organization consisting of international and interdisciplinary work and family researchers. Practitioners and policy makers are also welcome to join. The organization provides an open access work and family subject matter repository, networking among members, and holds a conference every two years.[154]

In 2001, the **American Association of University Professors (AAUP)** issued the *Statement of Principles on Family Responsibilities and Academic Work,*[155] and in 2004, AAUP devoted an entire issue of its bulletin *Academe* to the challenges in managing family care with an academic career.[156] AAUP provides extensive information about balancing family and academic work including model institutional policies.

Also in 2001, the **National Science Foundation (NSF)** began funding projects at higher education institutions and STEM-related not-for-profit organizations under the ADVANCE Program. The program was established to enhance the "representation and advancement of women in academic science and engineering careers, thereby contributing to the development of a more diverse science and engineering workforce."[157] With over $130 million in funding, many tools, resources, and products have emerged from over 100 institutions and organizations through this program. Frequently, these projects mobilize work-life-family initiatives on campus. In 2011, NSF released its NSF Career-Life Balance Initiative, which includes a "set of forward-looking policies and practices, that will help to increase the placement, advancement, and retention of women in STEM disciplines, particularly women who are seeking tenure in academe."[158]

The **National Clearinghouse on Academic Worklife** at the University of Michigan Center for the Education of Women was developed to provide resources for research, policy reports, demographic information, articles, and websites, with support from the Alfred P. Sloan Foundation.[159] Researchers developed and disseminated a helpful guide for *Designing and Implementing Family-Friendly Policies in Higher Education.*[160] Key research findings, surveys, and model policies are available through an extensive database, designed for administrators, researchers, faculty, graduate students, policy makers, and faculty unions.

The **Higher Education Recruitment Consortium (HERC)** was formed in 2000. According to the HERC website,

> Consortium member institutions share a commitment to hiring the most diverse and talented faculty, staff, and executives. Hiring decisions often involve two careers. HERC provides jobseekers with the most job opportunities and unsurpassed search technology, enabling dual-career couples to find the right jobs within a commutable distance of one another.[161]

Since 2003, the ACE in collaboration with the Alfred P. Sloan Foundation has been examining the structural and cultural changes necessary to increase flexibility in faculty careers through the **Alfred P. Sloan Awards for Faculty Career Flexibility.**[162] Research provides convincing evidence that higher education institutions

> can demonstrate a strong business case for providing flexibility for their tenure-track and tenured faculty. Flexibility constitutes an effective tool for recruiting and retaining talented faculty. Career flexibility is especially critical to retaining some of the most qualified PhDs in academe. Acquiring the best talent is essential to an institution's ability to achieve excellence and maintain its competitive advantage in a global environment.[163]

Under the umbrella of this program, ACE established an initiative to explore faculty retirement transitions. Monetary awards were given to 15 institutions representing three Carnegie classifications for their innovative best practices supporting faculty in retirement transitions. The outcome of these awards has been the enhanced understanding of effective policies and practices that can facilitate the retirement transition for faculty and their institutions.[164]

As discussed in Chapter 1, during 2005, the ACE issued a groundbreaking report titled *An Agenda for Excellence: Creating Flexibility in Tenure-Track Faculty Careers* that addressed critical work-life dilemmas in the academy. Briefly mentioned, this report was endorsed by a national panel of presidents and chancellors from major research universities across the country, and it was the first national call for institutional leaders to implement flexible career policies and practices to help faculty manage work and life demands more effectively. As noted in the report, flexibility is essential for U.S. higher education institutions to compete internationally by attracting and retaining the most talented tenured and tenure-track faculty. The report includes recommendations for using flexible career policies and practices and reviewing and changing institutional structures that prevent scholars from entering, thriving in, and retiring from academic with dignity and financial security. The ACE's national challenge in 2013 for higher education leaders to promote and support work-life balance faculty, as a strategy for retaining a 21st-century workforce, is a strong signal to higher education leadership that they need to get on board with these national trends.

Additionally, numerous recently published scholarly works have built on work funded by the Sloan Foundation to call for more serious attention to work-life-family balance of faculty and staff.[165]

> "The Alfred P. Sloan Foundation has played a vital role in developing the field of work-family scholarship through its Workplace, Workforce, and Working Families program. In 2003, the Foundation partnered with the American Council on Education to raise awareness throughout higher education of the need to create, implement, or enhance policies and procedures designed to support faculty lives throughout their careers."[166]

CONCLUSION

Work and life challenges are very real for faculty, staff, and students. It is imperative for leading higher education institutions to respond to these challenges in order to facilitate success and effectiveness for the vitality and sustainability of the university and college. Individuals are generally more attached to organizations that offer family-friendly policies, regardless of the extent to which they personally use them.[167] Thus, a supportive work-life environment should not be seen as the sole province of faculty mothers but, rather, as an inclusive culture that can benefit everyone, regardless of gender, race, age, orientation, or career status. Work-life initiatives and strategies for higher education is a burgeoning area of research and practice, and by further exploring the trends in that research as well as some of the best resources available, academic leaders can shape a work-life culture at their own institutions.

Questions for Discussion and Reflection

1. What work-life concerns are you aware of among your faculty and staff?

2. How might you approach a faculty/staff member who seems to be struggling with managing work and family obligations?

3. Which of the aforementioned organizations might be good fit to provide work-life support and resources for you or your department?

4. Do you have faculty/staff approaching retirement? How can you help them with this transition?

5. What professional development opportunities would be most useful for your faculty/staff? How can you make those opportunities available?

NOTES

1. Drago, R., & Colbeck, C. (2003). *The mapping project: Exploring the terrain of U.S. colleges and universities for faculty and families.* University Park: The Pennsylvania State University; Koppes Bryan, L. L., Schneider, S., & Linaberry, E. (2013) *What managers' behaviors support employees & their work-life effectiveness in higher education.* Baltimore, MD: University of Baltimore; Mason, M.A., & Goulden, M. (2002). Do babies matter? The effect of family formation on the lifelong careers of academic men and women. *Academe, 88*(6), 21–27; Mason & Goulden (2004); Williams, J. (2000). How the tenure track discriminates against women. *The Chronicle of Higher Education, 27,* B10.

2. Gappa et al. (2007); Quinn, K., & Shapiro, R. (2009). Balance@UW: Work-family cultural change at the University of Washington. In J. Lester & M. Sallee (Eds.), *Establishing the family-friendly campus: Models for effective practice* (pp. 18–36). Sterling, VA: Stylus; Trower (2012).

3. Akroyd, D., Bracken, S., & Chambers, C. (2011). A comparison of factors that predict the satisfaction of community college faculty by gender. *The Journal of the Professoriate, 4*(1), 74–95; Wolf-Wendel, L., Ward, K., & Twombly, S. B. (2007). Faculty life at community colleges: The perspective of women with children. *Community College Review, 34*(4), 255–281; Hagedorn,

L.S., & Laden, B.V. (2002). Exploring the climate for women as community college faculty. *New Directions for Community Colleges, 118,* 69–78.

4. Petersen Brus, C. (2006). Seeking balance in graduate school: A realistic expectation or a dangerous dilemma? *New Directions for Student Services, 115,* 31–45.

5. Bianchi, S.M., Casper, L.M., & Berkowitz King, R. (2005). *Work, family, health, and well-being.* Mahwah, NJ: Lawrence Erlbaum Associates; Clark, R.A., Nye, F.I., & Gecas, V. (1978). Husbands' work involvement and marital role performance. *Journal of Marriage and the Family, 40*(1), 9–21; Haller, M., & Rosenmayer, L. (1971). The pluridimensionality of work commitment: A study of young married women in different social contents of occupational and family life. *Human Relations, 24*(6), 501–518; Jones, A.P., & Butler, M.C. (1980). A role transition approach to the stresses of organizationally induced family role disruption. *Journal of Marriage and the Family, 42*(2), 367–376; Kossek & Lambert (2005); Philipsen & Bostic (2010); Pitt-Catsouphes et al. (2006); Poelmans, S.A.Y. (Ed.). (2005). *Work and family: An international research perspective.* Mahwah, NJ: Lawrence Erlbaum Associates, Inc.; Pleck, J.H. (1977). The work-family role system. *Social Problems, 24*(4), 417–427; Safilios-Rothschild, C. (1970). The influence of the wife's degree of work commitment upon some aspects of family organization and dynamics. *Journal of Marriage and the Family, 32*(4), 681–691; Zedeck, S. (Ed.). (1992). *Work, families, and organizations.* San Francisco, CA: Jossey-Bass.

6. Kirchmeyer, C. (2000). Work-life initiatives: Greed or benevolence regarding workers' time? In C. Cooper & D. Rousseau (Eds.), *Trends in organizational behavior* (pp. 79–93). New York, NY: John Wiley & Sons.

7. Carlson, D.S., Witt, L.A., Zivnuska, S., Kacmar, K.M., & Grzywacz, J.G. (2008). Supervisor appraisal as the link between family-work balance and contextual performance. *Journal of Business Psychology, 23*(1–2), 37–49; Dollwet, M., Schneider, S., & Koppes, L.L. (2010). *Effects of transformational and servant leadership on employee work-life balance.* Poster presentation for the Southeastern Psychological Association Annual Conference, Chattanooga, TN.

8. Dollwet et al. (2010).

9. Marks, S.R., & MacDermid, S.M. (1996). Multiple roles and the self: A theory of role balance. *Journal of Marriage and the Family, 58*(2), 417–432.

10. Greenhaus, J.H., & Beutell, N.J. (1985). Sources of conflict between work and family roles. *The Academy of Management Review, 10*(1), 76–88; Greenhaus, J.H., & Powell, G.N. (2006). When work and family are allies: A theory of work-family enrichment. *Academy of Management Review, 31*(1), 72–92; Grzywacz, J.G., Carlson, D.S., Kacmar, K.M., & Wayne, J.H. (2007). A multi-level perspective on the synergies between work and family. *Journal of Occupational and Organizational Psychology, 80*(4), 559–574; Mesmer-Magnus, J.R., & Viswesvaran, C. (2005). Convergence between measures of work-to-family and family-to-work conflict: A meta-analytic examination. *Journal of Vocational Behavior, 67*(2), 215–232; Wayne, J.H., Grzywacz, J.G., Carlson, D.S., & Kacmar, K.M. (2007). Work-family facilitation: A theoretical explanation and model of primary antecedents and consequences. *Human Resource Management Review, 17*(1), 63–76.

11. Koppes & Swanberg (2008).

12. Rose, K. (2006). *Work-life effectiveness: Bottom-line strategies for today's workplace.* Scottsdale, AZ: WorldatWork; Valcour, M. (2007). Work-based resources as moderators of the relationship between work hours and satisfaction with work-family balance. *Journal of Applied Psychology, 92*(6), 1512–1523.

13. Inam, H. (2013). Forget work life balance—seven paradigm shifts for The New 24/7 normal. *Forbes.* Retrieved from www.forbes.com/sites/hennainam/2013/10/07/forget-work-life-balance-seven-paradigm-shifts-for-the-new-247-normal/

14. Inam (2013), p. 1.

15. American Council on Education (2013a).

16. Rose (2006), p. 16.

17. Valcour (2007), p. 1513.
18. Emory University. WorkLife Resource Center. Retrieved from www.worklife.emory.edu/
19. Retrieved from www.coache.org.
20. Trower (2012).
21. Trower (2012), p. 78.
22. Trower (2012).
23. Anderson, D. M., Morgan, B. L., & Wilson, J. B. (2002). Perceptions of family-friendly policies: University versus corporate employees. *Journal of Family and Economic Issues, 23*(1), 73–92.
24. Wolf-Wendel & Ward (2006); Ward, K., & Wolf-Wendel, L. (2004). Academic motherhood: Managing complex roles in research universities. *The Review of Higher Education, 27*(2), 233–257; Akroyd et al. (2011); Wolf-Wendel et al. (2007); Hagedorn et al. (2002); Hart, J. (2011). Non-tenure track women faculty: Opening the door. *The Journal of the Professoriate, 4*(1), 96–124.
25. Carlson, D. S., Kacma, K. M., Holliday Wayne, J., & Grzywacz, J. G. (2006). Measuring the positive side of work-family interface: Development and validation of a work-family enrichment scale. *Journal of Vocational Behavior, 68*(1) 131–164; Karatepe, O. M., & Magaji, A. B. (2008). Work-family conflict and facilitation in the hotel industry. *Cornell Hospitality Quarterly, 49*(4), 395–412; Quick, J. D., Henley, A. B., & Campbell Quick, J. (2004). The balancing act—At work and at home. *Organizational Dynamics, 33*(4), 426–438.
26. Rose (2006).
27. Kossek, E. E., & Ozeki, C. (1998). Work-family conflict, policies, and the job-life satisfaction relationship: A review and directions for organizational behavior-human resources research. *Journal of Applied Psychology, 83*(2), 139–149.
28. Frone, M. R. (2000). Work family conflict and employee psychiatric disorders: The national comorbidity survey. *Journal of Applied Psychology, 85*(6), 888–895.
29. American Psychological Association. (2000). *Women in academe: Two steps forward, one step back. Report of the Task Force on Women in Academe.* Retrieved from www.apa.org/pi/women/programs/academe/taskforce-report.pdf; Halpern, D. (2008). Nurturing careers in psychology: Combining work and family. *Educational Psychological Review, 20*(1), 57–64; Lee, C. M., Reissing, E. D., & Dobson, D. (2009). Work-life balance for early career Canadian psychologists in professional programs. *Canadian Psychologist, 50*(2), 74–82; Hagedorn, L. S., & Sax, L. J. (2003). Marriage, children, and aging parents: The role of family-related factors in faculty job satisfaction. *Journal of Faculty Development, 19*(2), 65–76; Young, D. S., & Holley, L. C. (2005). Combining caregiving and career: Experiences of social work faculty. *AFFILIA, 20*(2), 136–152; Mason & Goulden (2002).
30. Mason & Goulden (2004).
31. Aumann, K., & Galinsky, E. (2011). *The state of health in the American workforce: Does having an effective workplace matter?* Retrieved from http://familiesandwork.org/downloads/StateofHealthinAmericanWorkforce.pdf
32. University of Kentucky Human Resources Office of Work-Life. (2012). *Work-life: Making a difference. Observations from the 2012 UK@Work survey;* Koppes, L. L., Sugarman, R., Ferlan, M., & Moore, D. (2007). *Shifting sands, changing tides: Strategic partnerships for culture change.* Paper presented at the Annual Conference of College and University Work/Family Association 13th National Conference, Santa Barbara, CA.
33. Mason et al. (2009).
34. West & Curtis (2006).
35. The Center for WorkLife Law (2013).
36. U.S. Department of Education, National Center for Education Statistics, Earned Degrees Conferred, 1869–70 through 1964–65; Projections of Education Statistics to 2016; Higher Education General Information Survey (HEGIS), "Degrees and Other Formal Awards Conferred" surveys, 1965–66 through 1985–86; and 1986–87 through 2005–06 Integrated

Postsecondary Education Data System, "Completions Survey" (IPEDS-C:87–99), and Fall 2000 through Fall 2006.

37. Mason et al. (2009).

38. Burrelli, J. (2008). *Thirty-three years of women in S&E faculty positions.* National Science Foundation Division of Science Resources Statistics, Survey of Doctorate Recipients, NSF 08–308.

39. West & Curtis (2006).

40. The Center for WorkLife Law (2012).

41. Digest of Educational Statistics. (2010). Retrieved from http://nces.ed.gov/pubsearch/pubsinfo.asp?pubid=2011015

42. Armenti, C. (2004). May babies and posttenure babies: Maternal decisions of women professors. *Review of Higher Education, 27*(2), 211–231; Misra, J., Hickes Lundquist, J., & Templer, A. (2012). Gender, work time, and care responsibilities among faculty. *Sociological Forum, 27*(2), 300–323; Sax, L. J., Hagedorn, L. S., Arredondo, M., & Dicrisi, F. A. (2002). Faculty research productivity: Explore the role of gender and family-related factors. *Research in Higher Education, 43*(4), 423–446.

43. Reddick, R. J., Rochlen, A. B., Grasso, J. R., Reilly, E. D., & Spikes, D. D. (2012). Academic fathering pursuing tenure: A qualitative study of work-family conflict, coping strategies, and departmental culture. *Psychology of Men & Masculinity, 13*(1), 1–15.

44. Armenti (2004).

45. Grant, L., Kennelly, I., & Ward, K. B. (2000). Revisiting the gender, marriage, and parenthood puzzle in scientific careers. *Women Studies Quarterly 1 and 2,* 62–85.

46. Mason et al. (2009).

47. Trower (2012).

48. Armenti (2004).

49. Mason & Goulden (2004).

50. Mason & Goulden (2004).

51. Perna, L. W. (2001). The relationship between family responsibilities and employment status. *Journal of Higher Education, 72*(5), 584–611; Trower (2012).

52. van Anders, S. M. (2004). Why the academic pipeline leaks: Fewer men than women perceive barriers to becoming professors. *Sex Roles, 9/10,* 511–521; Wolfinger, N. H., Mason, M. A., & Goulden, M. (2009). Stay in the game: Gender, family formation and alternative trajectories in the academic life course. *Social Forces, 87*(3), 1591–1621; Wolfinger, N. H., Mason, M. A., & Goulden, M. (2008). Problems in the pipeline: Gender, marriage, and fertility in the ivory tower. *The Journal of Higher Education, 79*(4), 388–405; Sandler, B. R., Silverberg, L. A., & Hall, R. M. (1996). *The chilly classroom climate: A guide to improve the education of women.* Washington, DC: National Association for Women in Education; Litzler, E., Lange, S. E., & Brainard, S. G. (2005). *Climate for graduate students in science and engineering departments.* Proceedings of the 2005 American Society for Engineering Education Annual Conference & Exposition; Williams, J. C., Alon, T., & Bornstein, S. (2006). Beyond the "chilly climate": A new model for eliminating bias against women and fathers in academe. *Thought & Action: The NEA Higher Education Journal,* 79–96.

53. Huang, P. (n.d.). *Gender bias in Academia: Findings from focus groups.* San Francisco, CA: The Center for WorkLife Law, p. 2.

54. Huang (n.d.).

55. Finkel, S. K., & Olswang, S. G. (1996). Child rearing as a career impediment to women assistant professors. *Review of Higher Education, 19*(2), 129–139.

56. Finkel, S. K., Olswang, S. G., & She, N. (1994). The implications of childbirth on tenure and promotion for women faculty. *Review of Higher Education, 17*(3), 259–270.

57. Williams, J., Glass, J., Correll, S., & Berdahl, J. L. (Eds.). (2013). The flexibility stigma [Special issue]. *Journal of Social Issues, 69*(2), 209–405.

58. The Center for WorkLife Law (2013), p. 6.

59. Trower (2012), p. 73.

60. Drago, R., Colbeck, C. L., Stauffer, K. D., & Pirretti, A., Burkum, K., . . . Habasevich, T. (2006). The avoidance of bias against caregiving. *The American Behavioral Scientist, 49*(9), 1222–1247.

61. The Center for WorkLife Law (2013).

62. Daly, K. J. (2008). Work-life issues for fathers. In K. Korabik, D. S. Lero, & D. L. Whitehead (Eds.), *Handbook of work-family integration* (pp. 249–264). London, UK: Elsevier.

63. Jacobs, J. A., & Gerson, K. (2004). *The time divide: Work, family, and gender inequality.* Cambridge, MA: Harvard University Press.

64. Zuzanek, J. (2000). The effects of time use and time pressure on child-parent relationships. *Health Canada Research Report.* Waterloo, Ontario, Canada: Optimum Publications.

65. De Ruijter, E., & Van der Lippe, T. (2007). Effects of work characteristics on household outsourcing as a strategy to combine work and home. *Work and Occupations, 34,* 205–230.

66. Ward & Wolf-Wendel (2012).

67. Mason, M. A., Wolfinger, N. H., & Goulden, M. (2013). *Do babies matter? Gender and family in the ivory tower.* New Brunswick, NJ: Rutgers University Press.

68. Trower (2012), pp. 68–69; Colbeck, C. L., & Drago, R. (2005). Accept, avoid, resist: How faculty members respond to bias against caregiving . . . and how departments can help. *Change, 37*(6), 10–17.

69. Mason & Goulden (2004), p. ix; Ward & Wolf-Wendel (2004, 2012).

70. Mason & Goulden (2002), p. 63.

71. Armenti (2004).

72. Mason & Goulden (2004).

73. Sax, L. J., Hagedorn, L. S., Arrendondo, M., & Dicrisi, F. A., III. (2002). Faculty research productivity: Exploring the role of gender and family-related factors. *Research in Higher Education, 43,* 423–446; Trower (2012).

74. Trower (2012).

75. Mason & Goulden (2004), p. 4.

76. Cuddy, A. J. C., Fiske, S. T., & Glick, P. (2004). When professionals become mothers, warmth doesn't cut the ice. *Journal of Social Issues, 64*(4), 701–718; Fuegen, K., Biernat, M., Haines, E., & Deaux, K. (2004). Mothers and fathers in the workplace: How gender and parental status influence judgments of job-related competence. *Journal of Social Issues, 60*(4), 737–754.

77. Philipsen & Bostic (2010).

78. Brandth, B., & Kvande, E. (2002). Reflexive fathers: Negotiating parental leave and working life. *Gender, Work and Organization, 9,* 186–203; Higgins, C. A., & Duxbury, L. E. (2006). Work-family conflict: A comparison of dual-career and traditional-career men. *Journal of Organizational Behavior, 13,* 389–411; Parasuraman, S., & Simmers, C. A. (2001). Type of employment, work-family conflict and well-being: A comparative study. *Journal of Organizational Behavior, 22,* 551–568; Philipsen & Bostic (2010).

79. Reddick et al. (2012).

80. Bond, J. T., Thompson, C., Galinsky, E., & Prottas, D. (2002). *Highlights of the national study of the changing workforce: Executive summary.* New York, NY: Families and Work Institute.

81. Haas, L., Allard, K., & Hwang, P. (2002). The impact of organizational culture on men's use of parental leave in Sweden. *Community, Work, and Family, 5*(3), 319–342.

82. The Center for WorkLife Law (2013).

83. Trower (2012).

84. Trower (2012).

85. Huang (n.d), p. 15.

86. Drago, R., Crouter, A. C., Wardell, M., & and Willits, B. S. (2001). *Faculty and Families Project: Final Report to the Alfred P. Sloan Foundation.* Report Work-Family Working Paper #01–02. University Park: Pennsylvania State University.

87. Williams, J., & Thomas, C. (2006). The growing concern of family responsibilities discrimination. *Women's Lawyer Review, 91*(2), 25–29.

55

88. Rose (2006).

89. Rose (2006).

90. Aumann et al. (2008).

91. National Alliance for Caregiving, University of Pittsburgh Institute on Aging, & MetLife Mature Market Institute. (2010). *The MetLife study of working caregivers and employer health care costs.* New York, NY: MetLife Mature Market Institute.

92. Aumann et al. (2008), p. 2.

93. Hammer, L. B., & Neal, M. B. (2008). Working sandwiched-generation caregivers: Prevalence, characteristics, and outcomes. *The Psychologist-Manager Journal, 11,* 93–112, p. 94.

94. Neal, M. B., Chapman, N. J., Ingersoll-Dayton, B., & Emlen, A. C. (1993). *Balancing work and caregiving for children, adults, and elders.* Newbury Park, CA: Sage.

95. National Alliance for Caregiving and AARP. (2004). *Caregiving in the U.S.* Washington, DC.

96. Fredriksen-Goldsen, K. I., & Scharlach, A. E. (2001). *Families and work: New directions in the twenty-first century.* New York, NY: Oxford University Press, p. 94. Hammer & Neal (2008); Fernandez. J. P. (1990). *The politics and reality of family care in corporate America.* Lexington, MA: D.C. Heath.

97. Neal, M. B., & Hammer, L. B. (2006). *Working couples caring for children and aging parents: Effects on work and well-being.* New York, NY: Taylor & Francis.

98. Mason et al. (2009).

99. Wolfinger et al. (2008).

100. Burrelli (2008).

101. Huang (n.d), p. 14.

102. Winkler, J. (2000). Faculty reappointment, tenure, and promotion: Barriers for women. *Professional Geographer, 52*(4), 737–750.

103. Trower (2012).

104. Schiebinger, L., Davies Henderson, A., & Gilmartin, S. K. (2008). *Dual-career academic couples: What universities need to know.* Stanford, CA: The Michelle R. Clayman Institute for Gender Research, Stanford University.

105. Wilson, R. (2013). Faculty couples, for better or worse. *The Chronicle of Higher Education.* Retrieved from http://chronicle.com/article/Faculty-Couples-for-Better-or/142481/

106. Schiebinger et al. (2008).

107. Wolf-Wendel et al. (2003).

108. Trower (2012).

109. Schiebinger et al. (2008).

110. Williams, J., & Norton, D. L. (2008). Building academic excellence through gender equity. *American Academic, 4*(1), 185–208.

111. Trower (2012).

112. Schiebinger et al. (2008).

113. Reynolds, B. W. (2013). The benefits of taking your pet to work. *Care2.* Retrieved from www.care2.com/greenliving/the-benefits-of-taking-your-pet-to-work.html?cid=email_na

114. Fisher, G. G., Bulger, C. A., & Smith, C. S. (2009). Beyond work and family: A measure of work/nonwork interference and enhancement. *Journal of Occupational Health Psychology, 14,* 441–456.

115. As cited in Bogese et al. (2010, March).

116. Gappa et al. (2007).

117. Cahn, S. M. (2008). *From student to scholar: A candid guide to becoming a professor.* New York, NY: Columbia University Press, p. 61.

118. Lang, J. M. (2005). *Life on the tenure track: Lessons from the first year.* Baltimore, MD: Johns Hopkins University Press, p. 52.

119. Davis, D., Duckett, S., Rietveld, B., Rosato, C., & Taylor, V. (2010, February). *Promoting work/life balance: A look at OSU's work/life potential.* The President's Commission on the Status of Women, Oregon State University.

120. The Center for WorkLife Law (2013).

121. Trower (2012), p. 102; Schuster, J. H., & Finkelstein, M. J. (2006). *The American faculty: The restructuring of academic work and careers.* Baltimore, MD: Johns Hopkins University Press.

122. McMillin, L. A., & Berberet, W. G. (2002). *A new academic compact: Revisioning the relationship between faculty and their institutions.* Bolton, MA: Anker Publication, p. 34.

123. Trower (2012).

124. Price, J., & Cotton, S. R. (2006). Teaching, research, and service. Expectations of assistant professors. *American Sociologist, 37*(1), 5–21.

125. The Center for WorkLife Law (2013).

126. The Center for WorkLife Law (2013).

127. American Council on Education (2010). *Review of faculty retirement literature.* Washington, DC.

128. American Council on Education (2010); Koppes Bryan, L. L., Cardona, M. M., Pitta, D., & Schneller, B. (2014). Leveraging the talents of faculty members to create an engaged retirement ecosystem at the University of Baltimore. In C. Van Ummersen, J. McLaughlin & L. Duranleau (Eds.), *Faculty retirement: Best practices for navigating the transition* (pp. 129–144). Sterling, VA: Stylus Publishing.

129. LaBauve, B. J., & Robinson, C. R. (1999). Adjusting to retirement: Considerations for counselors. *Adultspan: Theory Research & Practice, 1*(1), p. 2.

130. American Council on Education (2010).

131. Gappa et al. (2007), p. 64.

132. Berberet, J., Bland, C., Brown, B., & Ribsey, K. (2005). *Late career faculty perceptions: Implications for retirement planning and policymaking.* Retrieved from www.tiaa-crefinstitute.org/public/pdf/institute/research/dialogue/84.pdf

133. Ferren, A. S. (1998). *Senior faculty considering retirement: A developmental and policy issue. New pathways: Faculty career and employment for the 21st century working paper series inquiry #11*, p. 5.

134. Dorfman, L. T. (2009). Ten years later: A follow-up study of professors still working after age 70. *Educational Gerontology, 35*(11), 1032–1045; Dorfman, L. T. (2000). Still working after age 70: Older professors in academe. *Educational Gerontology, 26*(8), 695–713.

135. Berberet et al. (2005).

136. Firmin, M. W., & Craycraft, A. (2009). Life meanings for past and present: Case studies of four retired faculty. *Educational Research Quarterly, 32*(4), 17–35.

137. Goodman, J., & Pappas, J. G. (2000). Applying the Schlossberg 4s transition model to retired university faculty: Does it fit? *Adultspan: Theory Research & Practice, 2*(1), p. 15. Ekerdt, D. J. (1989). Retirement preparation. *Annual Review of Gerontology and Geriatrics, 9,* 321–356; Firmin & Craycraft (2009).

138. Ferren (1998).

139. Ferren (1998).

140. Ferren (1998), p. 7.

141. Ferren (1998), p. 7.

142. Evans, M. (2008). Sterling silver assets. *Times Higher Education.*

143. Firmin & Craycraft (2009).

144. Koppes Bryan et al. (2014).

145. American Council on Education (2010).

146. Dorfman, L. T., & Kolarik, D. C. (2005). Leisure and the retired professor: Occupation matters. *Educational Gerontology, 31*(5), 343–361.

147. Auerbach, A. J. (1984). *Professors in retirement: The emeritus college model*, p. 88.

148. Auerbach (1984), p. 22.

149. Chase, C. I., Eklund, S. J., & Pearson, L. M. (2003). Affective responses of faculty emeriti to retirement. *Educational Gerontology, 29*(6), p. 521.

150. American Council on Education (2010), p. 8.

151. Retrieved from www.acenet.edu/leadership/programs/Pages/Faculty-Retirement-Transitions.aspx

152. College and Work-Life-Family Association. (2013). *Mission*. Retrieved from www.cuwfa. org/mission
153. Sullivan et al. (2012).
154. http://workfamily.sas.upenn.edu/
155. Retrieved from www.aaup.org/AAUP/issues/WF/, Curtis, J.W. (Guest Ed.). (2004). Balancing family careers and family work. *Academe, 90*(6).
156. Retrieved from www.aaup.org/AAUP/issues/WF/
157. Retrieved from www.nsf.gov/crssprgm/advance/
158. Retrieved from www.nsf.gov/career-life-balance/brochure.pdf
159. Retrieved from www.academicworklife.org
160. Smith & Waltman (2006).
161. Higher Education Recruitment Consortium. (2013). Retrieved from www.hercjobs.org/about_herc/
162. Retrieved from www.acenet.edu/leadership/programs/Pages/Alfred-P-Sloan-Projects-for-Faculty-Career-Flexibility.aspx
163. Retrieved from www.acenet.edu/leadership/programs/Pages/Alfred-P-Sloan-Projects-for-Faculty-Career-Flexibility.aspx
164. Retrieved from www.acenet.edu/leadership/programs/Pages/Faculty-Retirement-Transitions.aspx
165. Gappa et al. (2007); Lester & Sallee (2009); Philipsen & Bostic (2010); Trower (2012); Ward & Wolf-Wendel (2012).
166. Retrieved from www.acenet.edu/leadership/programs/Pages/Alfred-P-Sloan-Projects-for-Faculty-Career-Flexibility.aspx
167. Grover, S., & Crocker, K. (1995). Who appreciates family-responsive human resource policies: The impact of family-friendly policies on the organizational attachment of parents and non-parents. *Personnel Psychology, 48,* 271–288.

Chapter 3

Emerging Practices and Strategies

Organizations have implemented various strategies to facilitate work-life satisfaction and effectiveness for the purpose of recruiting and retaining talented employees. For example, a "national sample of medium and large private-sector employers finds widespread adoption of flextime (68%), part-time work (53%), job sharing (46%), compressed work weeks (39%), and the occasional provision of on-site child care (7%)" to be the most commonly adopted strategies.[1] Nonetheless, the use of these strategies does not nearly equate to the prevalence of the issues. As discussed in Chapters 1 and 2, some faculty members report that they experience a negative stigma when using work-life policies and programs; thus, they do not take advantage of these opportunities for fear of career ramifications or other negative consequences. Additionally, surveys revealed that employees are often unaware of options available to them. Because faculty and staff perceive that academic leaders are the gatekeepers to these policies and programs, the low usage is frequently attributed to supervisors, managers, department chairs, or deans who are not supportive or do not have knowledge of the strategies and opportunities available at their institutions. A key responsibility of an academic leader, then, is to know the strategies, or, at the very least, to be able to refer the faculty or staff member to another unit that has in-depth knowledge of best practices. This chapter provides an overview of best practices and strategies that address work-life issues for faculty and staff. The following section begins with a brief overview of work-life infrastructures on campuses, moves to a discussion of policies, programs, and benefits as they pertain to various work-life issues, and concludes with the applicable work-life requirements that are mandated by state and federal laws.

WORK-LIFE INFRASTRUCTURES

Higher education institutions recognized for their work-life cultures and implementation of best practices have created infrastructures that institutionalize policies, programs, and benefits. Such infrastructures include staff, administrators, services, and offices devoted to facilitating a work-life culture. One defining characteristic of leading institutions with life and family–friendly campuses is the existence of a Human Resources (HR) professional with a strategic or change management focus and/or a chief of HR who is committed to work-life.[2] Universities employ a broad range of models, from work-life being diffused through human resources, to work-life being the focus of an entire unit staffed by work-life professionals, such as the Office of Work, Life, and Engagement at Johns Hopkins University. A benchmark survey revealed 15 different approaches to work-life infrastructure among 17 of 22 institutions with a work-life unit (Table 3.1).[3] These units often fall under the umbrella of Human Resources or Organizational Development (e.g., University of Toronto). Some universities have established structures in the Provost's Office; for instance, at the University of California at Los Angeles work-life is overseen by the Vice Provost for Faculty Diversity and Development. It is surprising when academic leaders have no knowledge of the work-life offices on their campuses—these leaders should know the institution's infrastructure. Indeed, it is those institutions with specific offices devoted to work-life that have outstanding reputations for implementing best practices among work-life professionals.

Table 3.1 Examples of Work-Life Infrastructures[4]

Brown University	Work-Life Friendly Initiative Through Dean of Faculty
Columbia University	Office of Work/Life
Cornell University	Office of Workforce Diversity and Inclusion
Duke University	Vice Provost for Faculty Diversity and Development
Emory University	WorkLife Resource Center
Harvard University	Office of Work Life (HR) and Senior Vice Provost for Faculty Diversity and Development
MIT	Work/Life Center
Northwestern University	Work/Life Office
UC Berkeley	Work/Life Office
UCLA	Vice Provost for Faculty Diversity and Development
University of Arizona	Life and Work Connections
University of Michigan	Work/Life Resource Center
University of Pennsylvania	Family Friendly Initiative Linked to Provost Office
University of Virginia	Work/Life Office
University of Southern California	Center for Work and Family Life

In addition to an organizational unit and staffing, some institutions have a work-life committee or advisory board consisting of faculty and staff. The purpose of this board is to provide oversight on work-life surveys, policies, benefits, and practices. Work-Life Directors can rely heavily on the advisory board for the members' perspectives and guidance. The members may include not only individuals with work-life needs but also scholars of work-life issues. Cornell University, for example, has a Provost's Advisory Committee on Faculty Work-Life. Such committees or boards can help mobilize the establishment and implementation of strategies and solutions as well as gain buy-in across campus.

An important function of work-life infrastructures is the **communication** of strategies and solutions. Many individuals who could benefit from work-life policies do not pursue their options because they are not aware of them. One common approach for relaying information is through a website. CUWFA recently completed a grant project funded by the Alfred P. Sloan Foundation, which discovered best practices for work-life websites. An outcome of this project was the identification of higher education institutions with "great" work-life websites (Table 3.2).

An academic leader understands the importance of communication and transparency; thus, if your institution does not have a work-life website, then you may want to work with your communications team to establish a webpage for your particular unit, which can highlight campus strategies as well as communicate your understanding and support of work-life issues to faculty and staff. Institutions also integrate policies into the faculty and staff handbooks, provide toolkits, and distribute procedures and forms. Several models of effective practice can also be found in the text titled *Establishing the Family-Friendly Campus: Models for Effective Practice.* [5]

Table 3.2 Great Work-Life Websites

Institutions With GREAT Work-Life Websites[i]

- Columbia University
- Emory University
- Massachusetts Institute of Technology (MIT)
- Middlebury College
- Northwestern University
- Stanford University
- University of Arizona
- University of Kentucky
- Virginia Commonwealth University

[i] CUWFA recently completed a grant project funded by the Alfred P. Sloan Foundation

"In terms of classical sociological concepts, then, we have taken a bureaucratically organized setting intended and designed to serve 'instrumental' needs—the formal, rigorous education of our students—and actively sought to build within it a substantial 'expressive' culture which makes it a pleasant place (usually: we are not perfect) within which to be and work and deal with challenges." (Dr. Timothy Wickham-Crowley, Department Chair, Georgetown University)

WORK-LIFE STRATEGIES

It is impossible to describe here all of the available strategies for facilitating work-life satisfaction and effectiveness. However, we offer a brief overview to introduce the wide range of possibilities and options. Most of these strategies have been established at the institution level; however, academic leaders can implement certain approaches at a unit level as well. Moreover, simply showing that you understand the policies and are concerned with the work-life needs of your faculty and staff can go a long way toward shaping a work-life culture and improving employee satisfaction and effectiveness.

Prevalence studies of university-based work-life efforts identify common programs, policies, and other initiatives.[6] The original basis for work-life offerings included dependent care, employee assistance, flexibility, and resource referral. From two studies conducted by the Center for the Education of Women at the University of Michigan, eight policies for faculty were featured: tenure-clock extension, modified duties, FMLA, leaves in excess of FMLA, paid dependent care leaves, phased retirement, reduced appointments, and dual-career assistance.[7] Some studies have been conducted to examine the effectiveness of policies in various institutions, including community colleges (Table 3.3).[8]

Workplace and Career Flexibility

Faculty

Evidence-based research studies reveal that higher education institutions

can demonstrate a strong business case for providing flexibility for their tenure-track and tenured faculty. Flexibility constitutes an effective tool for recruiting and retaining talented faculty. Career flexibility is especially critical to retaining some of the most qualified PhDs in academe. Acquiring the best talent is essential to an institution's ability to achieve excellence and maintain its competitive advantage in a global environment.[9]

Following is an overview of policies that allow for flexibility with regard to tenure and work assignments. It is important to briefly note here that the most effective policies are those to which eligible faculty are entitled (opt out), rather than discretionary (opt in). In the latter case, the faculty members must apply for the policy through the department chair or other senior administrator, which can deter individuals from making the requests; consequently, they do not use the policies.

Table 3.3 Alfred P. Sloan Award for Faculty Career Flexibility: Strategies

Strategies for Research, Master's, and Baccalaureate Institutions, Alfred P. Sloan Awards for Faculty Career Flexibility[i]	
Strategies for Research Institutions At least half of the 55 research universities in 2005 that applied for this award indicated the following policies and practices were available to faculty.	• Tenure-clock adjustment • Active Service Modified Duties (ASMD) or Partial Relief from Duties, with no reduction in pay • Paid leaves for biological or adoptive mothers • Paid leaves for biological or adoptive fathers • Parental leave for same-sex and opposite-sex couples when their partner gives birth • Disability policy for serious illness or injury • Memoranda of Understanding (MOUs) stating faculty member's expectations during leaves • Part-time appointments for tenure-track and tenured faculty • Health insurance for same-sex partners • Phased retirement • Seminars and workshops for graduate students to consider careers in academe • Courses in one or more departments that examine the interactions of work, personal, and family life
Strategies for Master's Institutions At least half of the 56 master's large universities and colleges in 2007 that applied for this award indicated the following policies and practices were available to faculty.	• Tenure-clock adjustment • Active Service Modified Duties (ASMD) or Partial Relief from Duties, with no reduction in pay • Paid leaves for biological or adoptive mothers • Disability policy for serious illness or injury • Memoranda of Understanding (MOUs) stating faculty member's expectations during leaves • Committee to identify problems and recommend actions regarding the recruitment, retention, and/or career satisfaction of faculty from under-represented groups • Tracking tenure outcomes for faculty who stop the tenure clock • Course offerings that examine the intersection of work, personal, and family life

(*Continued*)

Table 3.3 (*Continued*)

Strategies for Baccalaureate Institutions At least half of the baccalaureate colleges (arts & sciences classification) in 2008 that applied for this award indicated the following policies and practices were available to faculty.	• Tenure-clock adjustment • Active Service Modified Duties (ASMD) or Partial Relief from Duties, with no reduction in pay • Paid leaves for biological or adoptive mothers • Paid leaves for biological or adoptive fathers • Parental leave for same-sex and opposite-sex couples when their partner gives birth • Disability policy for serious illness or injury • Memoranda of Understanding (MOUs) stating faculty member's expectations during leaves • Health insurance for same-sex and opposite-sex partners • Phased retirement • Committee on family-friendly and/or career flexibility issues

[i] American Council on Education. (2005, 2007, 2008). *Strategies for Research, Master's, and Baccalaureate Institutions, Alfred P. Sloan Awards for Faculty Career Flexibility*. Retrieved from www.acenet.edu/leadership/programs/Pages/Past-Initiatives-in-Faculty-Career-Flexibility.aspx

■ Tenure-Clock Stoppage or Extension

Faculty members have the right to request that a period of time, usually one year, will not be counted as part of the probationary period for tenure. They may request to either stop the tenure clock or extend the clock because of life-changing circumstances, primarily the birth or adoption of a child. Some institutions, such as the University of Baltimore, have policies that cover faculty who experience other life-changing events, such as divorce, custody disputes, family illness, or death. The COACHE Survey revealed an average rating of 3.98 (from 1 = Very unimportant to 5 = Very important) for the importance of "Stop-the-clock for parental or other family reasons." According to the University of Michigan report, 43% of 255 institutions surveyed had a tenure-clock extension policy.[10]

Successful strategies for flexibility with tenure including the following:

• "Schools and departments individually consider whether to lengthen the probationary period, given that a university does 'not need a one-size-fits-all approach';
• Tenure extensions are granted for reasons other than childbirth;
• Flexible work arrangements are introduced;
• Department chairs, external reviewers, and tenure and promotion committee members are made aware of the details pertaining to tenure-clock stoppage and reminded that higher expectations should not result from this situation."[11]

■ Reduced or Part-Time Appointment

This strategy allows faculty members to work either temporarily or permanently at a less-than-full-time appointment and includes proportional salary and work adjustments. One approach might offer a faculty appointment at .50 FTE with eligibility for full benefits. This type of appointment allows for faculty members to manage family obligations or pursue other life activities. At some institutions, faculty may choose to reduce their full-time appointments on a temporary basis while facing a life event, and they then have the option of returning to the full-time status. A good example is a reduced teaching load for the semester during which a new child enters the family, either through birth or adoption. Of 255 institutions surveyed, an average of 14% offered some type of reduced appointment.[12]

■ Shared Faculty Positions

Both partners share a single tenure-track position. This strategy is especially helpful when partners want to work at the same institution.

■ Active Service Modified Duties

This strategy creates flexibility in the faculty member's workload by changing job responsibilities for one semester or term, without any changes in pay. The most common adjustment is a reduction in teaching with the expectation that the time devoted to the classroom would be reassigned to other responsibilities that allow for more flexibility in scheduling. Some institutions may simply reduce the work assignment for a finite period, while others may leave the arrangement open ended. Eighteen percent of the 255 institutions surveyed implemented a modified duties policy.[13]

■ Flexibility in Scheduling, Meeting Times, Office Hours, and Other Activities

These strategies create flexibility in a variety of ways. For example, faculty members are provided with flexibility when establishing their teaching schedules as a way to help manage work and family responsibilities. Academic leaders are also sensitive to meeting times that can be problematic for faculty and staff with families (e.g., 5:00 p.m.).

■ Career Flexibility

The institution facilitates flexibility throughout the careers of faculty and staff members in recognition that family and personal responsibilities change at different points in our lives. The ACE recommends the following best practices for career flexibility:[14]

• On- and off-ramps (i.e., entering and stopping out from the academic career), through leave policies;

• Shortened time for tenure, with prorated standard of productivity;

65

- Delayed entry or re-entry opportunities (including practices that foster later-than-usual starts).

■ Retirement Transitions

The number of faculty retirement programs and policies that cover pre- and postretirement for faculty has been growing.[15] To best meet the needs of retiring individuals, institutions will need to move beyond simply finding ways for faculty to feel secure about their finances and health coverage, and work to help faculty find outlets through which to continue their "positive accomplishments." Fortunately, many of the ways through which faculty may continue these efforts are beneficial to their institutions.

As noted earlier, the ACE is examining how institutions currently support the culminating stages of a senior faculty member's career.[16] The ACE is especially interested in three areas of retirement transitions: (1) the development of a legacy; (2) the transition into retirement; and (3) the continuing contribution to the campus community in postretirement. Strategies to facilitate retirement transitions include the following:

- Institutional approaches to encourage faculty retirement so that institutions may "renew" their tenured faculty;[17]
- Retirement incentives such as the UC Voluntary Early Retirement Incentive Programs (VERIPS);[18]
- Use of retired faculty to teach or fulfill institutional needs;[19]
- Use of periodic performance appraisals, postretirement employment, and other strategies for re-engaging older faculty members;[20]
- Use of phased retirement;
- Awareness and perceptions of retirement plans by faculty;
- Resources for faculty as they plan for retirement;[21]
- Good institutional responses to assist with the transition, including retirement celebrations.[22]

Staff

Within higher education, less attention has been given to strategies for staff. In other work sectors, however, research studies and surveys have demonstrated the benefits of a flexible workplace for all employees:

By definition, the term "flexible" means there is no "one size fits all." The needs of a non-tenured academic mother with a newborn differ significantly from those of a staff member who wants to leave early for an exercise class.[23]

Here are some common strategies for creating a flexible workplace:

■ Flexible Work Arrangements (FWA)

These arrangements are used to design when, where, and how work is completed.

- Flextime: Staff members choose their arrival and departure times during a flexible time period;
- Compressed work weeks: A regular 40-hour-week schedule is compressed into fewer than 5 days, which creates extended weekends;
- Telecommuting: A common approach that allows an employee to work from another location, typically home, from one day a week or full time;
- Part-time work: A reduction of hours, which also implies a reduction in pay and benefits;
- Job sharing: Two staff members, working part-time, share the responsibilities of a single position;
- Seasonal schedule: Staff members work full-time hours for part of the year and work part-time hours for other parts of the year. For example, this approach is common for offices that are extremely busy during the nine-month academic year but slow down considerably during the summer months.

■ Career Flexibility

- Some institutions implement strategies that retain outstanding staff members while also allowing for flexibility. These approaches may include leaves of absence, reduced schedules, temporary departure from the workforce, or phased retirement programs.

The University of Washington provides these tips for implementing flexible work arrangements with staff:

■ "Perform workforce planning of the entire work team, evaluating the appropriateness of flexibility work arrangements for each position"
■ "Include the work team in the planning process"
■ "Always pilot new initiatives"
■ "Document details of the arrangements"[24]

Not all staff positions may allow for flexibility; however, before assuming that flexibility is not feasible, leaders may want to consider redesigning the work to allow for flexibility. Work redesign entails a process that examines how work is designed and structured, determines essential tasks, identifies waste or low-value time at work, and develops an efficient work flow.[25] For example, cross-training student services staff to better respond to the ebb and flow of student needs at different points in the semester (e.g., registration, advising) can provide for flexibility in staffing. Another example is moving certain processes online (advising through chat sessions or self-serve options for students, such as graduation checks), which can be reviewed by student services staff during flexible hours and don't require face-to-face meetings. A third example is changing an office's hours one day per week to open early or to stay open late to accommodate staff schedules.

Dependent Care/Caregiving

As noted previously, with the rise of dual-income earners working full time, child care is a prevalent issue. Today, in addition to children, however, dependents can be any individuals who rely on the care of others, including elders or adults with disabilities. As explained in Chapters 1 and 2, elder care is on the rise, resulting in the sandwiched generation, who are caring for both children and adults, often in the same household, which further exacerbates the caregiving responsibilities.

Child Care

The choice to have or to not have children affects the career trajectory for faculty, traditionally for women, and more recently, for men as well. Because child care was one of the early recognizable work-life issues, many of the most sophisticated policies, programs, and benefits have been developed to help faculty, staff, and students manage these responsibilities. The COACHE Survey revealed an average rating of 3.50 (from 1 = Very unimportant to 5 = Very important) for the importance of child care.[26] Thorough descriptions of all policies and program are beyond the scope of this chapter, but the following list highlights the key issues.

- Convenient and affordable quality child care for faculty and staff:
  - Establish on-site child-care facilities
  - Acquire grants to operate on-campus child-care facilities
  - Work with the state to obtain funding for child care
  - Partner with child-care facilities in the community

- Develop a child-care network
- Offer a child-care subsidy program
- Establish online posting systems for child care.

■ Convenient and affordable child care for students through the Child Care Access Means Parents in School (CCAMPIS) grant program (U.S. Department of Education Resource and Referral Services)

■ A baby-sitting coordinator who connects faculty and staff with students who want to provide this work

■ Back-up/emergency care

■ Care for sick children

■ Resource and referral for sick children

■ Care for school-age children/after-school care

■ Snow camps/days

■ Dependent care travel grants

■ Adoption supports

■ Lactation support

■ Pregnancy and childbirth leave

■ Primary caregiver leave or family sick leave

■ Reserving space in a childcare facility for candidates being recruited to the institution, guaranteeing a place for the child if the candidate joins the institution

■ Baby showers.

It is important to note that some institutions, such as Princeton University, provide similar accommodations for graduate students, while others, such as The Ohio State University and the University of Michigan, support a Student Family Office.

Another related issue for higher education institutions concerns children in the workplace. Iowa State University, for example, established a policy to welcome children to the university, minimize the risk of injury to children, and promote an environment conducive to accomplishing the university's family-friendly mission. At Iowa State, department chairs and directors have the authority to approve or deny the presence of non-student children on campus, including in the classroom.[27] Other institutions, however, prohibit non-student children on campus.

Elder/Adult Care

Elder care is a responsibility that can be relevant for all individuals regardless of gender, race, or ethnicity. Only in recent years has the care of elderly individuals been recognized as a caregiving or dependent care responsibility; thus, work-life friendly universities have been expanding their definitions of dependent care beyond child care. Unfortunately, because of lack of visibility and misunderstandings about elder care, leadership response to elder care has not always been friendly or supportive.

There are several strategies that institutions can implement to provide support for elder-caregivers, including the following:

- Elder-care consultation and referral
- Elder-care workshops/support groups
- Elder-care resource expo
- End-of-life supports (flexible work arrangements, personal and bereavement leaves, consultation and referral services, etc.)
- Subsidized emergency or respite in-home elder-care services
- Direct elder-care services
- Geriatric care managers
- Supports for community-based services
- Adult-care centers
- Intergenerational care programs.

With the aging society, a significant increase in elder caregiving by faculty and staff is expected, and academic leaders must be prepared to respond to those needs.

Child Care, Elder Care, and Domestic Partner Benefits

Because of the complexity of much of the information regarding benefits supporting work-life, it is best to rely on the Office of Human Resources benefits experts at your institution. Nonetheless, it is important for a work-life leader to know the appropriate individual for referral and resource. Two common specific work-life friendly benefits are as follows:

- Flexible spending accounts to pay for child care, elder care, health, vision, and dental coverage;
- Flexible benefit programs or cafeteria-style benefits that can be customized for each family.

Paid and Unpaid Leave

The value of time for faculty and staff cannot be overstated. Paid and unpaid leave often refers to the time spent away from work to be with family, friends, and self. The COACHE Survey revealed an average rating of 3.72 (from

1 = Very unimportant to 5 = Very important) for the importance of "Paid or unpaid personal leave during the pre-tenure period."[28] Some of the best institutional practices that can facilitate work-life effectiveness include the following:

- Annual Leave and Family Sick Leave
  It is standard policy that employees accrue annual/vacation leave; however, at most institutions, faculty who are not on 12-month contracts do not accrue this leave, making it difficult to manage life and family obligations during the academic year. In most cases, sick leave is available for both faculty and staff. Institutional policies vary with regard to the purpose of this type of leave; in some cases, the leave may be used only for oneself. At other institutions, policies are broader and include family sick leave. In fact, some states require employers to allow sick leave for dependents.

- Paid Parental Leave
  Various policies exist for helping mothers and fathers adjust to newborn or adopted infants and children. In most institutions, mothers may use sick leave to cover the birth of a child, or they might be required to take a short-term or long-term disability leave. Progressive work-life friendly institutions treat pregnancy leave as they treat other kinds of disability leave and offer parental leave policies on the basis of caretaking status, not biological sex (i.e., not only maternity leave).[29] Another consideration for supporting paid parental leave is to establish a central fund to cover instructors or other expenses. Deans or department chairs may hesitate to support leave from work if they have to cover the costs from their own budgets.

- Leave Without Pay
  Because time is highly valued, faculty and staff may be willing to take time off without pay. Policies that allow for taking leave without pay can help employees manage work and life responsibilities without jeopardizing their positions and careers. Of course, the Family and Medical Leave Act (FMLA) requires that employers allow for unpaid time off.

- Bereavement Leave
  Many institutions allow short periods of time off with pay for those who are bereaved by the death of an immediate family member. Typical leave is three days with paid time off.

- Shared Leave
  This program allows employees to donate part of their annual leave, sick leave, and/or personal holiday hours to co-workers whose leave has been depleted but who need to take leave for unusual circumstances.

Tips for a Shared-Leave Program[30]

■ Review shared-leave policies at the state and local levels as well as peer institutions;
■ Promote the importance of community and of supporting colleagues in need.

■ Paid or Release Time for Community Service
Although most faculty members are engaged in their communities as part of their work assignments, this may not be the case for staff members. Some institutions allow employees to volunteer during work hours. For example, an institution may hold a university community day in which faculty, staff, and students are assigned to various volunteer activities, or a department may work together in holding a drive for donations to a domestic violence shelter.

Dual-Career Assistance or Spousal/Partner Hiring

The statistics clearly reveal that dual-career partners are on the rise and are especially prevalent in higher education. Many partners meet in graduate school or at professional conferences, for example. In one study of 9,000 faculty employed by 13 leading research universities, researchers found that 72% of faculty have partners who work full time (36% of whom are academic partners, making them dual-career academic couples).[31] Most candidates now inquire about spousal/partner employment. It is not unusual for a talented scholar being recruited at a prestigious university to expect employment for his or her partner or spouse.

"Women academics are disproportionately impacted in dual career hiring because more academic women than men have academic spouses (particularly in science and engineering) and women are more likely than men to refuse a job offer because they have not found a suitable position for their partner. One challenge faced by dual career policies is avoiding the situation in which the non-recruited partner carries a stigma of being less qualified, and (in the case of a professor) being a financial and intellectual burden on their department."[32]

Work-life friendly institutions have sophisticated policies and programs in place that provide dual-career assistance. A dual-career hiring/assistance program or relocation office can serve as a centralized location for partner placement within the University or in the community. A proactive service or program allows administrators to address dual-career concerns early in the recruitment process to avoid wasting time and resources. These services also enhance the attractiveness of the institution as an employer. Here are some strategies for supporting dual careers:

- Establish a central office or department, or designate an individual (faculty/staff) in the Provost or Dean's Office with credibility and influence to negotiate dual-career arrangements;
- Provide the individual with the resources necessary to create opportunities both within and outside the university;
- Develop and publish a dual-career academic hiring protocol, using language that minimizes discrimination and stigma;
- Provide services to support resumes, career counseling, and networking;
- Offer bridge funding by the Provost's office to assist couples who both want to be on the faculty in a department that cannot provide two full-time positions;
- Provide funding for relocation issues;
- Give spouses and partners access to web-based searchable databases with access to prospective employers;[33]
- Provide ways to link spouses and partners with non-academic employers in the area.[34]
- Create a brochure and provide resources for new faculty to demonstrate the University's commitment to dual-career couples;[35]
- Coordinate all stakeholders or partners. For example, the University of Massachusetts, Amherst implemented a Partner Employment Program (PEP). With this program, partners of candidates for faculty may be hired as faculty, librarians, or administrative staff across the university. If the partner of the candidate is offered a position in a separate department, the funding for that position is provided equally by the Provost, the candidate's department, and the partner's department for a minimum of three years;[36]
- Join a consortium that helps find positions at nearby institutions. For example, the Higher Education Recruitment Consortium (HERC) provides assistance for dual-academic career couples.

Financial Support

Financial stress can have a significant impact on employee well-being, and several strategies exist to provide some relief for financial stress:

- Tuition assistance or remission allows for tuition discounting or full tuition remission for self, spouses, and dependents;
- Housing assistance may include assistance in the form of forgivable loans, or reduced housing rates for apartments or homes owned by the University;

- Child-care subsidies can help offset the high cost of child care for faculty and staff, depending on family size, income, and so forth;
- Dependent care travel grants offer financial assistance to reduce the burden of work-life costs associated with travel, such as extra dependent care at home while the caregiver is traveling, on-site care at a conference, or transportation costs for a caregiver or dependent;
- Work-life balance research grants are funds to support professional development. For instance, at Lehigh University, grants are provided to help untenured faculty members build and sustain research productivity when providing dependent care. Grants may be used for research, but they also may be used for expenses related to caregiving.[37] Similarly, the University of Washington offers a Transitional Support Program to help faculty members maintain their research productivity during life-changing events that could negatively impact their careers.
- Several other programs exist that may provide financial assistance or support, such as:
  - Financial and retirement planning consultation and programs
  - Commuter benefits
  - Adoption assistance
  - Long-term care insurance
  - Employee discounts
  - On-site credit unions.

Health and Wellness

Employees at higher education institutions may take for granted their access to on-site fitness centers, recreational facilities, or health and wellness programs. For example, the Worksite Wellness program at the University of Arizona offers heart health screenings, individual nutrition and fitness coaching, exercise classes, planned walking options, and newsletters.[38] Additional health and wellness activities on some campuses include the following:

- Health fairs/health education
- Education/informational materials
- Health risk assessment (blood work, strength testing, cardio testing, flexibility testing)
- Weight control programs
- Stress management programs
- Smoking cessation programs
- On-site exercise classes, massage, and yoga
- On-site medical and dental care
- Employee assistance counseling/consultation
- Walking tours or programs.

Professional Development

Work-life experts will advocate for the professional development of faculty and staff as a strategy to facilitate work-life effectiveness and satisfaction. Mentoring programs for junior faculty are especially important, as are institutional professional networking opportunities for women. Activities that facilitate the mixing of junior and senior faculty are helpful because senior faculty can provide mentoring and role modeling.[39] Some institutions have affinity groups, in which individuals with similar interests engage outside of work. Other workshops may include time-management training, research workshops, grant-writing workshops, distance-learning training, and pedagogical strategies.[40] An academic leader will take advantage of these different strategies to provide mentoring and support throughout faculty and staff careers.[41]

Other Work-Life Strategies

The following strategies, which are common on many campuses, may improve work and life satisfaction and effectiveness because of on-campus accessibility and reduced costs:

- Ombudsperson
- Workplace convenience services (e.g., on-site ATMs)
- U.S. post office or other mailing/shipping services
- Company store/bookstore
- Take-home meals from student union
- Libraries and museums
- Theatre and music
- Recreational activities (tennis courts, canoes, kayaks, racquetball, etc.)
- Pet-care resources, insurance, and pets in the workplace.

On the other hand, work-life services not typical for campuses but offered in the corporate world include concierge services, handy services, dry cleaning, and on-site manicures, pedicures, and haircuts, to name a few!

Training for Deans and Department Heads/Chairs/Other Staff Supervisors

Institutions serious about facilitating work-life cultures know that the gatekeepers of implementing relevant programs and policies are administrators, especially deans, department heads and chairs, and other supervisors. Their responses, discussed further in Chapter 4, can determine whether and how policies are understood and implemented.[42] Unfortunately, these individuals do not always know what strategies exist for various situations. As explained in Chapter 6, Boise State University, University California, Berkeley (UC Berkeley), and Oregon State University are three institutions that have created toolkits to train administrators and leaders on the financial and recruitment benefits for supporting work-life as well as educate them about the university services that facilitate a work-life culture.[43] The University of Washington conducts specific leadership workshops, and UC Berkeley provides a "School for Chairs" where

> Chairs are taught to discount resume gaps attributable to parenthood, mentor new parents through the tenure process, help find a second job for dual-career couples, create a more family-responsive climate through small changes such as ending faculty meetings by 5 p.m., and ensure that stopping the clock or taking family leave does not count against candidates.[44]

The University of California, Davis (UC Davis) provides a mentoring program for department chairs that guides them in being more family-life responsive. Without appropriate training and knowledge, an academic leader could unknowingly violate state and/or federal laws, as discussed in the next section.

APPLICABLE WORK-LIFE REQUIREMENTS MANDATED BY STATE AND FEDERAL LAWS

Few federal and state laws exist that directly address work-life issues, but if these laws are violated, then institutions could face serious consequences. Many claims for family responsibilities discrimination (FRD)/caregiver discrimination are brought under Title VII of the Civil Rights Act of 1964. FMLA provides some protections, along with the Americans with Disabilities Act, Equal Pay Act of 1963, and Employee Retirement Income Security Act (ERISA). State and local laws, too, provide protections against caregiver bias. As agents for the institution, our acts represent the university; thus, it behooves academic leaders to be familiar with relevant laws.

Title VII of the Civil Rights Act (CRA) of 1964

Although the focus of this book is not on gender disparity, and others have written extensively about the gender differences in the academy, female faculty and staff members frequently face larger challenges than male faculty and staff when balancing work, family, and life obligations as noted earlier.[45] Research and practice consistently demonstrate that women and men are treated differently in the realm of work-family-life responsibilities, which can create gender-based discrimination. Differential treatment is a violation of Title VII of the Civil Rights of 1964, which prohibits sex discrimination.

Some institutions have developed strategies to control gender-based biases. An online training or face-to-face workshop may be offered, especially within the context of recruitment and hiring. Gender bias training can be offered to faculty search committees along with recruitment and toolkits for the searches. Many institutions closely monitor the search processes, which may include having an equity advisor serve on each search committee or the use of standardized evaluation tools. Gender bias training for all faculty is essential, especially with regard to advancement, recruitment, and retention decisions.[46]

Federal Family Medical Leave Act (FMLA) of 1993

The FMLA allows eligible faculty and staff to take up to 12 weeks of unpaid leave within a leave year for their own serious health condition, the serious health condition of a family member, or the care of a newborn or newly placed adoptive or foster child. FMLA provides job protection, job restoration, and continuation of medical and dental benefits during the leave period. To be eligible, employees must have been employed for at least 12 months and have worked at least 1,250 hours in the 12 months immediately preceding the date that the leave begins. Additionally, FMLA prohibits discrimination or retaliation against employees who have taken FMLA-protected leave.[47] Other policy guidelines may be specified for your institution.

Federal Pregnancy Discrimination Act

The Pregnancy Discrimination Act of 1978 amended Title VII of the 1964 CRA to prohibit sex discrimination based on pregnancy. The Act provides protections in the areas of hiring, pregnancy and maternity leave, health insurance, and fringe benefits.[48] Women who are affected by pregnancy-related conditions or are pregnant must be treated in the same way as other applicants or workers with similar abilities or limitations. The easiest solution is to apply the same requirements to pregnancy leave as are applied to other medical leaves. For example, a violation can occur when women faculty are required to find instructors to teach their courses while on maternity leave, yet this same requirement is not applied to professors who take medical leave for other reasons, such as cancer.[49]

Federal Breastfeeding Law

Section 4207 of the Patient Protection and Affordable Care Act amended the Fair Labor Standards Act (FLSA), or federal wage and hour law. Employers are required to provide reasonable break time and a private, non-bathroom place for mothers to express breast milk during the work days for one year after the child's birth.[50] Additional criteria are provided to make spaces appropriate.

State Laws

It is important for academic leaders to know that many states have established specific requirements pertaining to work-family-life. Some family leave laws exist at the state level, such as the Oregon Family Leave Act (OFLA), and other

> "Know your university's policies and procedures— it gives you options." (Dr. Rebecca Warner, Senior Vice Provost for Academic Affairs, University of Oregon)

states have specific breastfeeding laws. Work-life leaders should know the expectations of their particular states.[51]

RECOMMENDATIONS

The following recommendations support the development, implementation, and advocacy of the aforementioned work-life policies, services, benefits, and activities. Additional specific strategies for academic leaders are presented in Chapter 6.[52]

- Establish formal written policies and official practices. Informal policies increase the risk of discrimination and mistreatment;
- Address issues that discourage faculty and staff from using work-life policies;
- Develop policies as opt-out (entitlement) rather than opt-in (discretionary), which provides the expectations that faculty and staff are to use the policies available to them. With an opt-in policy, faculty must request or negotiate with department chairs to use the policy or program, which can be uncomfortable especially with an uninformed administrator;[53]
- Strengthen transparency, communication, and outreach. Ensure that written policies are communicated to everyone; for instance, this can be accomplished through a user-friendly website. If your institution does not have a work-life website, work with the director of college communication to link the college's webpage;
- Designate personnel/staff, such as an associate dean or associate chair, to oversee work-life and family issues in your unit;
- Extend beyond FMLA to provide leave and release time options that are more focused on addressing faculty and staff parents;
- Recognize and respond to work-life needs throughout the career and life cycle, including early career, mid-career, late career, and retirement transitioning;
- Review, evaluate, and adjust the workload of faculty and staff members;
- Create guidelines for family-responsive meeting times by establishing a set of hours that would be ideal to schedule important meetings and functions while minimizing conflicts with family responsibilities;
- Conduct ongoing evaluation of available policies and programs, and learn from the research and experiences of others;
- Ensure that practice supports policy;
- Show support beginning with leadership at the top.

Additionally, several effective policies and programs for the retention and advancement of women have been offered, and we contend that these strategies can benefit all faculty members regardless of gender (Table 3.4).

Table 3.4 Effective Policies and Programs for Retention and Advancement of Women in Academia[54]

Categories of Effective Policies and Programs	Specific Policies and Programs Within Each Category
Find Out What Your Needs Are	For example, surveys of faculty and staff to assess work-life needs and effectiveness of policies and programs
Parental Leaves and Stop-the-Clock Policies	Maternal and parental leave • Treat pregnancy leave the same as other kinds of disability leave • Design parental leave policies on the basis of caretaking status, not sex • Provide central funding for leave Stop-the-clock option • Stop the tenure clock for new parents • Broader application of stop-the-clock policies "Opt-out" instead of "opt-in" policies
Dual-Career Support	A dual-career academic couple hiring protocol Wording that minimizes discrimination and stigma An official within the Office of the Provost with appropriate credibility and influence to help broker dual-career arrangements Provide the official with the resources necessary to cultivate opportunities • Bridge funding • Interdepartmental coordination • Coordination with local institutions
Mentoring and Networking Programs	Mentoring programs to support junior faculty • Automatic mentor assignment • Women mentoring women network Institute professional networking opportunities for women • Women's faculty forum
Child-Care Needs	Convenient and affordable child care Dependent care travel grants
Part-Time Tenure Track Alternative	Temporary and permanent part-time tenure track
Control Bias	[See Chapter 6 of this guide for strategies]
Flexibility Benefit Programs	Cafeteria-style benefits
Practice Supports Policy	Trained family leave specialist Leadership from the top • Joint statements or publicized statements by leaders Strengthen transparency, communication, and outreach • Develop clearly stated and well-publicized family-responsive policies • Monitor policy usage

CONCLUSION

This chapter offers an overview to familiarize academic leaders with strategies to facilitate work-life effectiveness and satisfaction. As effective leaders, we need to know the options and either strive for their implementation or advocate for their inclusion on campus. As emphasized throughout this guide, as academic leaders, we have a responsibility to shape and influence a work-life culture by communicating our support and implementing best practices and policies.

Questions for Discussion and Reflection

1. Does your department or unit have a mentoring program? Is the program effective? Who, among your staff or faculty, might be suited to lead the development or revision of such a program?

2. Who is the local campus expert on work-life policies? What is your relationship with this individual?

3. How can you become aware of and initiate conversations about the work-life needs of your faculty and staff without violating their privacy?

4. What are the work-life policies specific to your state?

5. What small step can you take today to improve the work-life culture within your department or unit?

NOTES

1. Kelly, E. L., Kossek, E. E., Hammer, L. B., Durham, M., Bray, J., Chermack, K., ... Kaskubar, D. (2008). Getting there from here: Research on the effects of work–family initiatives on work–family conflict and business outcomes. *The Academy of Management Annals, 2*(1), 305–349, pp. 305–307.
2. Friedman, D. E., Rimsky, C., & Johnson, A.A. (1996). *College and university reference guide to work-family programs.* New York, NY: Families and Work Institute. Retrieved from www.eric.ed.gov/ERICWebPortal/recordDetail?accno=ED406939
3. Tufts University Arts, Sciences and Engineering Faculty Task Force on Work/Life Balance. (2012, February). *Report of the Tufts University Arts, sciences and engineering faculty task force on work/life balance.* Boston, MA: Tufts University.
4. Tufts University (2012).
5. Lester & Sallee (2009).
6. Friedman et al. (1996); Alliance for Work-Life Progress, an Affiliate of WorldatWork (2006). *State of the work-life profession: April 2006.* Scottsdale, AZ: Author; Koppes & Civian (2010); Nuter (2011).
7. August, L., Miller, J., & Hollenshead, C. (2007). *Research brief: Family-friendly policies in higher education.* Ann Arbor, MI: The Center for the Education of Women, University of Michigan.
8. Bowman, L., & Feeney, M. (2011). *Laundry and lab time: Do family-friendly policies affect academic work outcomes?* Presentation for the Midwest Political Science Conference, Chicago, Illinois; Gerten, A. (2011). Moving beyond family-friendly policies for mothers. *Affilia: Journal of*

Women and Social Work, 26(1), 47–58; Hill, M. S., Nash, A., & Citera, M. (2011). Parenthood in academia: What happens when there is no policy? *Wagadu, 9,* 113–139; Quinn, K. (2010). Tenure clock extension policies: Who uses them and to what effect? *NASPA Journal About Women in Higher Education, 3*(1), 182–206; Pribbenow, C. M., Sheridan, J., Winchell, J., Benting, D., Handelsman, J., & Carnes, M. (2010). The tenure process and extending the tenure clock: The experience of faculty at one university. *Higher Education Policy, 23,* 17–38; Sallee, M. (2008). Work and family balance: How community college faculty cope. *New Directions for Community Colleges, 142,* 81–91; Townsend, B. K. (2008). Community colleges as gender-equitable institutions. *New Directions for Community Colleges, 142,* 7–14; Welch, J., Wiehe, S. E., Palmer-Smith, V., & Dankoski, M. E. (2011). Flexibility in faculty work-life policies at medical schools in the big ten conference. *Journal of Women's Health, 20*(5), 725–732.

9. American Council on Education. (2013c). *Alfred P. Sloan projects for faculty career flexibility.* Retrieved from www.acenet.edu/leadership/programs/Pages/Alfred-P-Sloan-Projects-for-Faculty-Career-Flexibility.aspx

10. Smith & Waltman (2006).

11. Philipsen & Bostic (2010), pp. 117–118.

12. Smith & Waltman (2006).

13. Smith & Waltman (2006).

14. American Council on Education (2013c).

15. Berberet et al. (2010); Tizard B. (2004). Support for retired academic staff: University policies and practices. *Oxford Review of Education, 30*(2), 257–263.

16. American Council on Education (2010). *Review of faculty retirement literature.* Washington, DC.

17. Clark, R. L., & d'Ambrosio, M. B. (2005). Recruitment, retention, and retirement: Compensation and employment policies for higher education. *Educational Gerontology, 31*(5), 385–403; Senese, J. D. (2008). The institutional challenges of full-time faculty retirement: Has the expedition accomplished all that it promised and that it should accomplish? *Academic Leadership, 6*(3).

18. Gustman, A. L., & Steinmeier, T. L. (1991). The effects of pensions and retirement policies on retirement in higher education. *The American Economic Review, 81*(2), 111–115; Yakoboski, P. (2005, October). Findings from the retirement confidence survey of college and university faculty, *TIAA-CREF Institute Trends and Issues.* Retrieved from www.tiaa-cref.org/public/pdf/institute/research/trends_issues/tr1031051.pdf; Durbin, N. E., Gross, E., & Borgatta, E. F. (1984). The decision to leave work: The case of retirement from an academic career. *Research on Aging, 6*(4), 572–592; Ghent, L. S., Allen, S. G., & Clark, R. L. (2001). The impact of a new phased retirement option on faculty retirement decisions. *Research on Aging, 23*(6), 671–693; Weiler, W. C. (1981). Simulation of institutional incentive plans for faculty early retirement using a behavioral model of retirement decision-making. *Research in Higher Education, 15*(2), 129–139.

19. Bellack, J. P. (2004). One solution to the faculty shortage: Begin at the end. *Journal of Nursing Education, 43*(6), 243–244; Walz et al. (1991).

20. Falk, N. L. (2007). Strategies to enhance retention and effective utilization of aging nurse faculty. *Journal of Nursing Education, 46*(4), 165–169; Uhlenberg, P. (1992). Population aging and social policy. *Annual Review of Sociology, 18,* 449–474; Schrank, H. T., & Waring, J. M. (1989). Older workers: Ambivalence and interventions. *Annals of the American Academy of Political and Social Science, 503,* 113–126; Huston, T. A., Norman, M., & Ambrose, S. A. (2007). Expanding the discussion of faculty vitality to include productive but disengaged senior faculty. *Journal of Higher Education, 78*(5), 493–522; Wood, M., & Johnsrud, L. K. (2005). Post-tenure review: What matters to faculty. *Review of Higher Education, 28*(3), 393–420.

21. Murphy, C. H. (2009). Retiring in a time of economic uncertainty. *Academe, 95*(5), 36–38.

22. Leslie, D. W. (2005). New ways to retire. *New Directions for Higher Education, 132,* 5–7; Goodman & Pappas (2000).

23. Abramson, S. (2013). Creating flexible work policies: One size does NOT fit all. *Women in Higher Education 22*(8), p. 1.
24. Lester & Sallee (2009), p. 27.
25. Alliance for Work-Life Progress. (2006). *Introduction to work-life effectiveness: Successful work-life programs to attract, motivate and retain employees.* Retrieved from www.worldatwork.org/adim/seminars/html/seminars-w1.jsp
26. Trower (2012).
27. Iowa State University. (2009). *Children in the workplace.* Retrieved from www.policy.iastate.edu/policy/children/workplace
28. Trower (2012).
29. The Center for WorkLife Law (2013).
30. Lester & Sallee (2009), p. 33.
31. The Center for WorkLife Law (2013).
32. The Center for WorkLife Law (2013), pp. 20–21.
33. Philipsen & Bostic (2010).
34. Philipsen & Bostic (2010).
35. Philipsen & Bostic (2010).
36. The Center for WorkLife Law (2013).
37. Lester & Sallee (2009).
38. Lester & Sallee (2009).
39. Porter, R. (2004). Off the launching pad: Stimulating proposal development by junior faculty. *Journal of Research Administration, 35*(1), 6–11.
40. Trower (2012).
41. Trower (2012).
42. Ward & Wolf-Wendel (2012).
43. President's Commission on the Status of Women (2010). *Promoting work/life balance: A look at OSU's work/life potential.* Corvallis: Oregon State University.
44. The Center for WorkLife Law (2013).
45. Bain, O., & Cummings, W. (2000). Academe's glass ceiling: Societal, professional/organizational, and institutional barriers to the career advancement of academic women. *Comparative Education Review, 44*(4), 493–514; Bingham, T., & Nix, S. (2010). Women faculty in higher education: A case study on gender bias. *The Forum on Public Policy,* 1–12; Santos, G. G., & Cabral-Cardoso, C. (2008). Work-family culture in academia: A gendered view of work-family conflict and coping strategies. *Gender in Management: An International Journal, 23*(6), 442–457; Suitor, J. J., Mecom, D., & Feld, I. S. (2001). Gender, household labor, and scholarly productivity among university professors. *Gender Issues, Fall,* 50–67; Winkler (2000).
46. The Center for WorkLife Law (2013).
47. Family and Medical Leave Act, 29 U.S.C. § 2611 (1993).
48. U.S. Equal Employment Opportunity Commission (2008). *Facts about pregnancy discrimination.* Retrieved from www.eeoc.gov/facts/fs-preg.html
49. The Center for WorkLife Law (2013).
50. United States Breastfeeding Committee. (2013). Retrieved from www.usbreastfeeding.org; The Center for WorkLife Law (2013).
51. National Conference of State Legislatures. (2013). Retrieved from www.ncsl.org
52. Trower (2012); Ward & Wolf-Wendel (2012); The Center for WorkLife Law (2013).
53. The Center for WorkLife Law (2013).
54. The Center for WorkLife Law (2013).

Chapter 4

Facilitating Cultural Change

Scholars and practitioners strongly advocate that the best approach to facilitating work-life satisfaction and effectiveness is to cultivate an organizational climate or culture in which policies, programs, and benefits are the "way of doing things around here" and are no longer viewed as special programs or benefits. Although the terms organizational "culture" and "climate" are often used interchangeably, organizational culture is defined as the fundamental beliefs and values of an organization, while climate is the outward manifestation of those values such as the policies, procedures, benefits, and programs of the organization.[1] An organization's culture consists of three layers (Figure 4.1).[2] The innermost layer includes

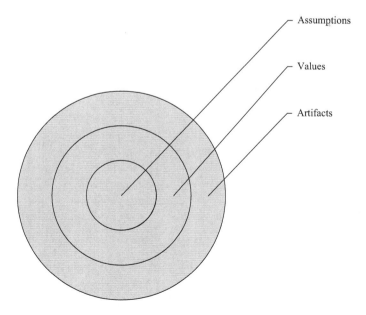

Assumptions

Values

Artifacts

FIGURE 4.1 The Three Layers of an Organizational Culture

the assumptions underlying the culture; these assumptions are deeply embedded, rarely discussed, and difficult to change. When identified, however, the assumptions can explain organizational practices. For example, what is the underlying assumption when an employee who takes a leave of absence to adopt a child is not promoted even though she or he may meet the qualifications? The middle layer of the organizational culture consists of the norms and ideologies, or values. Organizations profess that their values drive their operational practices and often share them when communicating the vision and mission. Examples of values are integrity, trustworthiness, and family centeredness. In other words, what matters? The external, or top layer, is the layer of artifacts. Artifacts are directly observable in the work environment, and they inform others about the organization's culture. For instance, an organization that values families may sponsor a family picnic. This layer is sometimes referred to as the climate.[3]

WORK-LIFE CULTURE

It is important to acknowledge that there are many cultures in higher education institutions.[4] Faculty and staff work within a broad academic culture as well as cultures specific to their various disciplines (e.g., psychology, physics, medicine, English). Cultures also vary by types of institutions, which range from large comprehensive research institutions to small liberal arts colleges. A work-life friendly culture is not a separate culture of its own; instead, it is a sum of all the parts of the institution. Research studies have documented the nature and importance of work environments that are supportive of life and families.[5] In one study, survey respondents stated that their comfort level and willingness to discuss work, life, and family balance was a function of their department's culture.[6]

Several researchers have used Schein's conceptualization of organization culture when defining a work-life culture (Table 4.1).[7] For example, three dimensions of a work-family culture were discerned from the research: (1) expectations about time at the organization that may interfere with family obligations, (2) managerial support for managing work-family responsibilities, and (3) consequences for one's career as a result of using work-family programs and benefits.[8] Workers in a culture that is perceived to be work-life friendly are more likely to participate in work-sponsored, parental leave policies,[9] and departments that are life-friendly are essential for the continued vitality of any university or college.

In organizations, a work-life culture develops over time and evolves through several stages.[10] In the first stage, a limited work-life program is implemented, which focuses on specific issues, such as dependent care or child care. In the second stage, a broad-based diverse work-life program is designed and developed. In this case,

Table 4.1 Definitions of Work-Life Cultures

- A work-life culture is one in which managers and supervisors recognize that professional and personal lives are not mutually exclusive and acknowledge that individuals want to be appreciated for being workers and understood as human beings with life obligations.[i]
- A work-life culture includes the extent to which the organization supports and values the integration of employees' personal lives with their professional lives through shared assumptions, beliefs, and values.[ii]
- A work-life culture exists when "Its overarching philosophy or belief structure is sensitive to the family needs of its employees and is supportive of employees who are combining paid work and family roles."[iii]
- A work-life culture is when the artifacts, values, and assumptions (three levels of culture) influence an employee's capability to manage work and family.[iv]

[i] Koppes (2008), see endnote 107 in Chapter 1.
[ii] Thompson et al. (1999), see endnote 110 in Chapter 1.
[iii] Warren & Johnson (1995), p. 163, see endnote 7 in Chapter 4.
[iv] Lewis (1997), see endnote 7 in Chapter 4.

however, strategies are implemented on an ad hoc basis. The Alliance for Work-Life Progress (AWLP), an affiliate of WorldatWork, advocates that a successful work-life program is one that implements best practices within a work-life portfolio. This portfolio consists of seven categories of work-life strategies and solutions:

- Workplace flexibility
- Health and well-being
- Creative use of paid and unpaid time off
- Dependent care (child, elder/adult)
- Financial support
- Community involvement
- Managing cultural challenges.[11]

Organizations may implement four strategies during the second stage of developing a work-life program:

- Time-based strategies to help employees manage their time, (e.g. flexible scheduling and leave policies);
- Information-based strategies that assist employees with decision making by providing appropriate information. (e.g., options for elder care);
- Money-based strategies that provide financial support to employees (e.g., housing assistance);
- Direct service strategies delivered directly to the workers (e.g., on-site child care).[12]

Table 4.2 Dimensions of Work-Life Culture

- Organizational time demands (work creep)
- Career consequences (caregiver discrimination, gender bias)
- Managerial support
- Work climate for sharing concerns
- Work climate for making sacrifices
- Climate for boundary separation
- Respect for an employee's non-work life[i]

[i]pp. 16–18; Thompson, C.A., Andreassi, J., & Prottas, D. (2003). *Work-family culture and climate.* Paper presented at the NICHD/Sloan Foundation Conference on Workplace/Workforce Mismatch, Washington DC.

In the third stage, these work-life strategies become embedded in the organization's culture (Table 4.2), to reflect concerns for employees' lives outside of work. Finally, stage four is realized when work-life becomes the way of doing things as work processes, systems, structures, and procedures are continuously re-evaluated and re-defined.[13] For instance, if flexibility becomes embedded in the culture, policies, and programs of the university or college, then faculty members can design work arrangements to align with their current personal responsibilities.[14] Higher education institutions designated as "Great Colleges to Work For" by *The Chronicle of Higher Education* have embraced a work-life culture through the achievement of stage four.[15]

A Non Work-Life Culture

As mentioned throughout this text, faculty have a tendency to under use work-life-family policies[16] because of a perceived unsupportive culture or chilly climate.[17] In particular, women with caregiving responsibilities report that some colleagues display a sense of hostility toward them.[18] Consequently, faculty members avoid using policies for fear of repercussion, known as bias avoidance.[19] We noted previously that women faculty members do not take leave for childbirth or caring for newborns and also do not use tenure-clock stoppage policies because they believe they would be hurt professionally by such a choice.[20]

Although some women have been subjected to a chilly culture for quite some time, researchers recently demonstrated that male faculty members who

27%–49% of employees believed that using flexibility could jeopardize their careers.[21]

strive for work-family balance face challenges as well. In one study, although more parents of both sexes were working, few parents felt comfortable using the family-friendly policies designed to ease their workload. This trend is persisting among men in academia as evidence grows that work culture and policies might not align with men's interests in achieving work-life satisfaction.[22] One study demonstrated that institutions had policies for maternity leave but less than half had policies in place for job assistance, flexible scheduling, and/or paternal leave, policies relevant to male academics.[23] Moreover,

> The changing times and the increased involvement in domestic affairs and parenting are not always easy . . . It is good that it is more acceptable now for male faculty to spend more time with their families; however, if one needs child care, and the wife's salary is low, dual-earner existence brings with it financial problems. In addition, on a day-to-day basis "it's a big coordination problem."[24]

Many faculty indicate their support for work- and family-friendly policies, yet, they often do not use them because of negative consequences.[25]

> Fathers as professors reported pervasive conflict and strain and a bias against active fathering.[26]

The underlying explanations for this negative climate are deeply ingrained beliefs about expectations for being a successful academic, that is, the ideal worker. As mentioned previously, the notion of an ideal worker was introduced in 1995 to describe an employee who is completely dedicated and committed to work without outside responsibilities or distractions.[27] Although this view is based on an outdated model of the family structure, employers continue to perceive the ideal worker as one who is single-mindedly committed to work above all else, and this attribute of employees is often seen as contributing to the development of efficient and effective workplaces.[28] In the 21st century, society has generally shifted away from this notion; however, the academy is still lagging behind.

Research studies examining the role of unconscious and implicit assumptions in making judgments consistently demonstrate that even the most conscientious individuals can have negative biases about caregiving and gender. Institutions must address these beliefs for a work-life friendly culture to exist. The following beliefs should be debunked:

1. "The traditional notion of a linear career trajectory without acknowledgement that careers can be flexible and diverse, yet still productive.

2. The perception of child leave and other policies as *accommodations* (thus potentially stigmatizing) rather than legitimate parts of a career trajectory.

3. The perception that work-life balancing policies benefit only faculty with children instead of faculty in diverse family constellations, living arrangements, and at various points in their careers.

4. The idea that institutions have no stake in helping faculty balance their work and family responsibilities."[29]

Discouraging problematic perceptions within the workplace is an effective first step toward creating a work-life culture. With regard to the presence or absence of such damaging ideas about work-life culture in academic departments, two types of departments typically exist. One is a department in which the chair has vague ideas and responds negatively, or not at all, when helping faculty manage work and family. The second department is "creative, proactive, and open about helping faculty get what they need to help them succeed as parents and as professors."[30] Researchers found a significant relationship between the usage of family-friendly policies and the perceptions of a department's supportiveness: "In departments thought to be 'very supportive' of maternal leave policies, 84 percent of women took a leave after childbirth. As those perceived to be 'somewhat supportive' of such policies, the percentage dropped to 57 percent."[31]

> "Fundamentally, the challenge is to change the culture on campus so that fear of bias is reduced, a critical mass of users exists, and career flexibility becomes the 'new normal.'"[32]

THE ROLE OF LEADERS IN TRANSFORMING CULTURE

A classic theory of organizational change reveals that an organization's culture exists in a larger context, and that leadership is the center of that context.[33] The larger context includes the external environment, the organization's mission and strategy, the organization's culture, and individual and organizational performance. At the center, leaders create and change cultures and the context. In order to affect change, the key issues for leaders are how to get at the deeper levels of a culture, how to assess the functionality of assumptions made at each level, and how to deal with the anxiety that is unleashed when those levels are challenged.

Although it is beyond the scope of this guide to review all leadership theories, transformational leadership theory is perhaps the most relevant to shaping a culture that facilitates work-life satisfaction and effectiveness.[34] Transformational leadership involves motivating and empowering followers to commit to and work toward the achievement of group/organizational goals. These leaders build trusting relationships with their followers and create an environment of shared values. Four core dimensions that are characteristic of transformational leadership were proposed.[35] The first, "Idealized (or charismatic) Influence" involves the leader being an admired, trusted, and respected role model for followers. Also essential to this dimension is the leader acting in a moral and ethical way and developing a shared vision and collective interests. Second, "Inspirational Motivation" involves the leader communicating and building relationships with followers. The leader inspires followers to work toward desired organizational goals. Third, "Intellectual Stimulation" refers to the leader encouraging followers to try new approaches and be creative. Finally, "Individualized Consideration" involves the leader giving individual attention to followers, thereby promoting their growth and achievement. These dimensions of transformational leaders are measured by the Multifactor Leadership Questionnaire (MLQ), and have been repeatedly validated.[36]

> "There should be no fear of retribution or firing because of a family issue." (Dr. Janette Brown, Executive Director of the Emeriti Center, University of Southern California)

With a positive leadership approach such as transformational leadership, academic leaders are more likely to shape a work-life culture because faculty and staff will perceive their leaders as being supportive of achieving a healthy balance between their work and personal lives: "Department chairs and deans have a central responsibility in understanding the importance of a family-friendly department and in implementing overall university policies, sharing resources, and reinforcing cultural practices to assist all faculty."[37]

> Cultural change "requires people to think differently as well as to act differently."[38]

FRAMEWORKS FOR CHANGE

In the organizational change literature, many frameworks or models exist that describe the steps or phases for planned change. For our purposes here, three frameworks are outlined (Table 4.3).[39] A synthesis of these frameworks is provided in Table 4.4 to present an overview of the steps involved when planning change. This table is followed by an overview of four specific examples for changing a higher education culture to be responsive to work-life challenges.

89

Table 4.3 Frameworks for Organizational Change

Author	Number of Steps or Phases
Lewin, 1947	3 stages
	Unfreezing
	Moving/Transforming
	Refreezing
Kotter, 1996	8-step path to success for change
	Establish a sense of urgency or the case for change
	Create a powerful guiding coalition
	Develop a vision and strategy for change
	Communicate the change vision/buy-in
	Empower others to act on the vision
	Generate short-term wins
	Don't let up; consolidate gains and produce more change
	Make change stick; institutionalize new approaches
Burke, 2008	4 phases
	The Prelaunch Phase
	The Launch Phase
	The Postlaunch Phase
	Sustaining the Change

Table 4.4 Synthesis of Three Frameworks for Change

Step/Phase 1: Unfreezing	3 processes to unfreeze (Lewin, 1947)	• Disconfirmation of the validity of the status quo • Induction of guilt or survival anxiety • Psychological safety
	Steps 1, 2, 3 (Kotter, 1996)	• Step 1: Establish a sense of urgency • Step 2: Form a powerful guiding coalition • Step 3: Create a vision
	The Prelaunch Phase (Burke, 2008)	• Leader self-examination • Self-awareness • Tolerance for ambiguity • Motives • Values • Gathering information from the external environment • Establishing a need for change • Providing clarity of vision and change
Step/Phase 2: Moving/ Transforming	Tangible changes are introduced and implemented (Lewin, 1947)	
	Steps 4, 5, 6 (Kotter, 1996)	• Step 4: Communicate vision/buy-in • Step 5: Empower others to act on the vision • Step 6: Create short-term wins

	The Launch Phase (Burke, 2008)	• Communication of the need for change • Initiate key activities • Deal with resistance
Step/Phase 3: Refreezing	Changes become relatively permanent; new behaviors are safe from regression (Lewin, 1947)	
	Steps 7, 8 (Kotter, 1996)	• Step 7: Don't let up: Consolidate improvements and produce more change • Step 8: Make change stick: Institutionalize new approaches
	Postlaunch Phase (Burke, 2008)	• Further implementation • Multiple leverage • Taking the heat • Consistency • Perseverance • Repeating the message
	Sustaining the Change (Burke, 2008)	• Dealing with unanticipated consequences • Momentum • Choosing successors • Launching yet again new initiatives

TRANSFORMING WORK-LIFE CULTURES IN HIGHER EDUCATION

The following four examples for changing a culture to be work-life friendly reveal that there is not only one model; a leader must consider which approach will work the best in her or his institution. The first two examples resulted in institution-wide change; the following two examples are applied to specific units or departments.

Institution-Wide Change

Implementation of Kotter's Model

The following steps of Kotter's model were implemented to mobilize institution-wide efforts at Johns Hopkins University (JHU).[40]

1. Establish a sense of urgency.
   To create the case for change, JHU held a daylong leadership conference that focused on work and family issues in academia generally and at JHU specifically. The conference had three primary goals: (1) enhancing leadership awareness, (2) committing to organizational change and intervention, and (3) emphasizing the importance of the approaches

and life-cycle theories that support work-life programs. Consequently, "the first leadership conference brought to the fore the issues of work-life that JHU was facing, promoting a sense of urgency among campus leaders who would be specifically responsible for supporting changes to create a more family-friendly campus."[41]

2. Form a powerful guiding coalition.

In addition to highlighting the work-life program staff who worked across campus in groups, teams, committees, and task forces, the vice president of HR sponsored the formation of a University-wide Work and Family Task Force (WFTF). The coalition also produced a report containing 16 recommendations that advocated for and guided significant changes reflecting work and family perspectives.

3. Create a vision.

Through collecting data, benchmarking with other institutions, reviewing work in other organizations, and attending to national policy and debates, a "picture of the realities of work and family life at Hopkins" was created.[42] A campus-wide vision was formed when the University used the task force recommendations and set priorities in the 5-year strategic plan.

4. Communicate the vision.

Many communication strategies were used including websites, newspapers, brochures, posters, pamphlets, information fairs, workshops, seminars, meetings, policy changes, and an online workshop for supervisors and staff.

5. Empower others to act on the vision.

Empowerment of others was accomplished through workshops, partnerships with other units (e.g., Career management; Provost's Committee on the Status of Women), and the development of a Worklife Advisory Committee.

6. Plan for and create short-term wins.

Short-term goals were established, each year gains were made, and recommendations were completed with directly observable changes. These goals were monitored by staff and the vice president of HR to ensure that the changes would be sustained.

7. Consolidate improvements and produce more change.

"To achieve the long-term change . . . attention must be paid to each step in the consolidation process. It was nearly 6 years from the end of the WFTF meetings to the development of the advisory committee leadership group. During that time, numerous work-life service programs were developed, policies and procedures were changed, and support groups, workshops, and presentations organized and publicized. The program also received a number of awards and other recognition for its work. Each of these reinvigorated the staff and created institutional recognition and support."[43] Participants also created a matrix of work-life programs to illustrate the supportive services available to all employees.

8. Institutionalize new approaches.
    To institutionalize the change, new approaches should be embedded in the operations and culture of the institution. At JHU, this was achieved by establishing new offices that integrated issues and services in ways that reflected work-life issues.

Five Phases for Building a Work-Life Culture

The following five phases[44] were implemented for building a work-life strategy and plan, which led to a perceived cultural shift at the University of Kentucky.[45]

1. Obtain organizational support for work-life effectiveness.
    Before moving forward with implementing change with strategies, it was first important to build the case for work-life effectiveness with relevant stakeholders, not only the senior leadership, but also faculty, staff, managers, supervisors, and HR professionals. One approach was to present the "business" goals of a work-life culture, such as reducing costs, recruiting and retaining talented faculty and staff, enhancing productivity, and achieving competitiveness with similar institutions. Additionally, identifying work-life issues specific to stakeholders helped them to personally understand the issues. Being prepared for and responding to resistance also helped with securing support. With the accomplishment of this step, leaders relied on organizational commitment to continue with the change efforts.

2. Form a work-life task force.
    The task force in this particular case was responsible for conducting a needs assessment and identifying work-life strategies and solutions. The members of this group were engaged with the staffing and work-life issues of the institution. With the achievement of this step, the task force members gained acceptance and commitment for strategies and enhanced buy-in and credibility.

3. Conduct a needs assessment.
    It is essential to understand the work-life needs of the faculty and staff. Therefore, the following seven steps were implemented:
    a. Analyzed institutional policies, benefits, programs, and culture
    b. Facilitated focus groups
    c. Developed and distributed a work-life culture survey
    d. Benchmarked with comparable organizations
    e. Reviewed demographic data
    f. Reviewed internal and external community resources
    g. Organized these findings.

In this situation, the data were organized into three themes: needs, organizational goals, and possible strategies and solutions.

4. Develop cultural change initiatives.
   Critical work-life issues were identified from the data analysis. These issues were then aligned with the institution's vision, mission, and goals. Finally, cultural change initiatives based on best practices were developed through input from many constituents.

5. Gain approval and implement.
   Approval for the cultural change initiatives was formally provided to send a message to all the employees regarding the leadership's commitment to creating a work-life culture. Communication strategies were immediately implemented, followed by the implementation of the initiatives with continuous evaluation and planning to maintain quality and consistency.

Unit/Department Change

University of Washington: Balance@UW

The University of Washington (UW) developed a comprehensive package of policies and programs titled Balance@UW to support the faculty in balancing their personal lives and professional careers. The University recognized the role of department chairs in supporting faculty and created and distributed a five-step brochure that transformational leaders could use to support cultural change in their respective areas.[46] The five steps are as follows:

1. Create readiness.
   Department members need to recognize the necessity of change and be ready for change to occur. This readiness can be created by providing an analysis or assessment of the department's work-life friendly culture and helping members realize their unconscious biases or faulty assumptions related to managing work-life obligations.[47]

2. Overcome resistance.
   Create a safe environment in which individuals can deal with the change. Members need to know that it is okay to move beyond their comfort zones without negative ramifications or consequences. The chair can establish this safe zone by creating ground rules for meetings and interactions that assure all opinions will be heard and respected and by having a zero tolerance policy regarding the proliferation of a hazing mentality or the repetition of disparaging comments.

3. Articulate a vision.
    Share a view of what the department would look like with a work-life friendly culture. For example, what will the department look like if all faculty can achieve their highest potential because their work-life balance is supported? What would the department look like if these flexible policies and work-life supports were used to recruit and retain the best and brightest faculty?
4. Obtain general commitment.
    Empower faculty to own the cultural change effort. Establish a faculty task force consisting of cross-generational members to generate strategies for change.
5. Institutionalize change.
    Impact the institutional culture as a whole by setting an example of best practices and policies. Influence the establishment of fair and equitable policies and practices at the institutional level.

University of California

At the University of California, a three-phase approach was implemented to create family-friendly departments.[48] The authors note, however, that this approach is only likely to be effective if baseline faculty accommodation policies exist.[49] Each phase consists of multiple steps, outlined as follows:

Phase 1: Assessment

Step 1: A department chair declares that understanding family friendliness is a major priority and goal for the department;
Step 2: A department chair reviews and assesses the department's current practices and climate. A committee can be formed to conduct interviews and meetings with faculty to seek information about the work-life needs of each faculty and staff member. If a formal survey is not conducted, the committee can meet with every individual. It is also important to be intentional about understanding the needs of staff as well as faculty;
Step 3: A department chair is sensitive to and about unconscious biases concerning caregiving and gender;
Step 4: A department chair is aware of and understands the variety of legal issues related to the role of academic leaders.

Phase 2: Implementation

Step 1: After identifying the work-life needs, leaders must then gain an in-depth understanding of current programs, policies, and benefits, so they can provide appropriate guidance to others. The department should ensure that all members know their options when facing work-life issues;

Step 2: A department chair actively highlights, advertises, and supports the department's family-friendly policies and procedures, benefits, and resources for all faculty;

Step 3: A department chair is proactive about recruiting and hiring diverse faculty for the department, including those who have temporarily slowed down their career for family caregiving reasons;

Step 4: A department chair ensures that transparency is established and maintained in the promotion and tenure process.

Phase 3: Devil-Is-in-the-Details

Step 1: A department chair makes the use of family-friendly policies the standard for conducting business in the department rather than viewing such policies as exceptions or "special privileges";

Step 2: A department chair maintains zero tolerance for discriminatory and disparaging comments and behaviors;

Step 3: A department chair implements small changes that can have a significant impact on the culture of the department;

Step 4: A department chair periodically assesses the effectiveness of the efforts toward work-life friendliness.

THE IMPORTANCE OF IDENTIFYING WORK-LIFE NEEDS

Several similar steps are apparent throughout these four examples. One of the most important steps is the identification of work-life issues in order to determine how to best meet employees' needs. This step is especially important in institutions where a gap seems to exist between the practice and the policy. Thus, to influence cultural change, it is essential to know the institution's workforce. Institutions striving for a work-life culture or climate have most likely gathered data about their members' satisfaction as well as issues about the climate and culture. For example, the University of California system has conducted extensive surveys on faculty work and family balance, sharing their data through articles such as "Do Babies Matter? Parts I and II" and "Why Graduate Students Reject the Fast Track."[50] The data are used to inform institutional policy that enhances campus climate related to family needs. These surveys were used as exemplars for the three rounds of the ACE/Alfred P. Sloan Faculty Career Flexibility Awards.

What data are available that will inform you about your faculty and staff? Demographic information such as age, gender, race/ethnicity, and family status by rank, job classification, and years of service, can reveal work-life needs. You can certainly locate university-level data that is applicable, especially through the Office of Institutional Research, Office of the Provost, or the Office of HR. Relevant data for work-life can be found in research centers, offices, committees, and/or departments across campus. Helpful units on campus may include the following:[51]

- Commission on the Status of Women
- Institutional Research
- Faculty Affairs
- Academic Personnel
- Human Resources
- Institutional Diversity and Equity
- Advisory Groups or Boards
- Faculty Senates or Councils
- Administrative Councils
- Work-Life Committees or Taskforces
- Strategic Planning.

Additionally, other reports such as faculty and staff satisfaction surveys can be useful. As noted earlier, a committee or task force can meet with faculty and staff about work-life issues as an approach to creating a comfortable climate for discussing this information. It is also helpful for leaders to meet with individual faculty members to learn about their personal and family lives.

Ultimately, leaders must be effective orchestrators of data collection, dissemination, and use in the complex, loosely coupled world that is an academic institution. This requires (1) political readiness (helping people understand who want to know what and why); (2) technical and operational readiness (an infrastructure to support data gathering and effective dissemination); and (3) agreement on definitions (a common vocabulary so everyone is measuring the same things).[52]

Nonetheless, data use must be approached thoughtfully:[53]

- "Be careful what data you ask for because anxieties will rise.
- Remember that data are not neutral.
- Clarify your data and analysis needs with data providers prior to collecting and displaying data.
- Model the behavior that you want others to show.
- Recognize the symbolic functions data serve that are not directly tied to decisions."[55]

"To find out whether existing policies are being used, and if not why not, is an important step towards competitiveness, in an environment where academic institutions have accepted that candidates shop around for the most family-responsive institution."[54]

GUIDING PRINCIPLES AND LESSONS LEARNED

In addition to implementing steps or phases to transform cultures, there are several principles that can be followed to facilitate a cultural shift that aligns with the institution's mission, goals, and values. For example, the Boston College Work and Family Roundtable for Employers recommend the following guiding principles to help shape a work-life culture:

- "The institution and leadership recognize the strategic value of addressing work and personal life issues.
- The work environment supports individual work and personal life effectiveness.
- The management of work and personal life effectiveness is a responsibility shared by the institution and the employees.
- The institution develops relationships to enhance external work and personal life resources.
- The institution helps strengthen policies that benefit both employers and individuals in public policy."[56]

Moreover, Kathleen Christensen of the Alfred P. Sloan Foundation offers the following lessons gleaned from the institutions that received the ACE/Alfred P. Sloan Awards for Faculty Career Flexibility:[57]

- "Know your internal and external culture, know and communicate policies, and be aware of biases against using policies.
- Engage leaders by initiating flexibility practices in the provost's office, and linking initiatives to the university mission.
- Train key gatekeepers, such as department chairs and promotion and tenure review committees.
- Initiate an awareness campaign to gain buy-in and foster transparency.
- Reward the implementation of flexibility practices, acknowledge family-friendly departments and leaders, and obligate central funds to work-life initiatives.
- Plan for the unexpected, such as turnover in leaders and budget cuts.
- Make the business case using a cost-benefit analysis and an intentional evaluation of policy usage on faculty and staff careers.
- Create a culture of inclusiveness, and extend leaves and benefits to all active and retiring faculty, regardless of age, gender, or lifestyle."

Changing any institutional culture is not an easy endeavor, nor is it a simple task. Examples of competencies to lead change are listed in Table 4.5.

As the literature has documented, various challenges may emerge throughout the change process. A few hurdles when leading change for a work-life friendly

Table 4.5 Professional Competencies for Department Chairs to Lead Change[58]

- Strategic leadership
- Vision and direction
- Communication
- Planning and decision making
- Credibility
- Dealing with resistance to change
- Managing conflict
- Dealing with difficult faculty/staff
- Dealing with senior leadership
- Navigating the human side of leadership

culture include, but are not limited to the following.[59] Effective leaders are aware of these hurdles and are prepared to overcome them.

- Resistance in fostering a work-life culture
- Determining readiness for the change
- Getting buy-in from leaders, faculty, staff, and HR professionals
- Fostering a culture that ensures fairness and equity, and is inclusive
- Determining the return on investment (ROI)
- Expecting to start big, but realizing the need to begin small with a pilot
- Facing outdated assumptions and expectations.

"The personal conversations matter—a lot. But it's the policies that end up ruling the day." (Dr. Ellen Schendel, Associate Dean, Grand Valley State University)

Additionally, Table 4.6 contains some lessons learned from various change efforts.

Table 4.6 Some Lessons Learned From Work-Life Culture Change Efforts[60]

- Leadership support
- Employee engagement
- Partnerships
- Flexibility in the timeline and process
- Use of technology
- Communication
- Short-term solutions and long-term strategies
- Managers and supervisors

CONCLUSION

There are many challenges and opportunities to leading the cultural changes that will make institutions or departments/units work-life friendly:

> Career flexibility must be achieved through *simultaneous* changes in policy and culture, and must be positioned as a means to an institutional end. It must be embraced by the top, driven by the chairs, and pursued without fear by the faculty. Equally important, career flexibility must be made available at all stages of the individual's career.[61]

With a work-life culture, you are helping faculty and staff to be the best that they can be!

Questions for Discussion and Reflection

1. With regard to work-life and family-friendly policies, what values does your department or organization project?

2. As a leader, how can you discourage bias avoidance and negative perceptions about work-life issues?

3. Consider your expectations for faculty and staff with regard to their work—are these expectations realistic?

4. How can you help everyone in your unit work toward a common vision or goal?

5. How would you describe your approach to academic leadership? How can you work to practice transformational leadership?

6. Do you know your workforce? For example: What proportion of your tenure-track faculty are women? What proportion are men?

7. How would you characterize your unit's culture? Is it supportive of work and life responsibilities?

NOTES

1. Schneider, B. (2000). The psychological life of organizations. In N. M. Ashkanasy, C. P. M. Wilderom, & M. F. Peterson (Eds.), *Handbook of organizational culture and climate* (pp. xvii–xxiii). Thousand Oaks, CA: Sage.
2. Schein (1990).
3. Schein (1990).
4. Trower (2012).
5. Allen (2001); Sanders, K., Willemsen, C. C., & Millar, J. M. (2009). Views from above the glass ceiling: Does the academic environment influence women professors' careers and experiences? *Sex Roles, 60,* 301–312.
6. Reddick et al. (2012).

7. Lewis, S. (1997). Family friendly employment polices: A route to organizational change or playing about the margins. *Gender, Work and Organization, 41*(1), 13–23; Thompson et al. (1999); Warren, J. A., & Johnson, P. J. (1995). The impact of workplace support on work-family role strain. *Family Relations, 44*(2), 163–169.

8. Thompson et al. (1999).

9. Thompson et al. (1999).

10. Galinsky, E., Friedman, D. E., & Hernandez, C. A. (1991). *The corporate reference guide to work-family programs.* New York, NY: Families and Work Institute; Rose (2006).

11. Alliance for Work-Life Progress (2006).

12. Lobel, S. A., & Kossek, E. E. (1996). Human resource strategies to support diversity in work and personal lifestyles: Beyond the "family-friendly" organization. In E. E. Kossek & S. A. Lobel (Eds.), *Managing diversity: Human resource strategies for transforming the workplace* (pp. 221–244). Oxford, UK: Blackwell.

13. Rose (2006).

14. Gappa et al. (2007).

15. Great Colleges to Work For 2013. (2013, July 22). *The Chronicle of Higher Education.* Retrieved from http://chronicle.com/article/Great-Colleges-To-Work-For/140369/#id=big-table

16. Ward & Wolf-Wendel (2012), p. 191; Finkel et al. (1994); Hochschild, A. R. (1997). *The time bind: When work becomes home and home becomes work.* New York, NY: Henry Holt; Ward & Wolf-Wendel (2004); Yoest, C. (2004). *Parental leave in academia.* Retrieved from http://faculty.virginia.edu/familyandtenure/institutional%20report.pdf

17. Riger, S., Stokes, J., Raja, S., & Sullivan, M. (1997). Measuring perceptions of the work environment for female faculty. *The Review of Higher Education, 21*(1), 63–78.

18. For a specific example of a faculty member not taking family leave, see Green, A. E. (2013, January 3). Not taking time off. *The Chronicle of Higher Education.* Retrieved from http://chronicle.com/article/Not-Taking-Time-Off/136433/

19. Drago, R., Colbeck, C., Stauffer, D., Pirretti, A., Burkhum, K., Fazioli, J., ... & Habasevich, T. (2005). The avoidance of bias against care-giving among faculty. *Academe, 91,* 22–25.

20. Finkel et al. (1994); Ward & Wolf-Wendel (2012).

21. Matos, K., & Galinsky, E. (n.d.). *Workplace flexibility in the United States: A status report.* Retrieved from http://familiesandwork.org/downloads/WorkplaceFlexibilityinUS.pdf

22. Van Deusen et al. (2008).

23. Perna (2001).

24. Philipsen & Bostic (2010), p. 154.

25. Drago et al. (2005); Finkel et al. (1994); Sullivan, B., Hollenshead, C., & Smith, G. (2004). Developing and implementing work-family policies for faculty. *Academe, 90*(6), 24–27; Yoest (2004).

26. Reddick et al. (2012).

27. Hochschild, A. (1995). The culture of politics: Traditional, postmodern, cold modern and warm modern ideals of care. *Social Politics: International Studies in Gender, State and Society, 2*(3), 331–346.

28. Ward & Wolf-Wendel (2012).

29. Philipsen & Bostic (2010), p. 125.

30. Ward & Wolf-Wendel (2012), p. 193.

31. Trower (2012), p. 72.

32. Christensen, K. (2009, Summer). Policies not enough. *CUWFA Newsbriefs,* p. 1.

33 Burke, W. W. (1994). *Organization Development,* 2nd ed. Reading, MA: Addison-Wesley.

34. Koppes Bryan, L., Schneider, S., & Linnabery, E. (under review). Work-life leadership: University staff perceptions of supportive supervisors.

35. Avolio, B. J., Walderman, D. A., & Yanimarina, F. J. (1991). Leading in the 1990s: The four Is of transformational leadership. *Journal of European Industrial Training, 15,* 9–16.

36. Bass, B. M., & Avolio, B. J. (1997). *Full range leadership development: Manual for the Multifactor Leadership Questionnaire.* Palo Alto, CA: Mind Garden; Tejeda, M. J. (2001). The MLQ revisited: Psychometric properties and recommendations. *The Leadership Quarterly, 12,* 31–52.

37. Frasch, K., Stacy, A., Mason, M. A., Page-Medrich, S., & Goulden, M. (2009). The devil is in the details. In J. Lester & M. Sallee (Eds.), *Establishing the family friendly campus* (pp. 88–104). Sterling, VA: Stylus; Quinn, K. (2007). Exploring departmental leadership: How department chairs can be transformative leaders. *InterActions: UCLA Journal of Education and Information Studies.* Retrieved from http://escholarship.org/uc/item/66t8h5k7, p. 89.

38. Eckel, P., Green, M. F., & Hill, B. (2001). *On change: Riding the waves of changes: Insights from transforming institutions.* Washington, DC: American Council on Education, p. 5.

39. Lewin, K. (1947). Frontiers in group dynamics. *Human Relations, 1,* 26–41; Kotter, J. P. (1996). *Leading change.* Boston, MA: Harvard Business School Press; Burke, W.W. (2008). Leading organization change. In W.W. Burke *Organization change: Theory and practice* (2nd ed.; pp. 239–272). Thousand Oaks, CA: Sage Publications.

40. Beauchesne, K. (2009). Hopkins 24/7. In J. Lester & M. Sallee (Eds.), *Establishing the family friendly campus* (pp. 72–87). Sterling, VA: Stylus.

41. Beauchesne (2009), p. 77.

42. Beauchesne (2009), p. 78.

43. Beauchesne (2009), p. 81.

44. Rose (2006); Seitel, S. (n.d.). Essential steps to designing a successful work-life program. Minnetonka, MN: WFCResources.

45. Koppes (2008); Koppes et al. (2007).

46. Cameron, K., & Ulrich, D. O. (1986). Transformational leadership in colleges and universities. In J. C. Smart (Ed.), *Higher education: Handbook of theory and research* (pp. 1–42). New York, NY: Agathon Press; Quinn (2007).

47. See Balance@UW for examples: www.washington.edu/provost/initiatives/

48. Frasch et al. (2009).

49. Frasch et al. (2009), p. 93.

50. Mason & Goulden (2002); Mason et al. (2009).

51. Sullivan et al. (2012).

52. Trower (2012), p. 161; Trower, C. A., & Honan, J. (2002). How might data be used. In R. P. Chait (Ed.), *The questions of tenure* (pp. 271–308). Cambridge, MA: Harvard University Press.

53. Trower & Honan (2002).

54. The Center for WorkLife Law. (2013).

55. Trower, C. A. (2012). Success on the tenure track: *Five keys to faculty job satisfaction.* Baltimore, MD: The Johns Hopkins University Press, p. 162.

56. Rose (2006), p. 31.

57. Christensen (2009).

58. Koppes, L. L. (2009, June). *Shifting sands, moving tides: Strategies for leading change.* Workshop for the Institute for Academic Leadership, State of Florida. Howey in the Hills, FL.

59. Koppes (2008).

60. Koppes (2008).

61. Christensen (2009), p. 2.

Chapter 5

Reflections of Academic Leaders

While the theory and research surrounding best practices are both useful and important, the experiences of academic leaders can lend a specificity and relevance to the material discussed in the previous chapters. This chapter includes a number of short narratives in which academic leaders, including department chairs, program directors, associate deans, vice provosts, and presidents share their experiences with work-life policies and practices. Identified by their colleagues as leaders who respond to faculty and staff work-life responsibilities, these individuals were asked to share both specific examples of work-life issues at their own institutions and more general strategies for becoming a leader who is responsive.

The institutions discussed here vary in terms of their mission, size, population, affiliation, and geography, ranging from small private schools to large state institutions. Nonetheless, the experiences shared by the contributors share a few common themes:

- Communication—of both work-life needs and institutional priorities
- Flexibility—at all levels of the institution
- Commitment—recognition that a work-life culture benefits everyone

To gather the information for these reflections, this project was submitted as a research study to the University of Baltimore Institutional Research Board for approval. The snowball sampling method was used to identify participants. We solicited names primarily through the CUWFA listserv, which consists of an extensive membership network. Additionally, others were identified through networking with colleagues. Specifically, we requested individuals *who not only understand the importance of work-life effectiveness and satisfaction, but who are also proactive, open, and creative about helping faculty and staff to succeed at work while also managing life responsibilities.* We attempted to seek representation of all the Carnegie Classifications, and as presented in Table 5.1, academic leaders of both private and public universities are listed, including master's colleges and universities, and research universities. The demographic characteristics of the sample are presented in Table 5.2.

Table 5.1 Academic Leaders in This Chapter

	Basic Carnegie Classification	Student Enrollment (as reported on website or by the leader)	Position
Institution: Private			
Bellarmine University	Master's Colleges and Universities (larger programs)	~3,500	President
Yale University	Research Universities (very high research activity)	~14,000	Deputy Provost for Faculty Development and Diversity
Yale University	Research Universities (very high research activity)	~14,000	Chief Diversity Officer
Johns Hopkins University	Research Universities (very high research activity)	~20,000	Vice President for Human Resources
DePaul University	Doctoral/Research Universities	~25,000	Assistant Dean
DePaul University	Doctoral/Research Universities	~25,000	Associate Vice President of University Advancement
George Washington University	Research Universities (very high research activity)	~20,000	Director of Honors Program
Georgetown University	Research Universities (very high research activity)	~17,000	Department Chair
University of Southern California	Research Universities (very high research activity)	~42,000	Executive Director
Institution: Public			
University of Houston-Clear Lake	Master's Colleges and Universities (larger programs)	~8,000	President
University of Houston-Clear Lake	Master's Colleges and Universities (larger programs)	~8,000	Vice President for Administration and Finance
Oregon State University	Research Universities (very high research activity)	~28,000	Senior Vice Provost for Academic Affairs

University of California, Davis	Research Universities (very high research activity)	~33,000	Vice Provost for Academic Affairs
University of Southern Maine	Master's Colleges and Universities (larger programs)	~9,300	Academic Dean
Western Kentucky University	Master's Colleges and Universities (larger programs)	~20,000	Dean
Indiana University School of Medicine	Research Universities (very high research activity)	~2,000	Associate Dean for Faculty Affairs and Professional Development
Grand Valley State University	Master's Colleges and Universities (larger programs)	~24,000	Associate Dean
University of Delaware	Research Universities (very high research activity)	~20,000	Department Chair
SUNY Geneseo	Master's Colleges and Universities (smaller programs)	~5,000	Dean of Residential Living
Southern Connecticut State University	Master's Colleges and Universities (larger programs)	~11,000	Vice President for Student Affairs
Southern Connecticut State University	Master's Colleges and Universities (larger programs)	~11,000	Department Chair

Table 5.2 Demographic Variables of the Sample

Gender ($n = 21$)	83% female	17% male	
Race/Ethnicity ($n = 18$)	83% Caucasian	17% African American	
Age ($n = 17$)	Average = 54 years	Range: 40–67 years	
Marital Status ($n = 18$)	78% married	11% divorced	11% not married
Children Under 18 years of Age at Home ($n = 15$)	60% yes	40% no	Average age of children: 13 years (if provided)
Length in Current Position ($n = 16$)	Average = 7 years	Range: 1.5–23 years	

Private Universities and Colleges

Bellarmine University: President

Bellarmine University is an independent Catholic university in Louisville, Kentucky. A community of 3,500 students with a 12:1 student-faculty ratio, Bellarmine prides itself on great teaching and close student-faculty relationships. Thus, the entire campus was affected by the sudden death of a faculty member on campus. Dr. Joseph J. McGowan, who has served as University President for 23 years, describes how the University responded to the situation:

> The Student Counseling Center made arrangements for grief counseling sessions for students; Human Resources brought in the university's Employee Assistance Program counselor to assist staff and faculty; Campus Ministry provided spiritual and pastoral counseling support for students, faculty, and staff.

In addition, President McGowan and the academic and student life leadership team directly addressed the students in the faculty member's classes, and individuals from across campus reached out to the faculty member's family. These cross-campus efforts demonstrate a widespread commitment to work-life balance and the strong sense of community at Bellarmine. Dr. McGowan speaks highly of the work-life policies at his University, noting that they are rooted in its Catholic mission, "which honors hospitality and the intrinsic dignity and infinite value of each person in our community." Such policies include, among others, a wellness program, confidential mental health counseling, and generous, inclusive leave policies. With regard to managing work-life situations, Dr. McGowan notes the importance of soliciting input from faculty and staff about their needs, and recognizing the importance of each person as an individual in addressing his or her needs.

Yale University: Deputy Provost for Faculty Development and Diversity; Chief Diversity Officer

As an Ivy League University with about 14,000 graduate and undergraduate students, Yale prides itself on the quality of faculty across the disciplines. However, hiring and retaining women faculty in the STEM disciplines has emerged as a growing challenge. Deputy Provost for Faculty Development and Diversity, Dr. Frances McCall Rosenbluth, has made the nurturing of women scientists a priority for the University. Dr. Rosenbluth explains that for women faculty in the sciences, in particular, the demands of lab work can have serious implications for childcare, leading many women to leave tenure-track faculty positions, often dropping out during the postdoctoral years. Unable to undertake a large campus-wide initiative on childcare because of budget constraints, the University focused on the group with the most

106

need: tenure-track women in the sciences. Yale established an infant-care center in proximity to the science labs so that women postdocs and faculty could have their babies nearby and, therefore, were better able to relax and focus on their research. The center, which serves children up to 3 years old, filled instantly. Dr. Rosenbluth stressed the importance of bringing concerns about access to childcare facilities to the attention of building and planning committees, noting that such concerns were rarely on their list of priorities, despite their tremendous importance for the work-life culture on campus. The research expectations at Yale are high, and Dr. Rosenbluth stressed the need for communication between senior faculty and junior faculty about work-life needs, as generational gaps can produce significant differences in expectations. Other work-life policies include professional development workshops on a variety of topics related to teaching and research (using media, classroom performance, time management, etc.); a mentoring program in which junior faculty are matched with mentors both inside and outside their home departments; a center for retired faculty; and a generous parental leave policy. She also noted that Yale has recently received a NSF ADVANCE grant to study the effects of mentoring on postdoctoral students. Dr. Rosenbluth's commitment to work-life began when she was the chair of the Political Science Department, in which capacity she made an effort to schedule meetings for times that accommodated the family responsibilities of her faculty—a practice that became a model for departments across campus. As the Deputy Provost for Faculty Development and Diversity, she is now in a position to support broader initiatives to build a university-wide work-life culture.

Deborah Stanley-McAulay serves as Chief Diversity Officer at Yale University, overseeing a staff with a range of work-life needs. Ms. Stanley-McAulay notes that she has reached out to her staff about work-life issues when she notices a decline in productivity—the result of which has been the creation of flexible work arrangements for several members of her department. Regarding one staff member who works from home one day each week, Ms. Stanley-McAulay attests,

> I think the best test of whether the employee is being productive, is when I walked to her workspace to have a face-to-face discussion, after a series of e-mail exchanges, to realize that she is not in the office today; however, she was totally plugged in and present. In this situation, the employee is 110% productive, the decision to support this request has strengthened our working relationship.

Ms. Stanley-McAulay notes that trust, collaboration, and communication are key to establishing a workplace where individuals can both be productive and manage their work-life needs. Moreover, she explains that other effective strategies include frequently checking in with staff, re-evaluating individual situations, and adjusting if necessary.

Johns Hopkins University: Vice President for Human Resources

Charlene Moore Hayes is Vice President for Human Resources at Johns Hopkins University, a Research I university with nearly 20,000 graduate and undergraduate students, located in Baltimore, Maryland. She has had considerable experience with work-life both in her own office and in working across the University. For instance, she describes how taking advantage of available technology made it possible for her Executive Assistant to work remotely for six weeks while accompanying her teenage daughter (who was too young to live in the dormitories) on a summer intensive program with the prestigious Alvin Ailey Dance Company in New York City. The organization and efficiency of her Executive Assistant, Ms. Hayes explains, enabled her office to continue running smoothly during this period. In her role as Vice President for Human Resources, Ms. Hayes worked with the Benefits Office to create a proposal for a "disability retirement option" for faculty or staff who had worked at JHU for at least 10 years. She recognized the need for this policy when a faculty member with more than 25 years of service was forced to retire before the official retirement age of 55, because of ill health. Despite his long period of service to the University, this early retirement meant that the faculty member's children would not be able to benefit from JHU's dependent tuition grant program. Recognizing the problem with this situation—in which a faculty member with just 10 years of service but having reached the official retirement age could benefit from the grant, but longer serving faculty members could not—Ms. Hayes intervened to create a more equitable policy. She notes that it was important to review and revise the official policy, rather than just grant an exception in the case of a particular faculty member. Indeed, through such policies, JHU has established a comprehensive work-life culture to "address issues that might arise at any point in the lifespan," including a breastfeeding support program, extensive online resources (http://hopkinsworklife.org/), and training for supervisors and managers on work-life issues. Ms. Hayes advises academic leaders to

> adopt the perspective that supporting work-life-family friendly culture is key to maintaining a high performing employee base. If the institution makes a commitment to help families address the myriad issues that arise in day-to-day life, employees can better focus on the work at hand, become more engaged, and be much more productive.

DePaul University: Assistant Dean; Associate Vice President of University Advancement

Located in Chicago, DePaul is the nation's largest Catholic university with almost 25,000 students. Assistant Dean in the Kellstadt Graduate School of Business, Dr. Christa Hinton oversees advising and success for students and also models good work-life practices for her staff. In describing her experience helping a staff member negotiate an earlier-than-expected maternity leave, Dr. Hinton stressed the importance of remaining calm and supportive and working collaboratively to consider the impact on the individual staff member as well as the staff as a whole. Sharing information about the situation with the entire office, she explains, both underscored her support for the staff member and helped avoid any confusion or miscommunication. She notes that she is most likely to support the work-life needs staff members who have been professional and honest in their work and behavior; indeed, she asserts, "I lead by example, and I let them know that I TRUST them. . . . Additionally, I expect that they are professionals, and that means giving them the opportunity to make their own decisions about their days." Dr. Hinton offers a few specific suggestions for academic leaders: "Trust your team; Self-awareness is extremely important; Open communication fosters great relationships; If you do not like to manage people, it is probably best that you don't." As Dr. Hinton's suggestions reveal, becoming an effective work-life leader first involves assessing one's own strengths, priorities, and values.

Erin Moran, Associate Vice President in the Office of University Advancement at DePaul University, works with a large staff, managing several aspects of university advancement, including fundraising and events. One of her staff members had to take on illness-related caregiving and end-of-life care for a parent, yet because she had not been employed by the University for at least one year, she was not eligible for FMLA. Ms. Moran provided emotional support for the staff member and also worked to keep their other colleagues informed about the situation. As the caregiving need became greater, she helped the staff member manage her flextime so that she could accommodate her caregiving responsibilities and attend to her own health. Ms. Moran notes, "the best thing I could do (both as a manager and as a human being) was to give her the space to be with her father while he was still living." She also explains that work-life has implications beyond individual situations and is part of a broader culture in which leaders are responsible for modeling good behavior, such as keeping reasonable hours or taking a break from e-mail:

> I tell them that the goal is not to work longer hours, but to do excellent work. If they can't do excellent work without working many hours of overtime, I tell them that that is indicative of either a time management problem or a performance problem.

A work-life culture, then, can also address concerns about overworking and productivity:

> I find that it's really important to address overworking as much as underworking. We tend as a society to think that overworking is a badge of honor, and

109

before we know it, everyone in the office is living at work and is plugged into their e-mail account all day and all night. The problem with that is that many people do not work as effectively, collegially, or creatively when they work that many hours. The entire office environment gets polluted with bad morale and a disaffected team, which is the last thing a manager wants to see.

In describing her relationship with her administrative assistant of eight years, Ms. Moran explains that they agreed upon a schedule in which her assistant could leave work in time to pick up her children from school. The assistant balances this time by arriving early in the morning and sometimes working from home in the evening. Ms. Moran points out the substantial benefits to such an arrangement: "If we can accommodate the reasonable needs of our staff members while getting our jobs done, it costs us nothing to allow them that leeway."

George Washington University: Director of Honors Program

The largest higher education institution in Washington, DC (more than 20,000 students), George Washington University is marked by a student body that is highly engaged with the politics and lifestyle of their urban home. Director of the University Honors Program, Dr. Maria Frawley, oversees the administration of a highly selective program (fewer than 5% of GWU students are admitted), which includes various honors courses, undergraduate research, and a high level of faculty-student interaction. As an administrator, Dr. Frawley needed to accommodate an extended maternity leave that coincided with the start of the semester and affected new student orientation. Together with her colleagues in the University Honors Program, Dr. Frawley was able to devise a solution in which the staff member worked from home and additional staff reworked their schedules to cover the absence. She cites both flexibility and teamwork as key elements of a successful work-life culture: "my sense is that professional people operate by a version of 'The Golden Rule'—they will help cover for others knowing that others will cover for them to get work done." Dr. Frawley also explains that projecting herself "as a person who understands that we all strive to balance work with home life" helps her staff to be "confident" that she will be receptive to their needs. The University Honors Program encourages a balance of individualism and community among its students, and this same philosophy extends to the work environment for the Program staff.

Georgetown University: Department Chair

A Catholic University in Washington, DC, with about 17,000 students—among whom are 7,500 undergraduates who reside on or near the main campus— Georgetown is "formally, institutionally committed as a university to '*cura personalis,'* or care for the whole person within our gates (and not just the students)" notes Sociology Department Chair, Dr. Timothy Wickham-Crowley. Dr. Wickham-Crowley continues, explaining that within such a culture, the most effective approach to work-life

> is simple decency and concern for "the whole person"—those alongside whom you must and do work—will go a long way. . . . Any administrator or authority-wielder within Georgetown can always point to that motto to justify the good treatment of others in ways that go far beyond the merely bureaucratic.

Working within a department marked by collegiality among a diverse group of faculty, staff, and students is a point of pride for Dr. Wickham-Crowley, who describes his department as one where work-life requests are "reasonable" and met with sympathy, understanding, and flexibility.

Dr. Wickham-Crowley describes two situations in which he led the department to meet the needs of faculty members with children. In one case, a mid-semester birth necessitated creative scheduling and team-teaching with an adjunct faculty member. Advance planning, careful organization of the syllabus, and extensive collaboration among the two faculty members ensured a positive experience for the students. In another instance, a faculty member frequently needed to bring her newborn son to the office, often accompanied by a caregiver. As Chair, Dr. Wickham-Crowley was alert for any discomfort that this might cause among other faculty members (excess noise, etc.) but noted that he heard "no whisper of complaints," and, indeed, appreciated the "breath of fresh air that a baby brings to more staid surroundings." Dr. Wickham-Crowley explains that he was particularly sensitive to this situation because, earlier in his career, he had witnessed a negative model of work-life in which a Chair deemed the presence of children in the workplace to be "unprofessional," thereby creating substantial childcare problems for a professional staff member. Learning from this negative experience enabled Dr. Wickham-Crowley to both meet the needs of one particular faculty member and create a supportive work-life culture for the entire department. Dr. Wickham-Crowley notes that a tradition of goodwill has grounded the department's work-life culture, which continues to evolve to accommodate the changing needs of its members. He also frames the matter in terms of his academic expertise:

> In terms of classical sociological concepts, then, we have taken a bureaucratically organized setting intended and designed to serve "instrumental" needs—the formal, rigorous education of our students—and actively sought to build within it a substantial "expressive" culture which makes it a pleasant place (usually: we are not perfect) within which to be and work and deal with challenges.

University of Southern California: Executive Director

A large private institution with 42,000 students, the University of Southern California employs over 3,500 faculty and over 12,000 staff. Dr. Janette Brown serves as Executive Director of the Emeriti Center, which serves "the university's retirees and pre-retirees in living healthy and purposeful lives by providing essential information, resources, services, advocacy, privileges, and support." In this capacity, she oversees a staff that attends to the work of the Center and also chairs the Center's Executive Committee, which draws membership from an interdisciplinary group of retired faculty and staff leaders. Her work-life challenges include supporting two staff members who are caring for aging parents as well as raising young children. Dr. Brown worked with these two staff members to create a flexible work schedule that accommodates caregiving needs. She explains, "It is important that staff can take care of family members and/or health first. Once these issues are resolved, then staff members can concentrate on their jobs." This commitment to creating a work-life supportive community is part of Dr. Brown's overall approach to leadership. Indeed, she notes that her Center's focus on retired and pre-retired faculty and staff requires sensitivity to work-life issues, and they have adopted the motto: "Colleagues for Life." The Center has created quality resources for their population, including programs on healthy aging, educational and enrichment courses, opportunities to teach, funds to continue research and publication, and referrals for financial and legal services, which are freely available on their website: http://emeriti.usc.edu/resources/. She emphasizes the Center's commitment to work-life issues: "There should be no fear of retribution or firing because of a family issue." The culture fostered by Dr. Brown in the Emeriti Center acknowledges both the needs of the individuals served by the USC Emeriti Center and the needs of those who work there.

Public Universities and Colleges

University of Houston-Clear Lake: President; Vice President for Administration and Finance

If you visit the University of Houston-Clear Lake (UHCL), you might find the President scooping ice cream. An urban upper-level undergraduate and graduate university with just over 8,000 students, UHCL serves a primarily adult student population, with an average age of 31. President William A. Staples and Vice President (VP) for Administration and Finance, Michelle Dotter, have served together at UHCL for 19 years. Their strong commitment to the community and work-life initiatives is woven throughout the fabric of the University. "People are our most important asset," asserts President Staples, and he notes that as academic leaders, he and Ms. Dotter can foster a work-life culture—including professional development, relationship development, health, and assistance—even if they are not always directly involved in the implementation of such initiatives. President Staples and VP Dotter are very involved across campus, however, participating regularly in events, including the ice cream social, Veterans Day celebration, Halloween contest, and a spring break breakfast, during which faculty and staff teams play games such as Pictionary. President Staples also sends a personal birthday card to every employee on campus (an idea, he notes, borrowed from Southwest Airlines). Although the demands of work and family are high, "showing people that you care about them," is a priority at UHCL. Professional Development efforts are also robust, and President Staples and Ms. Dotter described several programs, including "stepping up to supervisor" and "leaders in action" that foster leaders at all levels of the institution. This scaffolding of leadership helps to ensure effective practices across the campus. To mark National Work and Family Month in October, UHCL held a program on the relationship between physical and mental health. Other health-related programs include fitness release, flu shots, and a support group for cancer patients and caregivers. The administration notes that such initiatives are small but send a strong message about the University's commitment to its employees. The campus community has also had several fundraisers to support individuals and families in times of financial stress (death, illness, etc.). President Staples explains that, as the University President, he needs to be front and center on work-life initiatives and that academic leaders must understand and believe in the value of such initiatives if they are to become part of the institutional culture. Both President Staples and VP Dotter noted the importance of recognizing that individuals have lives and identities outside of the workplace and that only looking at one aspect of an individual provides a "limited perspective" that shortchanges both the employee and the institution. They noted that academia might learn from the model of tech companies, such as Google, which structure their work culture around work-life and build support of the whole person into their organization and its services. The payoff for such attention to work-life—through major institutional change or small, daily interactions—is tremendous and, President Staples notes, makes "good common sense."

Oregon State University: Senior Vice Provost for Academic Affairs

South of Portland, Oregon, Oregon State University (OSU) is home to more than 28,000 students. A large research University, OSU has strong connections to both its northwestern home and several nearby colleges and universities. Senior Vice Provost for Academic Affairs, Dr. Rebecca Warner, regularly reaches out to neighboring institutions in creating partnerships and promoting the work-life culture at OSU. Warner identifies herself as a "feminist leader" and notes that it is important for all academic leaders to be "out front" about their values and priorities. Her sensitivity to work-life issues was based largely on her own experience as a department chair dealing with the illness and loss of her mother. She notes how her colleagues helped with her grading and encouraged her to use FMLA time to care for her mother—and herself. As Senior Vice Provost for Academic Affairs, Dr. Warner is now in a position to institutionalize a work-life culture. OSU offers a number of programs, including a Leadership Academy for Department Chairs, resource guides for aging adults, and tenure-clock extensions for those using FMLA. She also works closely with the University's General Counsel and Human Resources to ensure the fair and legal use of work-life accommodations. She drew on such resources in one situation in which she was faced with the devastation of a faculty member after the loss of her husband—also a faculty member at OSU. Dr. Warner carefully considered the University's responsibilities to the couple and was able to retroactively remove the late faculty member from sabbatical to provide additional financial support for his widow. She also offered emotional support to help the faculty member become reintegrated into life on campus. Dr. Warner notes that the work-life culture at OSU energizes everyone around campus and is a visible part of campus life, "not something that's just isolated in an office." Moreover, work-life initiatives are linked to the broader mission of OSU, which involves a commitment to transformational curriculum that explores sites of difference, power, and discrimination. In her role as an academic leader, Dr. Warner is committed to not only the development of a work-life culture but also the institutionalization of such a culture in ways that are relevant and sustainable.

University of California, Davis: Vice Provost for Academic Affairs

Dr. Maureen Stanton is Vice Provost for Academic Affairs at the University of California (UC), Davis. Part of the UC System, Davis has 33,000 students enrolled across four undergraduate colleges and six graduate/professional schools. Dr. Stanton was asked to intervene in the case of a tenure-track faculty member whose caregiving responsibilities were raising concerns about her ability to meet the research standards expected for tenure. The faculty member's parent did not live locally; thus, she was traveling to provide care on a near-weekly basis. The department chair contacted Dr. Stanton to investigate opportunities to help this faculty member succeed, specifically, the possibility of a tenure-clock extension. Dr. Stanton granted the tenure-clock extension and also worked with the department chair to develop strategies for mentoring the tenure-track faculty member with regard to her scholarship and research. She notes that work-life policies regarding tenure-clock extensions are most frequently used by faculty members who are new parents, yet Dr. Stanton has been advocating for greater awareness and use of this policy in other caregiving situations. This is particularly important, she explains, because such caregiving obligations fall disproportionately upon women and under-represented minorities. Dr. Stanton notes that work-life is a priority at UC Davis, which has a work-life website that includes information on both system policies and campus programs, as well as suggestions for language to use in preparing requests for leave or tenure-clock extensions: https://academicaffairs.ucdavis.edu/programs/work-life/index.html. One of the most distinctive programs at UC Davis, Dr. Stanton explains, has been the establishment of Faculty Work-Life Advisors, all of which have benefited from the work-life policies. These faculty can then work with other faculty and academic leaders to educate them about work-life at the University. Dr. Stanton also cites UC Davis's participation in the NSF ADVANCE Institutional Transformation program, noting that effective work-life is part of broader campus transformation: "Changes in campus culture, including awareness of unconscious biases and behaviors that negatively affect women and faculty of color are essential components of this transformation process."

University of Southern Maine: Academic Dean

Dr. Joyce Taylor Gibson is Dean of Lewiston-Auburn College at the University of Southern Maine (USM)—a multi-campus institution with 9,300 students. Lewiston-Auburn College has a distinct identity within the University, providing undergraduate and graduate degrees through its unique interdisciplinary curriculum. Dr. Gibson was able to help a faculty member negotiate a flexible work schedule and leave to care for an ill parent who lived across the country. In working with her colleague, she stressed the importance of not only allowing time for caregiving and travel but also for handling the stress associated with such caregiving. The colleague was most appreciative of this additional consideration, which had not been part of the initial request but proved extremely useful because "it was impossible to imagine that the time was needed to take care of self after returning from caring [for a] parent." Her familiarity with the University's policies enabled Dr. Gibson to provide her colleague with the most beneficial information and support for this situation. Faced with morale issues resulting from financial strain, Dr. Gibson checks in frequently with her Liaisons (department chairs) and staff to help address potential wellness concerns. USM also supports a Health Educator on campus, and Dr. Gibson promotes the related programs and workshops. Even with minimal resources, Dr. Gibson notes that she can model good work-life behaviors, "I try to model behavior that honors family time, but also make efforts to encourage staff to take compensatory time to be with their families, to take longer vacations." This modeling is part of a broader culture that is both engaged with the community and family friendly. Dr. Gibson advises academic leaders to seek out resources and opportunities, recommending that they use local and national data to build a case for

115

the creation and/or implementation or work-life policies, conduct research on the practices of other institutions, and pursue relevant grants, such as the NSF ADVANCE Grant.

Western Kentucky University: Dean

Dean of the College of Science and Engineering at a mid-sized Regional State University, Dr. Cheryl L. Stevens had to advocate for a faculty member in a challenging work-life situation. The faculty member relocated to take a tenure-track job at the institution, bringing along her two young children, while her husband stayed in another part of the country because arrangements for a spousal hire could not be made. The faculty member faced challenges as both a temporarily single parent and a foreign-born woman living in a fairly homogeneous community, yet her department was not sensitive to those challenges. Dr. Stevens describes her role as helping others "navigate the academic environment a little more easily or efficiently," and she became involved in this situation when the department chair shared concerns about the faculty member's ability to receive a favorable review regarding her progress toward tenure because her family obligations were making it difficult for her to meet the department's research expectations. Dr. Stevens tried to help place the faculty member's children in the campus daycare facility to alleviate some of the stress of childcare, but she was not able to secure them a spot. Working with the chair to explain the importance of work-life balance and need for flexibility was more productive, however, as was matching the faculty member with a mentor from outside her department—someone with whom she could feel "safe" because that person would not be evaluating her performance. These strategies, Dr. Stevens explains, are part of a broader investment in the success of faculty members at the University, and she advocates collaboration between faculty and administrators and mutual respect and understanding:

> If someone has a sick child, it usually doesn't really matter whether the updated CV, for example, is submitted today or tomorrow or next week from their home or their office. The job needs to be done within a certain time frame but if there is a problem, flexibility doesn't cost anything except some goodwill.

Indiana University School of Medicine: Associate Dean for Faculty Affairs and Professional Development

As Associate Dean for Faculty Affairs and Professional Development at Indiana University School of Medicine (IUSM), Dr. Mary Dankoski frequently encounters work-life issues as a faculty advocate regarding policy and organizational culture. With nine campuses across the state, IUSM educates the second-largest medical student body

116

in the United States—about 2,000 students. Located in Indianapolis (on the campus of Indiana University-Purdue University Indianapolis), Dr. Dankoski works closely with the Women's Advisory Council on initiatives such as extended and flexible tenure schedules, paid maternity leave, and training for administrators in best practices, including unconscious bias reduction. As a result of Dr. Dankoski's work, the university has successfully recruited a number of senior women leaders who then "act as recruitment magnets for more women faculty across all ranks." A medical school places unique demands upon its faculty, and IUSM has a strong commitment to institutionalizing work-life culture and career flexibility. This commitment has led to the inclusion of work-life support as an aspect of departmental review; department chairs receive an individual report summarizing their faculty members' perceptions of the chair's leadership and the department's climate, including elements related to work-life. This report is then incorporated into the chair's performance review. Dr. Dankoski also works with individual faculty, sometimes facilitating conversations with chairs and other administrators. For example, she describes one instance in which elder care was causing substantial personal and financial stress for a faculty member—a situation that was compounded by cultural expectations that caused the faculty member to feel obligated to care for her parent in her home. Dr. Dankoski helped the faculty member understand the options that were available to her and negotiate a workable situation within her home department.

Her administrative position enables Dr. Dankoski to truly advocate for work-life, and she notes that it is critical for administrators to be work-life advocates because

> Faculty are the single most important resource of an academic institution, and they are seeking flexible approaches for integrating personal and professional demands more than ever before—men and women, minority and majority, and faculty of all ages. This means that policies and practices must evolve if institutions are to recruit, retain, and advance the best and most diverse faculty community possible.

Her endeavors have certainly been fruitful. In 2009, IUSM received the Association of American Medical Colleges Group on Women in Medicine and Science Organizational Leadership Award, and in 2012 they secured a Sloan Foundation Award to Accelerate Career Flexibility for IUSM—both testaments to their support for work-life.

Grand Valley State University: Associate Dean

As Associate Dean of the Brooks College of Interdisciplinary Studies, Dr. Ellen Schendel serves as a resource for numerous faculty at a large state University and has become something of an unofficial resource for faculty members trying to understand the policies and processes surrounding maternity leave. Her own experience negotiating two maternity leaves has prompted faculty to come to her for advice on managing their own leave. Schendel notes that although her personal connections with faculty have enabled her to aid them, in the end, official policies are always most important. She states, "It's important to both advocate for effective policies and procedures and to have frank conversations with individuals and help them get to what will best work for them." Schendel also cites her work in faculty governance as essential to ensuring the quality of work-life policies, such as the maternity leave policy, on her campus. According to Schendel, ensuring the quality of these policies and promoting faculty awareness of them are among the most effective strategies for a work-life leader.

University of Delaware: Department Chair

The Women and Gender Studies Department at the University of Delaware includes a robust major with several concentrations. With 7 core faculty and more than 40 joint and affiliate faculty, the Department has grown substantially over the past 10 years and become an integral part of this public research institution—the largest in Delaware with almost 20,000 graduate and undergraduate students. Department Chair Dr. Monika Shafi draws on both her personal and professional expertise in articulating a work-life philosophy, noting

> we need to develop a more holistic approach to work life that sees the responsibilities of care and caregiving as an integral part of adult human life and not as an exceptional scenario requiring specific adjustment and strategies. . . . It is crucial to signal that family and personal life are not separate entities which has no place in the work environment but on the contrary to acknowledge the reality of care responsibilities.

Dr. Shafi employs a variety of strategies within her department to foster a work-life culture, including variable meeting and teaching times that accommodate school and daycare schedules, flexible leave policies, and informal conversations about work-life balance issues. Of course, Dr. Shafi notes, such conversations should not be intrusive, they should enable her to better meet the needs of the faculty.

SUNY Geneseo: Dean of Residential Living

As Dean of Residential Living at SUNY Geneseo, Dr. Celia Easton oversees a staff of 17 who work with the nearly 5,000 students (mostly residential) at this public liberal arts college. Dr. Easton describes several strategies for creating a work-life culture within her department. Most important, she notes, is establishing a culture of trust where individuals can work effectively and collaboratively: "An environment of trust is an environment that cultivates trust-worthiness." Granting accommodations and meeting individual needs is much easier and more straightforward, she explains, in such an environment. Dr. Easton notes that recognizing her own leadership style has been essential to building a work-life friendly department. Dr. Easton describes herself as "fair and sympathetic" yet "not outwardly enthusiastic"; thus, in hiring an Assistant Director, she sought someone whose personality and style would complement her own. The Assistant Director she chose is empathic with whom some staff members are more comfortable sharing work-life concerns. Having multiple leadership and interpersonal styles represented in the office enables the Dean of Residential Living and Assistant Director to work together to meet the needs of the staff. Dr. Easton also notes the broader family-friendly environment of the College. For instance, faculty and staff are encouraged to bring their families to the opening-day picnic, a practice that reminds students "about the broader lives of faculty and staff." The culture of trust established and fostered by Dr. Easton in the Office of Residential Living ensures that with some planning and collaboration, individuals can receive the work-life support they need to be successful.

Southern Connecticut State University: Vice President for Student Affairs; Department Chair

As Vice President for Student Affairs at Southern Connecticut State University—a public university with about 11,000 students in New Haven, Connecticut—Dr. Tracy Tyree has encountered a number of scenarios in which she has been able to advocate for and support work-life. Student Affairs and Residence Life, she explains, do not always lend themselves to traditional 9–5 schedules because student need is 24/7. Thus, working in these fields is "a lifestyle, not a job." This situation can create both opportunities and challenges for scheduling and helping staff meet their obligations at work and at home. At the same time, acknowledging and even welcoming overlap between work and home can be essential to managing both roles. Dr. Tyree noted how children are often welcome at campus events, such as Residence Life celebrations, and that the university president models the integration of work and family by bringing her own husband and children to appropriate campus events. Such role modeling by both integrating work and family and setting clear boundaries (i.e., needing to leave campus at a particular time to pick up children) is essential, states Dr. Tyree, and she tries to be as "upfront" as possible with her staff so they can offer mutual support for one another's work-life needs.

In describing her efforts to help a colleague negotiate an international adoption, she explained the importance not only of allowing for time spent at home with the new child, as one would for a traditional maternity leave, but also of the need for flexible scheduling to accommodate in-country visitations and travel. Dr. Tyree noted that it was a big deal for her colleague to undertake the process of international adoption, and she was supportive as both an interested colleague and friend and a flexible supervisor. This colleague was simultaneously caring for elderly parents, making her part of the "sandwiched generation" of caretakers responsible for both child and adult dependents. In addition to working with the colleague to adjust her schedule to accommodate these caregiving and eventually bereavement needs, Dr. Tyree provided support when the colleague returned to work. Indeed, she responded not just as a leader but also "as a human being" who recognizes that tragedies affect individuals within the workplace and offers compassion and flexibility. Work-life needs extend to everyone, regardless of marital status, children, or lifestyle, and Dr. Tyree notes that attention to these needs helps to create "a highly productive work environment" and a higher degree of loyalty, productivity, and commitment because "people respond to being cared about."

As Department Chair at Southern Connecticut State University, Dr. Therese Bennett manages a range of faculty concerns. When a faculty member had to extend her maternity leave, Dr. Bennett worked with her to provide coverage for classes. Dr. Bennett notes that she was able to manage the situation in a way that worked for both the faculty member and the department by maintaining frequent contact with the faculty member. Dr. Bennett herself works to balance her family life (she has two children) and her work responsibilities and notes that maternity leave, in particular, poses a unique set of challenges for faculty members:

> Leaving a faculty position mid-semester in order to take a six-week maternity leave is not at all comparable to leaving any other job for maternity leave, since the faculty member still has to plan the entire course, has to leave instructions for the people covering her classes, usually has to respond to e-mail questions from both the faculty and students during her maternity leave, and possibly has to come back to submit grades.

Dr. Bennett believes that administrators need to be informed about the particular challenges facing faculty members who are parents and talk with those faculty members to gain a better sense of their needs.

Questions for Discussion and Reflection

1. What common strategies are used by these leaders?

2. What did you learn from these reflections about ways to support work-life satisfaction and effectiveness?

3. What strategies would not work in your culture? Why?

4. What strategies would work in your culture? Why?

5. What will you do to improve your leadership in shaping the work-life culture at your institution?

Chapter 6

Strategizing Solutions

As demonstrated throughout this text, the academic leader plays a key role in shaping a work-life culture that is supportive of and friendly to faculty, staff, and students. Decisions about access to benefits are often left to the discretion of the leaders or supervisors,[1] and although supportive policies and benefits exist, unsupportive leaders can offset their intended effects. Thus, the discrepancy between supportive policies and the unsupportive implementation of policies can create a culture that has the inadvertent effect of creating more work-life stress, rather than alleviating such stress. In fact, reports from several organizations that have enacted life- and family-friendly workplace policies and practices indicate that these policies and practices are likely useless without leader support.[2] Thus, as we have advocated throughout, leadership support has emerged as a crucial link between policy and practice that impacts whether an organizational culture is perceived as facilitating work-life satisfaction and effectiveness (see Table 6.1).[3]

Table 6.1 Factors That Matter Most for Work-Life Balance[4]

Factor 1: Quality of life	
Factor 2: Family-friendly campus [with leadership support]	
Factor 3: Flexibility	
Factor 4: Personnel dedicated to work-life and family issues	
Factor 5: Formal policies and official practices	• Modified duties • Tenure-clock flexibility, including part-time tenure • Provisions for dual-career couples • Child care, elder care, and domestic partner benefits

Being a leader who understands work-life obligations is being an effective leader. The purpose of this chapter is not to describe all the characteristics of effec-

> TIP: Know and understand your faculty and staff work-life challenges.

tive academic leaders, but rather to focus on specific strategies for responding to the work-life needs of faculty and staff. To contextualize this discussion, we first provide a brief overview of the scholarship on supervisory and leadership support followed by tools, tips, and suggestions.

EFFECTIVE ACADEMIC LEADERS

As noted on numerous occasions throughout this text, the breakdown of work-life friendly organizations often is due to leaders who are gatekeepers of policies, programs, and services. Indeed, some supervisors may discourage employees from using benefits that are supportive of family responsibilities. As described previously, supervisor bias against those who use work-life policies and procedures discourages employees from using them.[5] When leaders are supportive of work-life, employees are more likely to report positive outcomes such as employee satisfaction, performance, and commitment.[6] In organizations with work-life cultures, leaders understand that assisting employees with work-life issues has strategic value for the recruitment and retention of key employees.[7] Thus, in both higher education and corporate settings, organizations that foster a work-life culture tend to hire leaders who recognize employees' needs to effectively manage multiple work and family responsibilities.[8] These leaders understand the importance of employees using work and family-supportive benefits to better manage diverse work-life obligations.[9]

> "There is no primer on how to respond to this [the death of a faculty member on campus]. However, those involved in the early hours of addressing this sad event clearly understood the culture of the university and relied on their experience as well as their hearts in comforting the family and the university community." (President Joseph J. McGowan, Bellarmine University)

Perceptions of organizational and supervisor supportiveness were positively associated with perceptions of control over work and family matters, with such control, in turn, being linked with lower levels of work-family conflict and other psychological and physiological indicators of strain.[10] Similarly, the quality of the relationship one has with his or her supervisor was linked to reduced perceived role conflict and an increase in work-life balance.[11] Surveying a sample of employees within a large New Zealand organization, scholars found that managerial support was negatively related to work-family conflict and turnover intentions, and positively correlated with organizational commitment.[12] In addition, those employees who perceived they had more support from their supervisors made significantly more use of work-life balance initiatives, had lower time demands, and less perceived career damage.[13] Researchers continue to provide further verification that supervisors who are supportive of their employees' work-life issues positively influenced employee job attitudes, health, and well-being.[14] We also know from other studies that employees prefer leaders who will listen to their concerns, value them, and support them in their endeavors, and employees want to know that their work makes a significant contribution toward the organization's goals.[15] Thus, perceived organizational and supervisor support appear to be critical for employees to make use of work-life benefits and thereby achieve effective management of their work and personal lives.

Whereas most of the research conducted concerning work-life satisfaction and leader support has investigated employees' evaluations of their current supervisor only a few studies have addressed employees' preferences concerning specific supervisor behaviors.[16] For example, in one study, researchers used focus groups to examine critical supervisor behaviors that are perceived to be family-supportive by the employees of grocery stores. The researchers identified four main categories of supportive behaviors using factor analysis of the qualitative data gathered in their focus groups: Emotional Support, Instrumental Support, Role Modeling, and Creative Work-Family Management (Table 7.2).[17]

Table 6.2 Categories of Supportive Behavior[18]

Category	Behaviors
Emotional Support	The supervisor shows care and consideration to an individual employee's work and non-work issues, and the work situation creates perceptions that one is being cared for, that one's feelings are being considered, and that individuals feel comfortable communicating with the source of support when needed.
Instrumental Support	The supervisor helps with daily management and scheduling issues at an individual level and offers support as he or she responds to an individual employee's work and family needs in the form of day-to-day management transactions.
Role Modeling	The supervisor demonstrates the integration of work and non-work issues at the workplace through modeling behaviors on the job.
Creative Work-Family Management	The supervisor devises innovative strategies to solve unit-level conflicts between work and non-work and uses managerial initiated actions to restructure work.

123

More recently, these researchers validated a measure of Family Supportive Supervisor Behaviors (FSSB) on the basis of their original research and these categories.[19]

Although scholars and practitioners espouse the criticality of leader support, little research has been conducted to identify the specific supervisor behaviors in university settings that lead to employee work-life satisfaction and effectiveness. Moreover, administrators and managers generally are not trained on how their behaviors can foster a work-life culture within their units. Despite the fact that most faculty and many staff on campus report directly to academic department chairs, without easy access to clear and consistent information and appropriate training, chairs are not able to stay current in their knowledge of available resources, advocate for policy use by their faculty or staff, or implement campus work-life policies consistently.

> "I work in university fundraising. In my line of work, there is no reason that someone needs to be 'on call' to the extent that they never see their families. As I like to tell my team: 'We don't carry hearts around in coolers here. We can take a break.'" (Erin Moran, Associate Vice President, Office University Advancement, DePaul University)

In a recent survey of CUWFA members, some of the greatest barriers to accomplishing work-life initiatives on campus included a lack of funding, a decentralized structure, lack of staff resources, a lack of information on faculty/staff needs, *lack of support from senior administration and deans/department chairs, and a lack of understanding by senior leadership*.[20] Although university administrators are increasingly beginning to change their culture to become more work-life oriented, there is yet a long road ahead. Fostering a flexible workplace policy for both faculty and staff needs to be addressed in order to meet the growing demands within an academic setting.[21]

> TIP: Develop a standard of collegiality among faculty and staff that acknowledges and supports family identities. For example, host events including an annual picnic in which family members are invited. Additionally, respectful and collaborative behaviors supportive of work-life can be part of criteria for evaluating faculty and staff.

In a recent study, researchers conducted focus groups with university staff to identify supportive leadership behaviors.[22] At the outset of this research, the researchers wanted to know if the findings about leader behaviors in other organizations were relevant for higher education institutions. Several similar supervisor behaviors were identified in this study; however, other behaviors that were not included in the FSSB framework were discovered, leading the researchers to hypothesize that there are unique work-life considerations within the academic setting.

124

From the focus group results, a framework consisting of two overarching dimensions was inductively developed to capture the ways that leaders facilitated work-life satisfaction (Table 6.3). One dimension, the individual-level versus unit-level, relates to supervisor behaviors that are aimed towards either the individual or

Table 6.3 Work-Life Leader Behaviors (WLLB) in a University[23]

Dimensions	Leader Behaviors	Staff Responses
Individual-Level Personal-Life Focus (IPL)	Behaviors that focus on personal life issues for a specific individual. Characteristics and behaviors include *understanding; approachable; caring; offering pre-emptive support; following up with an employee; fostering trust; displaying humor; being inclusive of all employees; using the Golden Rule.*	• "She is very, very understanding. If it turns out I need to take leave, she supports me and will let me do what is necessary." • "I think if you have a boss with an open door policy that really helps." • "I had to tell an employee to take advantage of [EAPs]. Often employees don't want to let you down and don't want to take time off."
Individual-Level Work-Task Focus (IWT)	Behaviors that focus on resolving work issues for a specific individual. Characteristics and behaviors include *reassignment of workload; flexibility; helpful in assisting with work; providing constructive feedback about performance; stating clear expectations about job duties; giving reciprocity; holding job knowledge.*	• "My supervisor is very good about letting me take off. If I call in and say I'm not going to be there, my backup takes over." • "I have three little kids so I have all sorts of issues. My boss says we are the master of our own schedule." • "I know that my supervisor can back me up, and will do my work as needed."
Unit-Level Personal-Life Focus (UPL)	Behaviors that focus on the work unit as a whole to facilitate work-life satisfaction. Characteristics and behaviors include *fostering a climate that was caring, supportive, and family-oriented for everyone in the unit; treating employees consistently; demonstrating appreciation.*	• "I know the good, the bad, and the health and all about the kids ... we are a part of each other's lives." • "I can say from personal experience what I don't do but should do: let them know my employees are appreciated enough. Let people know they've done a good job, not just once a year for evaluation."
Unit-Level Work-Task Focus (UWT)	Behaviors that focus on the work unit as a whole to manage the work issues when employees have life responsibilities. Characteristics and behaviors include *flexibility; clear expectations about reasonable policies and guidelines; clear expectations of performance; fairness; consistency; equality; technical competence; appreciation; accountability*	• "Have policies that are common sense and good human judgments." • "I think treating everyone equally. Sometimes you see the boss is more lenient with someone than with another. Whatever the reason, age, gender, tenure ... that can cause lack of production."

the unit as a whole. The second dimension, life focus versus work focus, refers to the leader exhibiting helpful behaviors relating either to employees' personal matters or managing the work unit in order to accommodate employees. These two dimensions form four quadrants that were labeled as Work-Life Leader Behaviors (WLLB) in order to distinguish them from the FSSB categories.[24] The four categories of perceived helpful leader behaviors are individual-level personal-life focus (IPL), individual-level work-task focus (IWT), unit-level personal-life focus (UPL), and unit-level work-task focus (UWT).

In this study, overall, staff perceived the most helpful leader behaviors to be those that were aimed at them individually (e.g., asking follow-up questions about the family emergency, asking what he or she can do to help, reassigning workloads) as well as those that were aimed at the entire organizational unit (e.g., fostering a trusting overall work climate, having clear expectations regarding policies and guidelines). Thus, this research revealed that both an individual-level focus and unit-level focus are necessary for perceived leadership support. Focusing on increasing supervisors' supportiveness of their employees' work-life issues has proven to be effective in a long-term study.[25]

> TIP: Departmental climate (culture) change rests on wide-scale acknowledgement and acceptance of the diversity of faculty family structures, situations, and needs.[26]

EMERGING STRATEGIES FOR ACADEMIC LEADERS

Although few research studies of supportive leaders in university settings are available in the literature, leading work-life institutions have developed toolkits and guidelines for their academic leaders, as mentioned in Chapter 3. For example, UC Berkeley work-life professionals and faculty developed the "Creating a Family Friendly Department: Chairs and Deans Toolkit" for the University of California system's Faculty Family Friendly Edge initiative. This toolkit contains 10 essential steps for fostering a culture that values and supports the work and family needs of faculty (Table 6.4).

Oregon State University's toolkit is titled "Creating a Family Friendly Department: Toolkit for Academic Administrators" and Boise State University's toolkit is titled "Creating Work-Life Flexibility: A Toolkit for Chairs and Deans." The University of Washington provides a brochure

> TIP: Create a toolkit that provides strategies and best practices for facilitating a work-life friendly unit.

for department chairs that contains strategies for creating a responsive climate for flexibility within their departments. The brochure also includes the flexibility goals of the university. The University of Florida developed a Faculty Recruitment Toolkit required for search committee members as part of their certification

Table 6.4 Ten Essential Steps for Department Chairs and Deans[27]

1. Make becoming family [life] friendly a major priority and goal for your department [college].

2. Review and assess your department's [college's] current practices and climate around family friendliness.

3. Become conscious about unconscious bias issues concerning caregiving and gender.

4. Know the family [life] accommodation policies and laws that apply to your faculty [and staff].

5. Actively highlight, advertise, and support your department's [college's] family [work] accommodation policies and procedures for all faculty [and staff].

6. Make the use of family [life] accommodations the standard for conducting business in your department [college] rather than viewing them as exceptions or "special privileges."

7. Maintain "zero tolerance" for discriminatory and disparaging comments and behaviors.

8. Be proactive about recruiting and hiring diverse faculty for your department [college], including those who have temporarily slowed down their career for family caregiving [or other life changes] reasons.

9. Establish and maintain transparency in the promotion and tenure process, and advocate for your faculty who have used family accommodation policies through the promotion and tenure process.

10. Implement small changes that can have a significant impact on the culture of your department [college].

before sitting on the committee. The toolkit helps committee members to be receptive to individuals who participated in flexible policies throughout their careers. The content is similar across these toolkits, containing information on the importance of work-life friendly units, strategies for recruitment and hiring, advancement and tenure, best practices, policies, laws, and resources.

The COACHE survey results revealed several ways in which leaders could respond to work-life needs:[28]

- Hire personnel to staff or lead work-life services and initiatives
- Have written policies in areas of
  - Dual-career couples hiring
  - Early promotion and tenure
  - Parental leave
  - Modified duties
  - Part-time tenure option
  - Stop-the-tenure-clock provision.

- Communicate written policies
- Make written policies easily accessible
- Provide child care, elder care, lactation rooms, flexibility, and opportunities for social occasions in which kids can be included

Strategies to Overcome Resistance to Change

We have noted on several occasions in this text that academic leaders may not be supportive. Why would leaders resist? Frequently, department chairs, deans, provosts, and presidents are hesitant to shape work-life culture because the assumption is that the policies or strategies must be institution-wide and require a large financial investment. This may be true in some cases, but it is also possible to implement small changes that indicate a leader's understanding and support.

> TIP: Implement small changes that you have control of within your unit.

Another explanation for leader resistance is the existence of bias toward caregivers and others who have life responsibilities, previously described in this text. As mentioned in Chapter 3, an institution should be proactive in controlling these biases: "Gender bias in the academy can throw unfair obstacles in the paths of women with and without children and hamper fathers in their attempts to co-parent."[29] For example, the University of Florida requires that every member of a search committee

> participate in an online training module that discusses how to assess gaps in a candidate's resume. After faculty complete the online tutorial, they are required to take "refresher" courses every three years to maintain their knowledge of fair and effective recruiting practices.[30]

UC Davis informs reviewers that faculty who have taken a leave "be evaluated without prejudice" and Lehigh University states in its policy that faculty who have had tenure extensions must not be held to higher standards.[31]

Specific strategies for mitigating the impact of biases include the following:[32]

- Offer effective programs for chairs to heighten awareness of biases during hiring
- Offer gender bias training to faculty search committees
  - Online training and refresher courses
  - Recruitment tools tailored to each search
  - Interactive workshops for department chairs and search committees.

- Monitor the faculty search process
  - Appoint an equity advisor for each search committee
  - Institutionalize use of candidate evaluation tools for the faculty search process.
- Prevent gender bias during negotiation (double bind avoidance)
  - Resource negotiation, use of list of requested items
  - Confidential negotiation counseling for candidates.
- Promote advancement and retention
  - Offer programs to retain a diverse faculty (especially for women)
- Train department chairs to manage flexibility
  - Online faculty booklet for chairs and deans
  - Guidelines for family-responsive meeting times
  - School for chairs
  - Leadership workshops
  - Mentoring focused on family responsiveness.
- Eliminate bias: clearly communicate policies to internal and external tenure case reviewers
- Offer gender bias training to faculty
  - Peer-led workshops by request
  - Training activities available to all departments.

> TIP: Do not allow for family responsibilities or caregiver discrimination: Make sure policies are not biased against caregivers, develop anti-discrimination policies, etc.

Legal Do's and Don'ts

In Chapter 3, the laws that pertain to work, life, and family responsibilities were reviewed, and it is imperative that leaders understand that there may be legal ramifications if they do not support work-life satisfaction and effectiveness. Following are a few additional suggestions for academic leaders offered by Oregon State University, Boise State University, and UC Berkeley.

- Understand the variety of legal issues relevant to the role of the leader, including personnel decisions;
- Be aware of the legal realities of the chair role, as these can have significant negative consequences for the leader, the employees supervised, and the University;
- A leader of a unit or department is an agent of the institution, meaning her or his acts are attributable to the University;
- As a University agent, one of the major responsibilities is carrying out the University's policies and procedures. Having a working knowledge of the policies that affect faculty and staff is necessary. If conflicts arise and

are taken to course, the governing principles of the University will be used as a standard by which actions are judged;

- When making a decision that has the potential for legal risk, it is important that the leader inform and involve the next level of supervision (e.g., a chair informs the dean). The University's Office of General Counsel is available to consult with leaders;
- A wise leader will emphasize the central role of academic policy implementation in her or his actions and take care to harmonize decision making with the academic objectives of the unit and the University;
- Faculty and staff members who bring lawsuits against educational institutions can use comments made in the past by their colleagues or administrators.

Additionally, the Equal Employment Opportunity Commissions provides *Employer Best Practices for Workers With Caregiving Responsibilities.*[33]

"I lead by example, and I let them know that I TRUST them. . . . Additionally, I expect that they are professionals, and that means giving them the opportunity to make their own decisions about their days." (Dr. Christa Hinton, Assistant Dean, Kellstadt Graduate School of Business, DePaul University)

Strategizing Incremental Solutions

Through the ACE/Alfred P. Sloan Projects for Faculty Career Flexibility and the NSF ADVANCE Institutional Transformation grants, institution-level culture change has been made possible. There are now examples of how leaders can implement cultural change in higher education institutions (Table 6.5). These institution-wide changes can be daunting and time-consuming, especially at institutions that lack work-life staff or other entities (such as committees or advisory boards) to mobilize change efforts. However, this large-picture focus should not preclude an academic leader from implementing smaller manageable solutions on a daily basis.

As an academic leader, you can facilitate your unit's culture to be work-life friendly through changes that you can control and implement. Chairs and deans, in particular, are in positions to offer strategies and solutions (Tables 6.6 and 6.7).

In addition to a myriad of suggestions for facilitating a work-life culture, leaders can strategize solutions that can be implemented on a daily basis (Table 6.8). Showing understanding and concern can go a long way.

Table 6.5 The ACE/Alfred P. Sloan Projects for Faculty Career Flexibility: Findings From Winning Institutions[34]

Creating Flexibility	**Assess Where You Stand** Winning institutions have benefited from assessing where they stand on flexibility by benchmarking against other institutions. **Eliminate Bias** Once institutions determine which policies and practices they need to have in place, bias should be eliminated for both the users of the policies and the administrators who enforce those policies. **Offer Dual-Career Options** Winning institutions have found ways to support faculty with dual-career challenges.
Implementing Flexibility	**Awareness Campaign** Winning institutions found that widespread publicity of all flexible career policies and practices available was helpful in increasing knowledge and usage of these policies. **Training of Key Gatekeepers** Winning institutions found that essential to implementing their career flexibility plans was the training of key gatekeepers, such as department chairs, and the training of mentors or other advisors.
Evaluating Flexibility	**Measuring and Rewarding Usage** Winning institutions evaluate the use of faculty career flexibility policies to determine if policies are equitably enforced across departments on campus, and if there are negative career repercussions for faculty over time. **Evaluating Change** Looking at both the depth and breadth of change, ACE proposed four types of change (1) adjustments, (2) isolated change, (3) far-reaching change, and (4) transformational change.
Sustaining Flexibility	**Leadership From the Top** In order to sustain initiatives at the institutional level, colleges and universities must ensure that policies and programs apply to all individuals and deeply penetrate the culture of the institution. When these changes are pervasive and penetrating, they become transformational; therefore, changes in leadership do not affect a climate of continuing flexibility. **Addressing Cultural Change** Successful programs in altering the culture on a campus can facilitate transformational change. **Funding** Some departments are hesitant to support paid leave policies because of the costs associated with replacement instructors. Winning institutions centralize the funding for these purposes.

Table 6.6 Considerations for Department Chairs[35]

For All Faculty	• Departmental climate and the institutional mission influence faculty's daily work and family lives • Effective policies and practices and an accommodating culture encourage all faculty to be productive and successful • Be aware of and advocate for institution-wide policy • Call for department chair training • Break the silence • Share the wealth (share creative solutions) • Understand power differentials • Recognize that one size does not fit all • Adopt a life-course perspective • Offer support for child care and breastfeeding • Provide options for covering classes (modified duties, bank courses, team teaching, alternate formats)
Early-Career Faculty	• Provide clarity on promotion and tenure policies, including tenure-clock stoppage • Offer professional development for establishing successful teaching and research portfolios • Provide mentoring and help in navigating the university
Midcareer Faculty	• Midcareer faculty must manage family responsibilities while also pursuing opportunities for established faculty members • Regenerate academic careers through modified duties • Offer ongoing mentoring and support for faculty throughout the career • Clarify expectations for promotion to full professor • Provide professional development opportunities for administration

Table 6.7 Considerations for Deans[36]

- Implement competitive strategies for hiring and retaining faculty
- Ensure a positive work climate
- Provide an equitable and fair work environment with congruence between policy and climate
- Collect data regarding the status of faculty
- Advocate for policies on behalf of faculty and work climate
- Expand the conceptualization of what constitutes family-friendly policies

Table 6.8 Strategizing Incremental Solutions

- Maintain open communication and transparency
- Convey that your unit is a place where faculty with current or potential caregiving responsibilities can thrive
- Increase awareness through a website, brochures or discussions
- Appoint a work-life specialist or committee to champion changes
- Create an explicit plan to promote work-life-family friendliness within the unit
- Be strategic about changes
  - Timely and appropriate for unit's situation
  - Reasonable chance of success
  - Plans with least drastic changes
  - Sensitivity to values held by unit members
- Acknowledge the diversity of faculty needs
- Know the legal do's and don'ts
- Implement policy and best practices training for leaders in your unit, including search committees and P&T committees
- Provide information to external reviewers regarding P&T expectations and policies
- Include aspects of work-life culture in performance reviews of chairs, deans, etc.
- Implement family-friendly scheduling: Scheduling of faculty meetings, classes, seminars, and receptions should take into account demands of work and caregiving
- Mentor faculty: Junior faculty can benefit from mentoring by department chairs or senior faculty about combining and work, family, and life
- Provide professional development programs for faculty
- Make use of dual-career assistance, child-care support, and relocation assistance when recruiting finalists
- Establish Rainy Day Fund: Set aside funds in the event that temporary coverage may be needed for a faculty member who might have to take leave unexpectedly
- Provide travel funds: A travel fund available to faculty who must take a child along to research or conferences, or who need to hire additional help when they are away
- Give accommodations for pregnancy: During pregnancy, women may benefit from or need modifications of their position
- Give accommodations following leave: With a life-changing event, life circumstances might be different, determine course and committee assignments that may be more manageable
- Reduce course loads when a significant work-life event occurs
- Offer opportunities for faculty to socialize
- Ensure the practice supports policy
- Monitor policy usage
- Manage your boundaries between work and life spheres and help faculty and staff with boundary management[i]
- Don't be afraid to take reasonable risks
- Give voice to a sense of shared purpose about work-life
- Model the behaviors that you want others to exhibit
- Be patient and persistent

[i] Kossek, E.E., & Lautsch, B.A. (2012). Work–family boundary management styles in organizations: A cross-level model. *Organizational Psychology Review, 2*(2), 152–171.

CONCLUSION

When work-life and flexibility become embedded in the culture, policies, and programs of the university or college, then faculty and staff members can design work arrangements to align with their current personal responsibilities, which can result in enhanced work-life satisfaction.[37] According to the ACE's National Challenge for Higher Education, University Presidents commit to provide leadership to:

- "Advance excellence by developing flexibility as a tool to enhance recruitment, retention, and advancement of faculty within our institution;
- Actively communicate the institutional importance of workplace flexibility and implement policies and practices to keep pace with societal change while advancing gender, racial, and ethnic equity;
- Educate and support key academic leaders (department chairs, deans, etc.) in developing and strengthening their skills for managing career flexibility; and
- Develop workplaces in which flexibility is an integral part of the culture of the institution, where flexibility is broadly and equitably implemented and available to faculty at every phase of their career from recruitment to retirement."[38]

With this guide, it is our hope that leaders will begin or continue to shape cultures that will enhance the success of faculty, staff, and students. Our vision is that every higher education institution will embrace a culture where members can succeed and that work processes, systems, structures, and procedures supporting work-life become the way of doing things in the academy.

Questions for Discussion and Reflection

1. What are two research findings about the role of leaders in supporting work and life responsibilities of employees that are relevant to your institution?

2. What are the legal responsibilities of academic leaders with regard to work-life-family challenges?

3. What are specific changes you can implement to shape a work-life culture at your institution?

4. What strategies are currently being implemented to facilitate work-life satisfaction and effectiveness?

5. What did you learn from this chapter?

134

NOTES

1. Kossek, E.Y., & Nichol, V. (1992). The effects of on-site child care on employee attitudes and performance. *Personnel Psychology, 45,* 485–509.
2. Galinsky et al. (1996).
3. Hammer et al. (2009); Koppes & Schneider (2009); Koppes et al. (2009); Koppes et al. (2010).
4. Trower (2012), pp. 82–91.
5. Drago (2007).
6. Allen (2001); Erdogan & Enders (2007); Koppes & Swanberg (2008); Thompson et al. (1999).
7. Koppes & Swanberg (2008).
8. Hammer et al. (2009); Hammer et al. (2007); Koppes & Civian (2010); Koppes & Swanberg (2008); Yen et al. (2004).
9. Allen (2001); Smith & Gardner (2007).
10. Thomas, L. T., & Ganster, D. C. (1995). Impact of family-supportive work variables on work-family conflict and strain: A control perspective. *Journal of Applied Psychology, 80,* 6–15.
11. Carlson, D. S., & Perrewé, P. L. (1999). The role of social support in the stressor-strain relationship: An examination of work-family conflict. *Journal of Management, 25*(4), 513–540.
12. Smith & Gardner (2007).
13. Butler, A., Gasser, M., & Smart, L. (2004). A social-cognitive perspective on using family friendly benefits. *Journal of Vocational Behavior, 65,* 57–70; O'Neill et al. (2009).
14. Kossek, E. E., & Hammer, L. B. (2008). Supervisor work/life training gets results. *Harvard Business Review, 86,* 36–47.
15. Ehlert, D. (2000). Love 'em or lose 'em: Secrets of employee retention. *Paperboard Packaging, 60,* 42–45.
16. Hammer et al. (2009).
17. Hammer et al. (2009).
18. Hammer et al. (2009), pp. 840–842.
19. Hammer et al. (2009); Kossek, E., Pichler, S., Bodner, T. & Hammer, L. (2011). Workplace social support and work-family conflict: A meta-analysis clarifying the influence of general and work-family specific supervisor and organizational support. *Personnel Psychology, 64,* 289–313; Hammer, L. B., Kossek, E. E., Anger, W. K., Bodner, T., & Zimmerman, K. L. (2010). Clarifying work-family intervention processes: The roles of work-family conflict and family-supportive supervisor behaviors. *Journal of Applied Psychology, 96*(1), 134–150.
20. Koppes & Civian (2010).
21. Santos & Cabral-Cardoso (2008).
22. Koppes Bryan et al. (under review).
23. Koppes Bryan et al. (under review).
24. Hammer et al.
25. Kossek & Hammer (2008).
26. The UC Faculty Family Friendly Edge. (2007). *Creating a family friendly department: 2006 chairs and deans toolkit.* Retrieved from http://ucfamilyedge.berkeley.edu/ChairsandDeansToolkitFinal7-07.pdf
27. Frasch, K., Mason, M.A., Stacy, A., Goulden, M., & Hoffman, C. (2007). *Creating a family friendly department: Chairs and deans toolkit.* Berkeley, CA: University of California Faculty Family Friendly Edge.
28. Trower (2012).
29. The Center for WorkLife Law (2013), p. 13.
30. American Council on Education (2013c).
31. American Council on Education (2013c).
32. The Center for WorkLife Law (2013).

33. U.S. Equal Employment Opportunity Commission. (2009). *Employer best practices for workers with caregiving responsibilities.* Retrieved from www.eeoc.gov/policy/docs/caregiver-best-practices.html

34. American Council on Education (2013c).

35. Wolf-Wendel, L., & Ward, K. (2013). *Work and family integration for faculty: Recommendations for chairs.* Retrieved from http://cgi.stanford.edu/~dept-ctl/cgi-bin/tomprof/posting.php?ID=1251

36. McDade, S.A., & Dannels, S.A. (2009). Shaping the work environment and family-friendly policies: A perspective from deans. In J. Lester & M. Sallee *Establishing the family-friendly campus* (pp. 105–124). Sterling, VA: Stylus.

37. Gappa et al. (2007).

38. American Council on Education (2013a).

Work-Life Resources

AARP Public Policy Institute (www.aarp.org/research/ppi): AARP is a nonprofit, non-partisan organization, with a membership of more than 37 million, that helps people ages 50 and older to have independence, choice, and control in ways that are beneficial to them and society as a whole. The Public Policy Institute informs and stimulates public debate on the issues we face as we age. The Institute promotes development of sound, creative policies to address our common need for economic security, health care, and quality of life.

Alliance for Work-Life Progress (www.awlp.org/awlp/home/html/homepage.jsp): AWLP advances work-life as a business strategy integrating work, family, and community. A component of WorldatWork, AWLP defines and recognizes innovation and best practices, facilitates dialogue among various sectors, and promotes work-life leadership. In 2012, Emory University, George Mason University, and the University of Arizona received the inaugural AWLP Seal of Distinction (along with 23 businesses), which recognizes employers who demonstrate leadership in work-life effectiveness.

American Association of University Professors (www.aaup.org/issues/balancing-family-academic-work/professional-associations-and-workfamily-issues): AAUP offers a listing of discipline-specific professional organizations and their findings on work/family issues.

American Association of University Women (www.aauw.org/): AAUW is a 501 (c) (3) charitable membership organization, with a nationwide network of nearly 100,000 members, 1,000 branches, and 500 college/university institution partners. It advances equity for women and girls through advocacy, education, philanthropy, and research.

American Association for Women in Community College (http://www.aawccnatl.org: AAWCC changes women's lives through education, service, and leadership development.

American Council on Education (www.acenet.edu): The ACE is a major coordinating body for all the higher education institutions in the United States. It seeks to provide leadership and a unifying voice on key higher education issues and to influence public policy through advocacy, research, and program initiatives. ACE also aims to foster greater collaboration and new partnerships within and outside the higher education community to help colleges and universities anticipate and address challenges and contribute to a stronger nation and a better world and offers the Toolkit for Administrators on Faculty Career Flexibility (www.acenet.edu/leadership/programs/Pages/Toolkit-Faculty-Career-Flexibility.aspx)

Association for Women in Science (www.awis.org/): The AWIS is "today's premiere leadership organization advocating the interests of women in science and technology. For nearly 40 years, the Association for Women in Science has fought for equity and career advancement for women—from the bench to the board room." Workshops are provided on achieving work-life satisfaction.

Boston College Center for Work and Family (www.bc.edu/centers/cwf/): This Center of the Carroll School of Management at Boston College helps organizations create effective workplaces that support and develop healthy and productive employees. The Center provides a bridge, linking academic research and corporate practice and engages employers, employees, and communities in joint efforts to ensure the mutual prosperity and well-being of employees and their families. The Center has identified nine elements that compose *Standards of Excellence* (www.bc.edu/centers/cwf) to assess an organization's work-life culture.

Boston College's New England Work and Family Association (www.bc.edu/centers/cwf/newfa.html): The New England Work & Family Association (NEWFA) was established in 1992 to help employers understand and address the complex work-life challenges facing today's workforce.

California Work & Family Coalition (www.workfamilyca.org/about): This coalition is a collaborative of unions and community groups protecting every Californian's right to a job and a life. The California Work & Family Coalition is one of 16 state coalitions in the Family Values @ Work consortium working for paid sick days, family leave insurance, and other policies that value families at work.

CareerWise (http://careerwise.asu.edu): Research findings are applied to science and engineering doctoral programs.

Center for Aging & Work (http://agingandwork.bc.edu/statistics): This center at Boston College is a Sloan Center database. It includes fact sheets, brief descriptions of research studies, PowerPoint-ready graphics, and a huge list of topics to search for. However, it is only available to those with an affiliation with the Center.

Center for the Education of Women (www.cew.umich.edu/index.htm): The CEW advocates for women in higher education and in the workplace and adds to knowledge of women's lives through ongoing research. CEW focuses on women's education, employment, careers, leadership growth and development, and well being.

The Center of WorkLife Law (www.worklifelaw.org): A Center of the UC Hastings College of Law, this center works with employees, employers, management-side employment lawyers, unions, and public policymakers to educate each group about the prevalence of Family Responsibilities Discrimination and develop effective measures to eliminate it.

Centre for Work + Life, University of South Australia (www.unisa.edu.au/Research/Centre-for-Work-Life/): "The Centre for Work + Life is a hub for innovative thinking about work, life, and improving the wellbeing of Australians. We focus on generating long-term change, tackling the big questions around how work in Australia intersects with households, community and social life."

Claremont McKenna's Berger Institute for Work, Family, and Children (www.cmc. edu/berger): The Berger Institute for Work, Family, and Children was established in 2001 to be a leading source of research on significant issues impacting the intersection between work and family. The Berger Institute focuses on quantitative research impacting business practices and families.

CLASP (www.clasp.org): Since 1969, CLASP has been a trusted resource, a creative architect for systems change, and one of the country's most effective voices for low-income people. They develop and advocate for federal, state, and local policies to strengthen families and create pathways to education and work.

Collaborative on Academic Careers in Higher Education (http://isites.harvard.edu/ icb/icb.do?keyword=coache): With data, COACHE members can launch a context-sensitive strategy to build a culture of success and maintain a vibrant faculty, for the benefit of everyone with whom faculty share their campuses. COACHE's tools are designed to generate actionable diagnoses. The results include peer comparisons and provide provosts and faculty affairs professionals with a road map for making sound investments in their faculty.

College and University Work-Life-Family Association (www.cuwfa.org): This membership organization of institutions of higher education in the United States and Canada has an excellent annual conference plus an invaluable active listserv that enables the sharing of information on all aspects of work-life.

Conference Board (www.conference-board.org): This is an independent, nonprofit, membership organization. It conducts research, convenes conferences, makes forecasts, assesses trends, publishes information and analysis, and brings executives together to learn from one another how to strengthen their performance and better serve society.

Connecticut Women's Education and Legal Fund (www.cwealf.org): Since 1973, CWEALF has worked to advance women's rights and opportunities in Connecticut. To achieve this, CWEALF's work is divided into three core programs: Legal Education, Public Policy and Advocacy, and Research and Evaluation. Through these programs, CWEALF initiates services to educate and empower women and girls to ensure they have the tools, knowledge, and avenues to reach their goals.

Corporate Voices for Working Families (www.cvworkingfamilies.org): This is a non-profit, nonpartisan organization, improving the lives of working families by developing and advancing innovative policies that reflect collaboration among the private sector, government, and other stakeholders. They combine research, collaboration, business best practices, legislative outreach, and advocacy to adopt policies that ensure the mutual success of businesses, individuals, and communities.

Diversity & Flexibility Alliance (http://dfalliance.com/): The Diversity & Flexibility Alliance is a national forum dedicated to the promotion and retention of women lawyers and work-life control for all attorneys. The Alliance combines research-based organizational solutions and individual strategies for leveraging talent in the legal profession. The goal of the Alliance is to advance best practices towards a more inclusive and diverse legal profession. Alliance members receive vital information about recruiting, retention, and development of attorneys, all with an eye toward solidifying the long-term financial health of their organization.

Families and Work Institute (www.familiesandwork.org): FWI is a nonprofit, nonpartisan, research organization that studies the changing workforce, family, and community. FWI is committed to finding research-based strategies that foster mutually supportive connections among workplaces, families, and communities.

Greater Good Science Center (http://greatergood.berkeley.edu/work_career): The Greater Good Science Center studies the psychology, sociology, and neuroscience of well-being; and teaches skills that foster a thriving, resilient, and compassionate society and has a specific section dedicated to Work and Career.

Higher Education Resource Services (HERS: http://www.hersnet.org) Professional development opportunities are provided for women in higher education management.

Higher Education Recruitment Consortium (www.hercjobs.org/index.html?site_id=793): HERC offers the largest database of higher education and related jobs in the world. They are a nonprofit consortium of over 600 colleges, universities, hospitals, research labs, government agencies, and related non- and for-profit organizations. Consortium member institutions share a commitment to hiring the most diverse and talented faculty, staff, and executives. Hiring decisions often involve two careers. HERC provides jobseekers with the most job opportunities and unsurpassed search technology, enabling dual-career couples to find the right jobs within a commutable distance of one another.

International Center for Work and Family, IESE Business School, University of Navarra, Barcelona, Spain (www.iese.edu/en/faculty-research/research-centers/icwf/): "The ICWF's mission is to promote Family Corporate Responsibility in business, in order to promote leadership, culture and reconciliation policies that facilitate the integration employees' work, family and personal life."

Labor Resource Center at UMass, Boston (www.umb.edu/lrc): The Labor Resource Center (LRC) is an undergraduate education and research center located within the College of Public and Community Service at the University of Massachusetts Boston. Their work centers on the belief that the labor movement, representing both organized and unorganized workers, is an essential force for economic and social justice.

MIT Workplace Center (http://web.mit.edu/workplacecenter/): The MIT Workplace Center was established in 2001 by the Alfred P. Sloan Foundation and the MIT Sloan School of Management to build—in theory and in practice—a mutually supportive relationship between the performance of firms and the well being of employees, their families, and communities.

National Alliance for Caregiving (www.caregiving.org/): "Established in 1996, The National Alliance for Caregiving is a nonprofit coalition of national organizations focusing on issues of family caregiving. Alliance members include grassroots organizations, professional associations, service organizations, disease-specific organizations, a government agency, and corporations. The Alliance was created to conduct research, do policy analysis, develop national programs, increase public awareness of family caregiving issues, work to strengthen state and local caregiving coalitions, and represent the US caregiving community internationally."

National Organization for Women (www.now.org): The National Organization for Women (NOW) is the largest organization of feminist activists in the United States. NOW has 500,000 contributing members and 550 chapters in all 50 states and the District of Columbia. Since its founding in 1966, NOW's goal has been to take action to bring about equality for all women.

National Partnership for Women & Families (www.nationalpartnership.org): The National Partnership for Women & Families is a nonprofit, nonpartisan organization based in Washington, D.C. Founded in 1971, the National Partnership works on public policies, education, and outreach that focus on women and families.

National Science Foundation ADVANCE Program (www.nsf.gov/crssprgm/advance/): "ADVANCE is an integral part of the NSF's multifaceted strategy to broaden participation in the STEM workforce, and supports the critical role of the Foundation in advancing the status of women in academic science and engineering."

9to5 (www.9to5.org): 9to5 is one of the largest, most respected national membership organizations of working women in the United States, dedicated to putting working women's issues on the public agenda.

Organisation for Economic Cooperation and Development, or OECD (www.oecdbetter lifeindex.org/topics/work-life-balance/) The OECD Better Life Index was created to compare well-being across countries, using 11 topics deemed essential, including work-life balance. OECD consists of 35 countries that are members, and the index is an indicator of work-life balance in most of the world's developed economics and several emerging economies.

Texas Workforce Commission (www.twc.state.tx.us): Texas Workforce Commission (TWC) is the state agency charged with overseeing and providing workforce development services to employers and job seekers in Texas.

UC Berkeley Faculty Family Friendly Edge (http://ucfamilyedge.berkeley.edu): This program hosts the significant landmark academic work/family research and related documents for the University of California System.

University of Kentucky Institute for Workplace Innovation (www.uky.edu/centers/iwin): The Institute for Workplace Innovation, at the University of Kentucky, is a research center with a mission to develop and disseminate knowledge about the 21st century workplace to create work environments that boost the bottom line, employee health, and work-life fit. Their research is informed by theory and guided by the need for innovative, practical solutions.

U.S. Department of Labor, Women's Bureau (www.dol.gov/wb/): This bureau was created by law in 1920 to formulate standards and policies to promote the welfare of wage-earning women, improve their working conditions, increase their efficiency, and advance their opportunities for profitable employment.

Wellesley Centers for Women (www.wcwonline.org): Since 1974, WCW has conducted interdisciplinary studies on issues such as gender equity in education, sexual harassment in schools, child care, adolescent development, gender violence, and women's leadership—studies that have influenced private practices and public policy.

Wharton Work/Life Integration Project (www.worklife.wharton.upenn.edu): The Wharton Work/Life Integration Project was founded in 1991 to produce knowledge for action on the relationship between work and the rest of life and promote an understanding of how students and alumni think about and value their interests in life: work, education, family, society, and the private self (mind, body, and spirit).

Women in Higher Education (www.wihe.com): This is a monthly source of news and views that provides an overview of issues affecting women on campus.

Work and Family Connection (www.workfamily.com/): Since 1990, WFC Resources has been the nation's #1 partner for employers wanting a more flexible, effective, and supportive workplace, and service providers who help them.

Work and Family Researchers Network (https://workfamily.sas.upenn.edu/): The Work and Family Researchers Network (formerly the Sloan Work and Family Research Network), is an international membership organization of interdisciplinary work and family researchers. The WFRN facilitates virtual and face-to-face interaction among work and family researchers from a broad range of fields and engages the next generation of work and family scholars.

Work, Family, & Health Network (http://projects.iq.harvard.edu/wfhn): Sponsored by Harvard University, the Work, Family & Health Network embarked on the most comprehensive evaluation of a work-family intervention undertaken to date. Their workplace solution focused on two elements of workplace change: family supportive supervisory behaviors and employees' control over when and where they work.

Working Family Center on Parents, Children and Work (http://wf.educ.msu.edu/): As part of a network of six Sloan Working Family Centers, the Sloan Center based out of the University of Chicago and currently working out of Michigan State University was founded to examine the issues facing working parents and their children by taking a different approach to conceptually defining the research issues and exploring new research methodologies.

Workplace Flexibility 2010 (www.law.georgetown.edu/workplaceflexibility2010/): This is a campaign designed to support the development of a comprehensive national policy on workplace flexibility.

Bibliography

This list contains references not cited in the endnotes throughout the guide.

AARP. (2001). *In the middle: A report on multicultural boomers coping with family and aging issues.* Retrieved from http://assets.aarp.org/rgcenter/il/in_the_middle.pdf

AARP/Society for Human Resources Management (2006). *Phased retirement and flexible retirement arrangements: Strategies for retaining skilled workers.* Washington, DC: AARP.

Abelman, S.W., & Cross, M.L. (2007). Postretirement medical coverage in Ohio. *Academe, 93*(3), 34–36.

Acker, S. (2007, February). Breaking through the ivy ceiling. *Academic Matters,* 10–12.

Advance Center for Institutional Change. (2005). *University of Washington faculty retention toolkit.* Seattle, WA: Author.

Aisenberg, N., & Harrington, M. (1988). *Women of academe: Outsiders in the sacred grove.* Amherst: University of Massachusetts Press.

Allen, N.J., & Meyer, J.P. (1990). The measurements and antecedents of affective, continuance, and normative commitment to the organization. *Journal of Occupational and Organizational Psychology, 63,* 1–8.

Allen, S.G. (2005). The value of phased retirement. In R.L. Clark & J. Ma, (Eds.), *Recruitment, retention, and retirement in higher education: Building and managing the faculty of the future.* Northampton, MA: Edward Elgar Publishing.

Allen, S.G., Clark, R.L., & Ghent, L.S. (2004). Phasing into retirement. *Industrial and Labor Relations Review, 58*(1), 112–127.

Allen, S.G., Clark, R.L., & Ghent, L.S. (2005). Managing a phased retirement program: The case of UNC. *New Directions for Higher Education, 132,* 47–60.

Allen, T.D., Herst, D., Bruck, C., & Sutton, M. (2000). Consequences associated with work-to-family conflict: A review and agenda for future research. *Journal of Occupational Health Psychology, 5,* 278–308.

Allen, T.D., & Russell, J.E. (1999). Parental leave of absence: Some not so family-friendly implications. *Journal of Applied Social Psychology, 29*(1), 166–176.

Alliance for Work-Life Progress. (2004). *Worklife definition*. Retrieved from www.awlp.org/

Alliance for Work-life Progress, an Affiliate of WorldatWork. (2006). *State of the work-life profession: April 2006*. Scottsdale, AZ: Author.

Allis, P., & O'Driscoll, M. (2008). Positive effects of nonwork-to-work facilitation on well-being in work, family, and personal domains. *Journal of Managerial Psychology, 23,* 273–291.

Allison, J. E. (2007). Composing a life in twenty-first century academe: Reflections on a mother's challenge. *NWSA Journal, 19*(3), 23–46.

Almedia, D. M., & McDonald, D. A. (2005). The national story: How Americans spend their time on work, family, and community. In J. Heymann & C. Beem (Eds.), *Unfinished work: Building equality and democracy in an era of working families* (pp. 180–203). New York, NY: New Press.

Altman, B. W., & Post, J. E. (1996). Beyond the "social contract:" An analysis of the executive view at twenty-five large companies. In D.T. Hall (Ed.), *The career is dead—long live the career: A relational approach to careers*. San Francisco, CA: Jossey-Bass.

American Council on Education. (2009, August 24). *ACE Sloan faculty career flexibility compendium report—BU cares*. Lisle, IL: Benedictine University.

American Psychological Association. (2004). *Public policy, work and families: The Report of the APA Presidential Initiative on Work and Families*. Retrieved from www.apa.org/pubs/info/reports/work-family.aspx

Anderson, E. (2002). *The new professoriate: Characteristics, contributions, and compensation*. Retrieved from www.acenet.edu/news-room/Documents/New-Professoriate-Characteristics-Contributions-and-Compensation-2002.pdf

Anderson, S. E., Coffey, B. S., & Byerly, R. T. (2002). Formal organizational initiatives and informal workplace practice: Links to work-family conflict and job-related outcomes. *Journal of Management, 173,* 1–24.

Arthur, G. (1998). The 'graying' of librarianship: Implications for academic library managers. *Journal of Academic Librarianship, 24*(4), 323–327.

Ashenfelter, O., & Card, D. (2001). *Did the elimination of mandatory retirement affect faculty retirement flows?* IZA Discussion Paper No. 402.

Association of Executive Search Consultants. (2006, July 4). *87% of executives feel that work-life balance considerations are critical in their career decision making process*. Retrieved from https://members.aesc.org/eWeb/docs/aesc/pressreleases_2002-2008/pressrelease2006070401.html

Austin, A. E. (1994). Understanding and assessing faculty cultures and climates. *New Directions for Institutional Research, 84,* 47–63.

Austin, N. D. (2012). *Assessing academic best practices in workplace flexibility for the college and university/work family association*. (Unpublished manuscript). Southern Connecticut University, New Haven, CT.

Avery, G. C. (2001). Situational leadership preferences in Australia: Congruity, flexibility and effectiveness. *Leadership and Organizational Development Journal, 22,* 11–18.

Avolio, B. J., & Gardner, W. L. (2005). Authentic leadership development: Getting to the root of positive forms of leadership. *The Leadership Quarterly, 16,* 315–338.

Avolio, B. J., Yammarino, F. J., & Bass, B. M. (1991). Identifying common methods variance with data collected from a single source: An unresolved sticky issue. *Journal of Management, 17,* 571–587.

Axel, H. (1996). *Building the case for workplace flexibility.* New York, NY: Conference Board.

Bailyn, L. (1997). The impact of corporate culture on work-family integration. In S. Parasuraman and J. H. Greenhaus (Eds.), *Integrating work and family: Challenges and choices for a changing world* (pp. 209–219). Westport, CT: Quorum.

Baldwin, D., & Bidgood, V. H. (1991). Effects of retirement on supply of accounting educators during the 1990s. *Journal of Education for Business, 67*(2), 84–89.

Baldwin, R. G. (1990). Faculty vitality beyond the research university: Extending a contextual concept. *Journal of Higher Education, 61*(2), 160–180.

Baldwin, R. G. (1998). Technology's impact of faculty life and work. *New Directions for Teaching and Learning, 76,* 7–21.

Baltes, B. B., Briggs, T. E., Huff, J. W., Wright, J. A., & Neuman, G. A. (1999). Flexible and compressed workweek schedules: A meta-analysis of their effects on work-related criteria. *Journal of Applied Psychology, 84,* 496–513.

Barron, D. (2003, September 26). Learning to be a department head. *The Chronicle of Higher Education,* C5.

Bass, B. M. (2000). The future of leadership in the learning organization. *Journal of Leadership Studies, 7,* 18–38.

Bass, B. M., & Avolio, B. J. (1997). *Multifactor Leadership Questionnaire Manual.* Palo Alto, CA: Mind Garden.

Bates, B. B., Briggs, T. E., Huff, J. W., Wright, J. A., & Neuman, G. A. (1999). Flexible and compressed workweek schedules: A meta-analysis of their effects on work-related criteria. *Journal of Applied Psychology, 84*(4), 496–513.

Baughman, R., DiNardi, D., & Holtz-Eakin, D. (2003). Productivity and wage effects of family-friendly fringe benefits. *International Journal of Manpower, 24*(3), 247–259.

Beehr, T. (1998). Research on occupational stress: An unfinished enterprise. *Personnel Psychology, 51,* 835–844.

Behson, S. J. (2002a). Coping with family-to-work conflict: The role of informal work accommodations to family, *Journal of Organizational Behavior, 16,* 3–27.

Behson, S. J. (2002b). Which dominates? The relative importance of work-family organizational support and general organizational context on employee outcomes. *Journal of Vocational Behavior, 61,* 53–72.

145

Behson, S. J. (2005). The relative contribution of formal and informal organizational work family support. *Journal of Vocational Behavior, 66,* 487–500.

Bellas, M. L. (1997). The scholarly productivity of academic couples. In M. A. Ferber & J. W. Loeb (Eds.), *Academic couples: Problems and promises* (pp. 156–181). Urbana: University of Illinois Press.

Bellas, M. L., & Toutkoushian, R. K. (1999). Faculty time allocations and research productivity: Gender, race, and family effects. *Review of Higher Education, 22,* 367–390.

Bennett, J. B., & Figuli, D. J. (1993). *Enhancing departmental leadership: The roles of the chairperson.* New York, NY: Rowman & Littlefield.

Berberet, J. (2005). Planning for the generational turnover of the faculty: Faculty perceptions and institutional practices. In R. L. Clark & J. Ma, (Eds.), *Recruitment, retention, and retirement in higher education: Building and managing the faculty of the future* (pp. 80–100). Northampton, MA: Edward Elgar Publishing.

Berg, P., Kalleberg, A., & Appelbaum, E. (2003). Balancing work and family: The role of high commitment environments. *Industrial Relations: A Journal of Economy and Society, 42*(2), 168–188.

Berger, J. O., & Chen, M. H. (1993). Predicting retirement patterns: Prediction for a multinomial distribution with constrained parameter space. *Journal of the Royal Statistical Society. Series D (The Statistician), 42*(4), 427–443.

Berkman, L. F., & Okechukwu, C. (2010). Managers' practices related to work-family balance predict employee cardiovascular risk and sleep duration in extended care settings. *Journal of Occupational Health Psychology, 15*(3), 316–329.

Berry, L. H., Hammons, J. O., & Denny, G. S. (2001). Faculty retirement turnover in community colleges: A real or imagined problem? *Community College Journal of Research & Practice, 25*(2), 123–136.

Bickel, J., & Brown, A. J. (2005). Generation X: Implications for faculty recruitment and development in academic health centers. *Academic Medicine, 80,* 205–210.

Biggs, J. H. (2006). The future train wreck: Paying for medical costs for higher education's retirees. *Change, 38*(6), 8–14.

Blair Loy, M., & Wharton, A. S. (2002). Employees use of work/family policies and the workplace social context. *Social Forces, 80*(3), 813–845.

Bland, C. J. (2002). One school's strategy to assess and improve the vitality of its faculty. *Academic Medicine, 77*(5), 368–376.

Bland, C. J., & Bergquist, W. H. (1997). *The vitality of senior faculty members: Snow on the roof—fire in the furnace.* J-B ASHE Higher Education Report Series. San Francisco, CA: Jossey-Bass.

Blau, P. (1964). *Exchange and power in social life.* New York, NY: Wiley.

Boatwright, K. J., & Forrest, L. K. (2000). The influence of gender and needs for connection on workers' ideal preferences for leadership behaviors. *Journal of Leadership Studies, 7,* 18–34.

146

Boles, J. S., Howard, W. G., & Donofrio, H. H. (2001). An investigation into the inter-relationships of work-family conflict, family-work conflict and work satisfaction. *Journal of Managerial Issues, 13*(3), 376–391.

Bombardieri, M. (2005, October 4). Reduced load lets faculty meld family, tenure track. *Boston Globe.* Retrieved from www.boston.com/news/education/higher/articles/2005/10/04/reduced_load_lets_faculty_meld_family_tenure_track/?page=full

Bond, J., Galinsky, E., Kim, S., & Brownfield, E. (2005). *2005 National Study of Employers.* New York, NY: Families and Work Institute.

Bonner, F. B. (2001). Addressing gender issues in the historically Black college and university community: A challenge and call to action. *Journal of Negro Education, 70*(3), 176–192.

Bottomley, W. N., Linnell, R. H., & Marsh, H. W. (1980). Differences in cost, tenure ratio, and faculty flow as a result of changed mandatory retirement ages. *Research in Higher Education, 13*(3), 261–272.

Bowers, D. G., & Seashore, S. E. (1966). Predicting organizational effectiveness with a four factor theory of leadership. *Administrative Science Quarterly, 11*(2), 238–263.

Bowles, H. R., Babcock, L., & Lai, L. (2007). Social incentives for gender differences in the propensity to negotiate for salary: Sometimes it does hurt to ask. *Organizational Behavior and Human Decision Processes, 103*(1), 84–103.

Boyar, S. L., Carr, J. C., Mosely, D. C., & Carson, C. M. (2007). The development and validation of scores on perceived work and family demand scales. *Educational and Psychological Measurement, 67,* 100–115.

Bracken, S. J., Allen, J. K., & Dean, D. R. (2006). *The balancing act: Gendered perspectives in faculty roles and work lives.* Sterling, VA: Stylus.

Brannick, M. T., Levine, E. L., & Morgeson, F. P. (2007). *Job and work analysis: Methods research and application for human resource management* (2nd ed.). Thousand Oaks, CA: Sage.

Breneman, D. (2006). A wake-up call? *Change, 38*(6), 1–14.

Broder, J. M., White, F. C., & Taylor, T. D. (1991). Determinants of agricultural economics faculty retirement. *American Journal of Agricultural Economics, 73*(3), 641–651.

Bronfenbrenner, U., McClelland, D., Wethington, E., Moen, P., & Ceci, S. J. (1996). *The state of Americans: This generation and the next.* New York, NY: Free Press.

Brown, M., Aumann, K., Pitt-Catsouphes, M., Galinsky, E., & Bond, J. T. (2010). *Working in retirement: A 21st century phenomenon.* New York, NY: Families and Work Institute.

Buckley, M. R., Fedor, D. B., Verres, J. G., Wiese, D. S., & Carraher, S. M. (1998). Investigating newcomer expectations and job-related outcomes. *Journal of Applied Psychology, 83,* 452–461.

Califano, J.A., Jr. (1978). The aging of America: Questions for the four-generation society. *Annals of the American Academy of Political and Social Science, 438,* 96–107.

Carlson, D. S. (1999). Personality and role variables as predictors of three forms of work-family conflict. *Journal of Vocational Behavior, 55,* 236–253.

Carlson, D. S., Kacmar, K. M., & Williams, L. J. (2000). Construction and initial validation of a multidimensional work-family conflict measure. *Journal of Vocational Behavior, 56,* 249–276.

Carnegie Foundation for the Advancement of Teaching. (1990). Early faculty retirees: Who, why, and with what impact? *Change, 22*(4), 31–34.

Case Western Reserve University. (2008). *Toolkit for equitable searches.* Retrieved from www.case.edu/diversity/faculty/toolkit.html

Casey, J., & Corday, K. (2009). Military families and work-family concerns. *Sloan Work and Family Research Network Newsletter, 11*(5), n.p.

Casper, J.W., Lilly, J.D., & Virick, M. (2007). Doing more with less: An analysis of work-life balance among layoff survivors. *Career Development International, 12*(5), 463–480.

Casper, L.M., & Bianchi, S.M. (2002). *Continuity and change in the American family.* Thousand Oaks, CA: Sage.

Cheung, F. M., & Halpern, D. F. (2010). Women at the top: Powerful leaders define success at work + family in a culture of gender. *American Psychologist, 65*(3), 182–193.

Chronicle of Higher Education. (2009). *Retired professors' groups play a variety of roles.* Retrieved from http://chronicle.com/article/Retired-Professors-Groups/49446/

Civian, J. (2009). Work/Life programs: Lifesavers in a scary economy. *Women in Higher Education, 18*(8), 1–3.

Clark, R.L. (2006). Employer-provided retiree health insurance: A dying employee benefit. *Change, 38*(6), 15.

Clark, R.L., & Hammond, P.B. (Eds.). (2001). *To retire or not? Retirement policy and practice in higher education.* Philadelphia: University of Pennsylvania Press.

Clark, R.L., & Ma, J. (Eds.). (2005). *Recruitment, retention, and retirement in higher education: Building and managing the faculty of the future.* Northampton, MA: Edward Elgar.

Clark, R.L., & Rappaport, A. (2001). The changing retirement landscape. *Pension Section News,* 14–19.

Clark, S.C. (2001). Work cultures and work/family balance. *Journal of Vocational Behavior, 58,* 348–365.

Clark, S.L. (1998). Female faculty in community colleges: Investigating the mystery. *Community College Review, 26*(3), 77–88.

Claxton, R.P., Rao, C.P., & Kurtz, D.L. (1993). Marketing faculty retirement plans: Findings, scenarios, and recommendations for an uncertain future. *Journal of Marketing Education, 15*(2), 21–29.

COACHE. (2007). *The collaborative on academic careers in higher education: Exemplary institutions by theme (2005–2007)*. Cambridge, MA: Harvard Graduate School of Education.

Comer, D. R., & Stites-Doe, S. (2006). Antecedents and consequences of faculty women's academic-parental role balancing. *Journal of Family and Economic Issues, 27,* 495–512.

Conley, V. M. (2005a). Demographics and motives affecting faculty retirement. *New Directions for Higher Education, 132,* 9–30.

Conley, V. M. (2005b). Exploring faculty retirement issues in public 2-year institutions. *Journal of Applied Research in the Community College, 13*(1), 59–72.

Conley, V. M. (2007). *Survey of changes in faculty retirement policies 2007.* Washington, DC: American Association of University Professors.

Cooke, T. J. (2001). "Trailing wife" or "Trailing mother"? The effect of parental status on the relationship between family migration and the labor-market participation of married women. *Environment and Planning A, 33*(3), 419–430.

Cooney, T. M., & Uhlenberg, P. (1989). Family-building patterns of professional women: A comparison of lawyers, physicians, and postsecondary teachers. *Journal of Marriage and the Family, 51,* 749–758.

Cooper, K. J. (2009). A disturbing trend. *Diverse: Issues in Higher Education, 26*(9), 20–21.

Corporate Voices for Working Families. (2005). *Business impacts of flexibility: An imperative for expansion.* Boston, MA: WFD Consulting.

Coser, L. A. (1974). *Greedy institutions.* New York, NY: Free Press.

Cotterell, N., Eisenberger, R., & Speicher, H. (1992). Inhibiting effects of reciprocation wariness on interpersonal relationships. *Journal of Personality and Social Psychology, 62,* 658–668.

Crane, B., O'Hern, B., & Lawler, P. (2009). Second career professionals: Transitioning to the faculty role. *Journal of Faculty Development, 23*(1), 24–29.

Crouter, A. C., Bumpus, M. F., Maguire, M. C., & McHale, S. M. (1999). Linking parents' work pressure and adolescents' well-being: Insights into dynamics in dual-earner families. *Developmental Psychology, 35,* 1453–1461.

Damiano-Teixeira, K. M. (2006). Managing conflicting roles: A qualitative study with female faculty members. *Journal of Family and Economic Issues, 27*(2), 310–334.

Davis, L. J. (2008, June 6). Where did I put my 'Foucault'? *The Chronicle of Higher Education,* B22–B23.

de Graaf, J. (Ed.). (2003). *Take back your time: Fighting overwork and time poverty in America.* San Francisco, CA: Berrett-Koehler.

Dickson, C. E. (2007, Summer). Building a legal case for work-life balance policies. *EAP Digest,* 16–19.

Didion, C. J. (1996). Dual-careers and shared positions: Adjusting university policy to accommodate academic couples. *Journal of College Science Teaching, 26*(2), 123–124.

149

Diener, E., Emmons, R.A., Larsen, R.J., & Griffin, S. (1985). The satisfaction with life scale. *Journal of Personality Assessment, 49,* 71–75.

Dierdorff, E. C., & Ellington, J. K. (2008). It's the nature of the work: Examining behavior-based sources of work-family conflict across occupations. *Journal of Applied Psychology, 93,* 883–892.

Dixon, M.A., & Sagas, M. (2007). The relationship between organizational support, work-family conflict, and the job-life satisfactions of university coaches. *Research Quarterly for Exercise and Sport, 78*(3), 236–247.

Dorfman, L.T. (2002). Stayers and leavers: Professors in an era of no mandatory retirement. *Educational Gerontology, 28*(1), 15–33.

Dorfman, L.T. et al. (1984). Reactions of professors to retirement: A comparison of retired faculty from three types of institutions. *Research in Higher Education, 20*(1), 89–102.

Dorfman, M. S. (1980). A faculty views its retirement benefit plan: An empirical observation and analysis. *Research in Higher Education, 13*(1), 49–60.

Doty, D. H., & Glick, W. H. (1998). Common methods bias: Does common methods variance really bias results? *Organizational Research Methods, 1,* 374–406.

Doyle, W. R. (2008). The baby boomers as faculty: What will they leave behind? *Change, 40*(6), 56–59.

Drakich, J., & Stewart, P. (2007, February). Forty years later, how are university women doing? *Academic Matters,* 6–9.

Dwyer, M.M., Flynn, A.A., & Inman, P. (1991). Differential progress of women faculty: Status 1980–1990. In J. Smart (Ed.), *Handbook of theory and research* (Vol. 7; pp. 173–222). New York, NY: Agathon.

Eaton, S. C. (2003). If you can use them: Flexibility policies, organizational commitment and perceived performance. *Industrial Relations, 42,* 145–167.

Edwards, J. R. (2001). Ten difference score myths. *Organizational Research Methods, 4*(3), 265–287.

Edwards, J. R., & Rothbard, N. P. (2000). Mechanisms linking work and family: Clarifying the relationship between work and family constructs. *Academy of Management Review, 25,* 178–199.

Edwards, J. R., & Rothbard, N. P. (2005). Work and family stress and well-being: An integrative model of person-environment fit within and between the work and family domains. In E. E. Kossek & S. J. Lambert (Eds.), *Work and life integration: Organizational, cultural, and individual perspectives* (pp. 201–232). Mahwah. NJ: Lawrence Erlbaum.

Ehrenberg, R. G. (1999). No longer forced out: How one institution is dealing with the end of mandatory retirement. *Academe, 85*(3), 34–39.

Ehrenberg, R. G. (2001). Career's end: A survey of faculty retirement policies. *Academe, 87*(4), 24–29.

150

Ehrenberg, R. G., & Rizzo, M. J. (2001). Faculty retirement policies after the end of mandatory retirement. *TIAA-CREF Institute Research Dialogue, 69*. Retrieved from www1.tiaa-cref.org/ucm/groups/content/@ap_ucm_p_tcp_docs/documents/document/tiaa02029407.pdf

Ehrhart, M. G. (2004). Leadership and procedural justice climate as antecedents of unit-level organizational citizenship behavior. *Personnel Psychology, 57*, 61–94.

Eisenberger, R., Armeli, S. Rexwinkel, B., Lynch, P. D., & Rhoades, L. (2001). Reciprocation of perceived organizational support. *Journal of Applied Psychology, 86*, 42–51.

Eisenberger, R., Huntington, R., Hutchinson, S., & Sowa, D. (1986). Perceived organizational support. *Journal of Applied Psychology, 71*, 500–507.

Ejiogu, A. M. (1985). Patterns of principals' leadership behavior preferred by teachers in secondary school in Lagos. *Journal of Teacher Education, 1*, 77–88.

Ekerdt, D. J. (1989). Retirement preparation. *Annual Review of Gerontology and Geriatrics, 9*, 321–356.

Elliott, M. (2003). Work and family role strain among university employees. *Journal of Family and Economic Issues, 24*, 157–181.

Etaugh, C., & Moss, C. (2001). Attitudes of employed women toward parents who choose full-time or part-time employment following their child's birth. *Sex Roles, 44*, 611–619.

Euster, G. L. (2004). Reflections upon university retirement: With thanks and apologies to James Joyce. *Educational Gerontology, 30*(2), 119–128.

Fairweather, J. S., & Rhoads, R. A. (1995). Teaching and the faculty role: Enhancing the commitment to instruction in American colleges and universities. *Educational Evaluation and Policy Analysis, 17*(2), 179–194.

Fleig-Palmer, M., Murrin, J., Palmer, D. K., & Rathert, C. (2003). Meeting the needs of dual career couples in academia. *CUPA-HR Journal, 54*(3), 12–15.

Fogg, P. (2001, October 19). Can department heads be trained to succeed? More colleges are offering orientation programs for new chairmen. *The Chronicle of Higher Education*, A10.

Foret, M., & de Janasz, S. (2005). Perceptions of an organization's culture for work and family: Do mentors make a difference? *Career Development International, 10*, 478–492.

Fothergill, A., & Feltey, K. (2003). I've worked very hard and slept very little: Mothers on the tenure track in academia. *Journal of the Association on Mothering, 5*, 7–19.

Foxall, M. et al. (2009). Faculty retirement: Stemming the tide. *Journal of Nursing Education, 48*(3), 172–175.

Fried, M. (1998). *Taking time: Parental leave policy and corporate culture.* Philadelphia, PA: Temple University Press.

Friedman, D. E., & Johnson, A. A. (1997). Moving from programs to culture change: The next stage for the corporate work-family agenda. In S. Parasuraman & J. H. Greenhaus (Eds.), *Integrating work and family: Challenges and choices for a changing world* (pp. 192–208). Westport, CT: Quorum.

Frone, M. R. (2003). Work-family balance. In J. C. Quick & L. E. Tetrick (Eds.), *Handbook of occupational health psychology* (pp. 143–162). Washington, DC: American Psychological Association.

Frone, M. R., Russell, M., & Barnes, G. M. (1996). Work-family conflict, gender, and health-related outcomes: A study of employed parents in two community samples. *Journal of Occupational Health Psychology, 1,* 57–69.

Frone, M. R., Russell, M., & Cooper, M. L. (1997). Relation of work-family conflict to health outcomes: A four-year longitudinal study of employed parents. *Journal of Occupational and Organizational Psychology, 70,* 325–335.

Froom, J. D., & Bickel, J. (1996). Medical school policies for part-time faculty committed to full professional effort. *Academic Medicine, 71*(1), 92–96.

Furstenberg, F. F. (1990). Divorce and the American family. *Annual Review of Sociology, 16,* 379–403.

Gahn, S., & Twombly, S. B. (2001). Dimensions of the community college faculty labor market. *Review of Higher Education, 24*(3), 259–282.

Galinsky, E. (2002). *Navigating work and family: Hands-on advice for working parents.* New York, NY: Families and Work Institute.

Galinsky, E., Bond, J. T., & Sakai, K. (2008). *2008 National Study of Employers.* Retrieved from http://familiesandwork.org/downloads/2008NationalStudyofEmployers.pdf

Galinsky, E., & Stein, P. J. (1990). The impact of human resource policies on employees, *The Journal of Family Issues, 11*(4), 368–383.

Gambles, R., Lewis, S., & Rapoport, R. (2006). *The myth of work-life balance: The challenge of our time for men, women and societies.* San Francisco, CA: Jossey-Bass.

Gappa, J. M., & MacDermid, S. M. (1997). Work, family, and the faculty career. *New pathways: Faculty career and employment for the 21st century working paper series, inquiry #8.* Washington, DC: American Association for Higher Education.

Gillespie, K. J., Robertson, D. L., & Associates. (2010). *A guide to faculty development* (2nd ed.). San Francisco, CA: Jossey-Bass.

Gilroy, M. (2009). The graying professoriate. *Education Digest, 74*(5), 62–64.

Ginsberg, R., & Davies, T. G. (2007). *The human side of leadership: Navigating emotions at work.* Westport, CT: Praeger.

Glass, J. L., & Finley, A. (2002). Coverage and effectiveness of family-responsive workplace policies. *Human Resource Management Review, 12*(3), 313–337.

Glass, J. L., & Riley, L. (1998). Family responsive policies and employee retention following childbirth. *Social Forces, 76*(4), 1401–1435.

Glazer, S. D., Redmon, E. L., & Robinson, K. L. (2005). Continuing the connection: Emeriti/retiree centers on campus. *Educational Gerontology, 31*(5), 363–383.

Glazer-Raymo, J. (1999). *Shattering the myths: Women in academe.* Baltimore, MD: Johns Hopkins University Press.

Glazer-Raymo, J. (2004). Women and retirement. *Academe, 90*(3), 32–36.

Gmelch, W. H., & Miskin, V. D. (1995). *Changing an academic department.* Thousand Oaks, CA: Sage Publications.

Goff, S. J., Mount, M. K., & Jamison, R. L. (1990). Employers supported childcare, work/family conflict, and absenteeism: A field study. *Personnel Psychology, 43,* 793–809.

Goldberg, W. A., Greenberger, E., Koch-Jones, J., O'Neil, R., & Hamill, S. (1989). Attractiveness of child care and related employer-supported benefits and policies to married and single parents. *Child and Youth Quarterly, 18,* 23–37.

Golden, L. (2005). The flexibility gap: Employee access to flexibility in work schedules. In I. U. Zeytinoglu (Ed.), *Flexibility in workplaces: Effects on workers, work environment and the unions* (pp. 38–56). Geneva, Switzerland: IIRA/ILO.

Goldstein, E. R. (2008, July 25). The profs they are a-changin'. *The Chronicle of Higher Education,* B4.

Graen, G., Novak, M. A., & Sommerkamp, P. (1982). The effects of leader-member exchange and job design on productivity and job satisfaction: Testing a dual attachment model. *Organizational Behavior and Human Performance, 30,* 109–131.

Grandey, A. A. (2001). Family friendly policies: Organizational justice perceptions of need-based allocations. In R. Cropanzano (Ed.), *Justice in the workplace: From theory to practice* (Vol. 2; pp. 145–173). Mahwah, NJ: Erlbaum.

Grandey, A. A., & Cordeiro, B. L. (2002, October 9). *Family-friendly policies and organizational justice.* Retrieved from https://workfamily.sas.upenn.edu/wfrn-repo/object/j4y9ov50xr2yw0p6

Grant-Vallone, E. J., & Donaldson, S. I. (2001). Consequences of work-family conflict on employee well-being over time. *Work & Stress, 15*(3), 214–226.

Grawitch, M. J., Gottschalk, M., & Munz, D. C. (2006). The path to a healthy workplace: A critical review linking healthy workplace practices, employee well-being, and organizational improvements. *Consulting Psychology Journal: Practice and Research, 3,* 129–147.

Grawitch, M. J., Kohler, J. M., & Trares, S. (2007). Healthy workplace practices and employee outcomes. *International Journal of Stress Management, 14,* 275–293.

Greenhaus, J. H., & Foley, S. (2007). *Handbook of career studies.* Thousand Oaks, CA: Sage.

Greenleaf, R. K. (1977). *Servant leadership.* New York, NY: Paulist Press.

Gropel, P., & Kuhl, J. (2009). Work-life balance and subjective well-being: The mediating role of need fulfillment. *British Journal of Psychology, 100,* 365–375.

Grubb, W. N. et al. (1999). *Honored but invisible: An inside look at teaching in community colleges.* New York, NY: Routledge.

Grundy, E. (1991). Ageing: Age-related change in later life. *Population Studies, 45,* 133–156.

Grzywacz. J. G., & Demerouti, E. (2012). *New frontiers in work and family research.* New York, NY: Routledge.

Haden, N. K. et al. (2008). The quality for dental faculty work-life: Report on the 2007 Dental School Faculty Work Environment Survey. *Journal of Dental Education, 72,* 514–531.

Hagedorn, L. S. (1994). Retirement proximity's role in the prediction of satisfaction in academe. *Research in Higher Education, 35*(6), 711–728.

Halpern, D. F. (2005a). How time-flexible work policies can reduce stress, improve health, and save money. *Stress and Health, 21,* 157–168.

Halpern, D. F. (2005b). Psychology at the intersection of work and family. *The American Psychologist, 60,* 397–409.

Halpern, D. F. (2006). How organizations can alleviate the traffic jam at the intersection of work and family. *The American Behavioral Scientist, 49,* 1147–1151.

Halpern, D., & Murphy, S. E. (Eds.). (2005). *From work-family BALANCE to work-family INTERACTION: Changing the metaphor.* Mahwah, NJ: Lawrence Erlbaum Associates.

Hammer, L. B., Neal, M. B., Newsom, J. T., Brockwood, K. J., & Colton, C. L. (2005). A longitudinal study of the effects of dual-earner couples' utilization of family-friendly workplace supports on work and family outcomes. *Journal of Applied Psychology, 90,* 799–810.

Hamovitch, W., & Morgenstern, R. D. (1977). Children and the productivity of academic women. *Journal of Higher Education, 48*(6), 633–645.

Hanson, G. C., Hammer, L. B., & Colton, C. L. (2006). Development and validation of a multidimensional scale of perceived work-family positive spillover. *Journal of Occupational Health and Psychology, 11,* 249–265.

Harenstam, A., & Bejerot, E. (2001). Combining professional work with family responsibilities: A burden or a blessing? *International Journal of Social Welfare, 10,* 202–214.

Harrington, B., & Ladge, J. J. (2009). Present dynamics and future directions for organizations. *Organizational Dynamics, 38*(2), 148–157.

Harris, A. A., & Prentice, M. K. (2004). The role exit process of community college faculty: A study of faculty retirement. *Community College Journal of Research & Practice, 28*(9), 729–743.

Hart, J. (2009). Family-friendly activism. In J. Lester & M. Salle (Eds.), *Establishing the family-friendly campus: Models for effective practice* (pp. 125–140). Sterling, VA: Stylus.

Harter, J. K., Schmidt, F. L., & Keyes, C. L. (2002). Well-being in the workplace and its relationship to business outcomes: A review of the Gallup Studies. In C. L. Keyes & J. Haidt (Eds.), *Flourishing: The positive person and the good life* (pp. 205–224). Washington DC: American Psychological Association.

Hartwell, T. D., Steele, P., French, M. T., Potter, F. J., Rodman, N. F., & Zarkin, G. A. (1996). Aiding troubled employees: The prevalence, cost, and characteristics of employee assistance programs in the United States. *American Journal of Public Health, 86*(6), 804–808.

Harvard Business Review. (2000). *Harvard business review on work and life balance.* Cambridge, MA: Harvard Business Review Press.

154

Hayes, W. (2003). *So you want to be a college professor?* Lanham, MD: Scarecrow.

Heelan, M.P., Major, D.A., Morganson, V.J., Oborn, K.L., & Vervive, J.M. (2009). Comparing telework locations and traditional work arrangements: Differences in work-life balance support, job satisfaction, and inclusion. *Journal of Managerial Psychology, 25*(6), 578–595.

Henderson, B.B., & Kane, W.D. (1991). Caught in the middle: Faculty and institutional status and quality in state comprehensive universities. *Higher Education, 22,* 339–350.

Hersey, P., & Blanchard, K.H. (1982). *Management of organizational behavior: Utilizing human resources.* Englewood Cliffs, NJ: Prentice Hall.

Hersey, P., Blanchard, K.H., & Johnson, D.E. (2001). *Management of organizational behavior: Leading human resources.* Upper Saddle River, NJ: Prentice Hall.

Hewlett, S.A. (2002). *Creating a life: Professional women and quest for children.* New York, NY: Miramax.

Heymann, J. (2000). *The widening gap: Why America's working families are in jeopardy—and what can be done about it.* New York, NY: Basic Books.

Hill, E.J., Hawkins, A.J., Ferris, M., & Weitzman, M. (2001). Finding an extra day a week: The positive influence of perceived job flexibility on work and family life balance. *Family Relations, 50,* 49–58.

Hill, E.J., Miller, B.C., Weiner, S.P., & Colihan, J. (1998). Influences of the virtual office on aspects of work and work/life balance. *Personnel Psychology, 51,* 667–683.

Hochschild, A. (1989). *The second shift: Working parents and the revolution at home.* New York, NY: Viking Press.

Holden, K.C., & Hansen, W.L. (1989a). Eliminating mandatory retirement: Effects on retirement age. *New Directions for Higher Education, 65,* 73–83.

Holden, K.C., & Hansen, W.L. (1989b). Retirement behavior and mandatory retirement in higher education. *New Directions for Higher Education, 65,* 33–49.

Hollenshead, C., & Waltman, J. (2005). *Family-friendly policies in higher education: Where do we stand?* Retrieved from www.cew.umich.edu/sites/default/files/wherestand.pdf

Hollenshead, C.S., Sullivan, B., Smith, G.C., August, L., & Hamilton, S. (2005, Summer). Work/family policies in higher education: Survey data and case studies of policy implementation. *The Challenge of Balancing Faculty Careers and Family Work: New Directions for Higher Education, 130,* 41–65.

Hoobler, J.M., Wayne, S.J., & Lemmon, G. (2009). Bosses' perceptions of family-work conflict and women's promotability: Glass ceiling effects. *Academy of Management Journal, 52*(5), 939–957.

Hopkins, D.S.P. (1974). Analysis of faculty appointment, promotion, and retirement policies. *Higher Education, 3*(4), 397–418.

Hopkins, K. (2005). Supervisor support and work-life integration: A social identity perspective. In E.E. Kossek & S.J. Lambert (Eds.), *Work and life integration: Organizational, cultural, and individual perspectives* (pp. 445–467). Mahwah, NJ: Lawrence Erlbaum Associates.

House, R. J., & Mitchell, T. R. (1974). Path-goal theory of leadership. *Contemporary Business, 3,* 81–98.

Hughes, G. C. (1981). Age 70 retirement for faculty: An institutional approach. *Research in Higher Education, 15*(3), 213–230.

Hughes, R. L., & Colarelli Beatty, K. (2005). *Becoming a strategic leader: Your role in your organization's enduring success.* Hoboken, NJ: John Wiley & Sons.

Hulbert, M.A. (2008). Lessons from the office: The organizational implementation of work-life policies. *Workat Work Journal, 44*–54.

Hutchens, R., & Grace-Martin, K. (2006). Employer willingness to permit phased retirement: Why are some more willing than others? *Industrial and Labor Relations Review, 59*(4), 525–546.

Hutchens, R. M. (2007). Phased retirement: Problems and prospects. *An issue in brief, work opportunities for older Americans, Series 8.* Boston, MA: Center for Retirement Research at Boston College.

Ikenberry, J. (2010). *Q1 2010 Higher Education Employment Report.* Retrieved from www.higheredjobs.com/documents/HEJ_Employment_Report_2010_Q1.pdf

Jacobs, J.A. (1999). Sex segregation of occupations: Prospects for the 21st century. In G. Powell (Ed.), *Handbook of Gender and Work* (pp. 125–143). Thousand Oaks, CA: Sage.

Jacobs, J.A. (2004). *Mommies and daddies on the fast track: Success of parents in demanding professions.* The Annals of the American Academy of Political and Social Science Series. Thousand Oaks, CA: Sage.

Jacobs, J.A., & Winslow, S. E. (2004). The academic life course, time pressures and gender inequality. *Community, Work and Family, 7*(2), 143–161.

Janson, N. (2005). Phased retirement policies. *New Directions for Higher Education, 132,* 31–46.

Jaschik, S. (2007, November 1). A satisfied full-time faculty. *Inside Higher Ed.* Retrieved from www.insidehighered.com/news/2007/11/01/faculty

Jaschik, S. (2009, January 6). Ignorance about 'stop the clock' policies. *Inside Higher Ed.* Retrieved from www.insidehighered.com/news/2009/01/06/stc

Johnson, G. E., & Stafford, F. P. (1974). The earnings and promotions of women faculty. *The American Economic Review, 64,* 888–903.

Johnson, H. P. (2000). Retirements on the rise. *Academe, 86*(3), 11.

June, A.W. (2008). University of North Carolina lets professors ease their way into retirement. *The Chronicle of Higher Education, 54*(40), A12–A13.

June, A.W. (2009). Minority Ph.D.'s, stay the course; you'll be needed as boomers retire. *The Chronicle of Higher Education, 56,* A11–A11.

156

June, A.W., McCormack, E., & Wheeler, D.L. (2008). Colleges explore new ways to manage retirements. *The Chronicle of Higher Education, 54*(40), A1–A11.

Jung, C.S., Swihart, D.L., & Thompson, D.A. (2009). Connecting work and life at the University of Arizona. In J. Lester & M. Salle (Eds.), *Establishing the family-friendly campus: Models for effective practice* (pp. 125–140). Sterling, VA: Stylus.

Kadilak, K.O., & Watts, D. (2006). Revisiting the work-life dialogue. *Workspan, 05/06,* 39–42.

Kanter, R.M. (1977). *Men and women of the corporation.* New York, NY: Basic Books.

Karin, M. (2009). Time off for military families: An emerging case study in a time of war … and the tipping point for future laws supporting work-life balance? *Rutgers Law Record, 33,* 46–64.

Keeney, J., Boyd, E.M., Sinha, R., Westring, A.F., & Ryan, A.M. (2013). From "work-family" to "work-life": Broadening our conceptualization and measurement. *Journal of Vocational Behavior, 82,* 221–237.

Kim, S. (2003). The impact of research productivity on early retirement of university professors. *Industrial Relations, 42*(1), 106–125.

Kimber, M. (2003). The tenured "core" and the tenuous "periphery": The casualisation of academic work in Australian universities. *Journal of Higher Education Policy and Management, 25,* 41–50.

Kinney, D.P., & Sharon, P.S. (1992). Age and teaching performance. *The Journal of Higher Education, 63*(3), 282–302.

Kinnunen, U., & Mauno, S. (1998). Antecedents and outcomes of work-family conflict among employed women and men in Finland. *Human Relations, 5,* 157–177.

Kinnunen, U., Vermulst, A., Gerris, J., & Makikangas, A. (2003). Work-family conflict and its relationships to well-being: The role of personality as a moderating factor. *Personality and Individual Differences, 35,* 1669–1683.

Kolodny, A. (1998). Creating the family-friendly campus. In C. Colner & D.H. George (Eds.), *The family track: Keeping your faculties while you mentor, nurture, teach, and serve* (pp. 284–308). Urbana: University of Illinois Press.

Koppes Bryan, L.L., & Schneider, S.K. (Chairs). (2011). *Decent work and beyond: Work-life effectiveness [work-family balance] in relation to positive employee work and personal outcomes.* Symposium for the 15th European Congress of Work and Organizational Psychology, The Netherlands.

Kossek, E.E., Baltes, B., & Mathews, R. (2011). How work-family research can finally have an impact in organizations. *Industrial and Organizational Psychology: Perspectives on Science and Practice, 4*(3), 352–369.

Kossek, E.E., & Friede, A. (2005). *The business case: Managerial perspectives on work and the family.* Retrieved from http://ellenkossek.lir.msu.edu/documents/businesscase.pdf

Kossek, E. E., Lautsch, B. A., & Eaton, S. C. (2006). Telecommuting, control, and boundary management: correlates of policy use and practice, job control, and work-family effectiveness. *Journal of Vocational Behavior, 68,* 247–267.

Kossek, E. E., Lewis, S., & Hammer, L. (2009). Work life initiatives and organizational change: Overcoming mixed messages to move from the margin to the mainstream. *Human Relations, 63*(1), 3–19.

Kossek, E. E., & Ozeki, C. (1999). Bridging the work-family policy and productivity gap: A literature review. *Community, Work & Family, 2,* 7–32.

Kossek, E. E., Ruderman, M. N., Braddy, P. W., & Hannum, K. M. (2012). Work-nonwork boundary management profiles: A person-centered approach. *Journal of Vocational Behavior, 8*(1), 112–128.

Kotter, J. P. (2002). *The heart of change: Real-life stories of how people change their organizations.* Boston, MA: Harvard Business School Publishing.

Kottke, J. L., & Sharafinski, C. E. (1988). Measuring perceived supervisory support and organizational support. *Educational and Psychological Measurement, 48*(4), 1075–1079.

Kowalski, S. D., Dalley, K., & Weigand, T. (2006). When will faculty retire? Factors influencing retirement decisions of nurse educators. *Journal of Nursing Education, 45*(9), 349–355.

Kreiner, G. E., Hollensbe, E. C., & Sheep, M. L. (2009). Balancing borders and bridges: Negotiating the work-home interface via boundary work tactics. *Academy of Management Journal, 52*(4), 704–730.

Kyvik, S. (1990). Motherhood and scientific productivity. *Social Studies of Science, 20*(1), 149–160.

LaPierre, L. M., Hackett, R. D., & Taggar, S. (2006). A test of the links between family interference with work, job enrichment and leader-member exchange. *Applied Psychology, 55*(4), 489–511.

Lambert, S. J. (2000). Added benefits: The link between work-life benefits and organizational citizenship behavior. *Academy of Management Journal, 43,* 801–815.

Leaming, D. R. (2007). *Academic leadership: A practical guide to chairing the department* (2nd ed.). Bolton, MA: Anker Publishing Company, Inc.

Leslie, D. W. (2005). The costs and benefits of phased retirement. *New Directions for Higher Education, 132,* 61–71.

Leslie, D. W., & Conley, V. M. (2005). Editors' notes. *New Directions for Higher Education, 132,* 1–4.

Leslie, D. W., Janson, N., & Conley, V. M. (2005). Policy-related issues and recommendations. *New Directions for Higher Education, 132,* 73–85.

Levering, R., & Moskowitz, M. (1993). *The 100 best companies to work for in America.* New York, NY: Currency/Doubleday.

Levine, J., & Pittinsky, T. (1997). *Working fathers.* Reading, MA: Addison-Wesley Publishing Company.

Lewis, S. (2003). Flexible working arrangements: Implementation, outcomes and management. In C. L. Cooper & I. T. Roberts (Eds.), *International review of industrial and organizational psychology* (Vol. 18; pp. 1–28).

Lewis, S., Izraeli, D., & Hootsmans, H. (Eds.) (1992). *Dual-earner families: International perspectives.* London, UK: Sage Publications.

Lewis, W. C. (1996). Retirement wealth, income, and decision making in higher education. *The Journal of Higher Education, 67*(1), 85–102.

Lobel, S. A. (1999). Impacts on diversity and work-life initiatives in organizations. In G. N. Powell (Ed.), *Handbook of gender and work* (pp. 453–476). Thousand Oaks, CA: Sage.

Lord, M. (2005). Phased retirement: Often a win-win situation. *TIAA-CREF Institute Trends and Issues.* Retrieved from www.tiaa-crefinstitute.org/public/pdf/institute/research/trends_issues/tr060105.pdf

Lozier, G. G., & Dooris, M. J. (1989). Elimination of mandatory requirement: Anticipating faculty response. *Planning for Higher Education, 17*(2), 1–14.

Lozier, G. G., & Dooris, M. J. (1991). Projecting faculty retirement: Factors influencing individual decisions. *The American Economic Review, 81*(2), 101–105.

Lucas, A. (2000). *Leading academic change,* San Francisco, CA: Jossey-Bass.

Luria, G., & Torjman, A. (2008). Resources and coping with stressful events. *Journal of Organizational Behavior, 30,* 685–707.

Lynch, P. D., Eisenberger, R., & Armeli, S. (1999). Perceived organizational support: Inferior versus superior performance by wary employees. *Journal of Applied Psychology, 84,* 467–483.

Major, D. A., & Cleveland, J. N. (2007). Strategies for reducing work-family conflict: Applying research and best practices from industrial and organizational psychology. In G. P. Hodgkinson & J. K. Ford (Eds.), *International review of industrial and organizational psychology* (Vol. 22; pp. 111–140). Chichester, UK: John Wiley & Sons.

Major, D. A., & Germano, L. M. (2006). The changing nature of work and its impact on the work-home interface. In F. Jones, R. Burke, & M. Westman (Eds.), *Work-life balance: A psychological perspective* (pp. 13–38). London, UK: Psychology Press.

Maloney, W. A. (2007). New report explores faculty retirement policies. *Academe, 93*(2), 14.

Mannix, M. (2001, November). Take me, take my spouse. *ASEE Prism, 11*(3), 26–28.

Marcus, J. (2007). Helping academics have families and tenure too: Universities discover their self-interest. *Change, 39*(2), 27–32.

Massachusetts Institute of Technology, News Office. (2001, January 30). *Leaders of 9 universities and 25 women faculty meet at MIT, agree to equity reviews.* Retrieved from http://web.mit.edu/newsoffice/2001/gender.html

Matthews, R. A., Kath, L. M., & Barnes-Farrell, J. L. (2010). A short, valid, predictive measure of work-family conflict: Item selection and scale validation. *Journal of Occupational Health Psychology, 15,* 75–90.

159

Mauch, J.E., Birch, J.W., & Matthews, J. (1990). The emeritus professor: Old rank—new meaning. *ASHE-ERIC Higher Education Report No. 2.* Washington, DC: School of Education and Human Development, the George Washington University.

McCormack, E. (2008). Community colleges hope to keep aging professors in the classroom. *The Chronicle of Higher Education, 54*(40), A14.

McMahan, S., & Sturz, D. (2006). Implications for an aging workforce. *Journal of Education for Business, 82*(1), 50–55.

Menall, L.A., Masuda, A.D., & Nicklin, J.M. (2010). Flexible work arrangements, job satisfaction, and turnover intentions: The mediating role of work-to-family enrichment. *The Journal of Psychology, 144*(1), 61–81.

Michael, J.S., & Hargis, M.B. (2008). Linking mechanisms of work-family conflict and segmentation. *Journal of Vocational Behavior, 73,* 509–522.

Milliken, F.J., Dutton, J.E., & Beyer, J.M. (1990). Understanding organizational adaptation to change: The case of work-family issues. *Human Resource Planning, 13*(2), 91–107.

Milliken, F.J., Martins, L.L., & Morgan, H. (1998). Explaining organizational responsiveness to work-family issues: The role of human resource executives as issue interpreters. *Academy of Management Journal, 41*(5), 580–592.

Morgan, H., & Milliken, F.J. (1993). Keys to action: Understanding differences in organizations' responsiveness to work-and-family issues. *Human Resource Management, 31*(3), 227–248.

Morrison, M.H. (1986). *Work and retirement in an aging society.* New York, NY: Daedalus.

Mulvany, R.H. (1992). Work-family conflict and the bottom line: Reassessing corporate policies and initiatives. In U. Sekaran & F.T. Leong (Eds.), *Women-power: Managing in times of demographic turbulence* (pp. 59–84). Newbury Park, CA: Sage.

Murphy, S.E., & Zagorski, D.A. (2005). Enhancing work-family and work-life interaction: The role of management. In D.F. Halpern & S.E. Murphy (Eds.), *From work-family balance to work-family interaction: Changing the metaphor* (pp. 27–47). Mahwah, NJ: Lawrence Erlbaum.

Murray, J.P., & Cunningham, S. (2004). New rural community college faculty members and job satisfaction. *Community College Review, 32*(2), 19–38.

National Academy of Sciences, National Academy of Engineering, and Institute of Medicine. (2006). *Beyond bias and barriers: Fulfilling the potential of women in academic science and engineering.* Washington, DC: National Academies Press.

National Center for Education Statistics. (2005). *2004 national study of postsecondary faculty report on faculty and instructional staff.* Washington DC: U.S. Department of Education.

Neil, G.I., & Kirby, S.L. (1985). Coaching styles and preferred leadership among rowers and paddlers. *Journal of Sport Behavior, 8,* 3–15.

Nettles, M., Perna, L.W., Bradburn, E.M., & Zimbler, L. (2000). *Salary, promotion, and tenure status of minority and women faculty in U.S. colleges and universities.* Retrieved from http://nces.ed.gov/pubs2000/2000173.pdf

160

Noor, N. M. (2002). Work-family conflict, locus of control, and women's well-being: Tests of alternative pathways. *Journal of Social Psychology, 142*(5), 645–662.

Norrell, J. E., & Norrell, T. H. (1996). Faculty and family policies in higher education. *Journal of Family Issues, 17*(2), 204–226.

Oi, W.Y. (1979). Academic tenure and mandatory retirement under the new law. *Science, 206*(4425), 1373–1378.

O'Laughlin, E. M., & Bischoff, L. G. (2005). Balancing parenthood and academia: Work/family stress as influenced by gender and tenure status. *Journal of Family Issues, 26*(1), 79–106.

Olsen, D., Maple, S.A., & Stage, F. K. (1995). Women and minority faculty job satisfaction: Professional role interests, professional satisfactions, and institutional fit. *The Journal of Higher Education, 66*(3), 267–293.

O'Meara, K., Lapointe Terosky, A., & Neumann, A. (2008). Faculty careers and work lives: A professional growth perspective. *ASHE Higher Education Report Series 34*(3). Hoboken, NJ; Wiley Periodicals, Inc.

O'Rand, A.M., & Agree, E. M. (1993). *Kin reciprocities, the familial corporation, and other moral economies: Workplace, family, and kin in the modern global context.* New York, NY: Springer Publishing Co.

Osterman, P. (1995). Work/family programs and the employment relationship. *Administrative Science Quarterly, 40,* 681–700.

Overman, S. (1999). Make family-friendly initiatives fly. *HR Focus, 76,* 13–15.

Pace, L.A., & Argona, D.R. (1989). Participatory action research: A view from Xerox. *American Behavioral Scientist, 32,* 552–565.

Palmer, J. L. (2006). Emeriti offers benefits over health saving accounts. *Change, 38*(6), 15.

Parker, L., & Allen, T.D. (2001). Work/family benefits: Variables related to employees' fairness perceptions. *Journal of Vocational Behavior, 58,* 453–468.

Parolini, J., Patterson, K., & Winston, B. (2008). Distinguishing between transformational and servant leadership. *Leadership & Organization Development Journal, 30,* 274–291.

Patterson, K., Grenny, J., McMillan, R., & Switzler, A. (2002). *Crucial conversations: Tools for talking when stakes are high.* New York, NY: McGraw-Hill.

Pencavel, J. (2001). The response of employees to severance incentives. *Journal of Human Resources, 36*(1), 58–84.

Perna, L.W. (2003). The status of women and minorities among community college faculty. *Research in Higher Education, 44*(2), 205–239.

Perna, L.W. (2005). Sex differences in faculty tenure and promotion: The contribution of family ties. *Research in Higher Education, 46*(3), 277–307.

Peterson, L. M. (2003). Half-full or half-empty? How institutional cooperation could turn a wave of faculty requirements into an opportunity. *Connection: The Journal of the New England Board of Higher Education, 17*(5), 24–25.

Phillipe, K.A. (Ed.). (1999). *National profile of community colleges: Trends and statistics* (3rd ed.). Washington, DC: American Association of Community Colleges.

Podsakoff, P.M., Bommer, W.H., Podsakoff, N.P., & MacKenzie, S.B. (2006). Relationships between leader reward and punishment behavior and subordinate attitudes, perceptions, and behaviors: A meta-analytic review of existing and new research. *Organizational Behavior and Human Decision Processes, 99*(2), 113–142.

Poelmans, S., Chinchilla, N., & Cardona, P. (2003). The adoption of family friendly HRM policies: Competing for scarce resources in the labour market. *International Journal of Manpower, 24*(2), 128–147.

Poole, M., Bornholt, L., & Summers, F. (1997). An international study of the gendered nature of academic work: Some cross-cultural explanations. *Higher Education, 34,* 373–396.

Powell, G.N., & Greenhaus, J.H. (2006). Is the opposite of positive negative? Untangling the complex relationship between work-family enrichment and conflict. *Career Development International, 11,* 650–659.

Presser, H.B. (2003). *Working in a 24/7 economy: Challenges for American families.* New York, NY: Russell Sage Foundation.

Quinn, K., Lange, S.E., & Olswang, S.E. (2004). Family-friendly policies and the research university. *Academe, 90,* 32–34.

Raabe, P.H. (1997). Work-family policies for faculty: How "career-and-family-friendly" is academe? In M.A. Ferber & J.W. Loeb (Eds.), *Academic couples: Problems and promises* (pp. 208–225). Urbana: University of Illinois Press.

Ralston, D.A. (1989). The benefits of flextime: Real or imagined? *Journal of Organizational Behavior, 10,* 369–373.

Rao, C.P., Kurtz, D.L., & Claxton, R. (1991). The impact of uncapping mandatory retirement and other factors affecting marketing faculty retirement plans. *Journal of Marketing Education, 13*(3), 7–13.

Rapoport, R., Bailyn, L., Fletcher, J.K., & Pruitt, B.H. (2002). *Beyond work-family balance: Advancing gender equity and workplace performance.* San Francisco, CA: Jossey-Bass.

Rees, A., & Sharon, P.S. (1991a). The end of mandatory retirement for tenured faculty. *Science, 253*(5022), 838–839.

Rees, A., & Smith, S.P. (1991b). *Faculty retirement in the arts and sciences.* Princeton, NJ: Princeton University Press.

Reimenschnieder, A., & Harper, K.V. (1990). Women in academia: Guilty or not guilty? Conflict between caregiving and employment. *Initiatives, 53*(2), 27–35.

Rhoades, G. (1998). *Managed professionals: Unionized faculty and restructuring academic labor.* Albany: State University of New York Press.

Rhoades, L., & Eisenberger, R. (2002). Perceived organizational support: A review of the literature. *Journal of Applied Psychology, 87,* 698–714.

Roman, P.M., & Blum, T.C. (2001). Work-family role conflict and employer responsibility: An organizational analysis of workplace responses to a social problem. In R.T.

Golembiewski (Ed.), *Handbook of organizational behavior* (2nd ed.; 415–444). New York, NY: Marcel Dekker.

Rosser, S.V., & Lane, E.O. (2002). Key barriers for academic institutions seeking to retain female scientists and engineers: Family-unfriendly policies, low numbers, stereotypes, and harassment. *Journal of Women and Minorities in Sciences and Engineering, 8,* 161–189.

Rosser, V.J. (2004). Faculty members' intentions to leave: A national study on their worklife and satisfaction. *Research in Higher Education, 45*(3), 285–309.

Rosser, V.J., & Townsend, B.K. (2006). Determining public 2-year college faculty's intent to leave: An empirical model. *Journal of Higher Education, 77*(1), 124–147.

Rothausen, T.J. (1999). "Family" in organizational research: A review and comparison of definitions and measures. *Journal of Organizational Behavior, 20,* 817–836.

Rothausen, T.J., Gonzalez, J.A., Clarke, N.E., & O'Dell, L.L. (1998). Family-friendly backlash—Fact or fiction? The case of organizations' onsite child care centers. *Personnel Psychology, 51,* 685–705.

Russell, R.F., & Stone, A.G. (2002). A review of servant leadership attributes: Developing a practical model. *Leadership and Organization Development Journal, 23,* 145–157.

Scahill, P.L., & Forman, J.B. (2002). Allowing phased retirement helps both employees and employers. *The Actuary, 36*(3), 13–14.

Schaufeli, W.B., & Enzemann, D. (1998). *The burnout companion to study and research.* London, UK: Taylor & Francis.

Schlossberg, N.K. et al. (1997). *Counseling adults in transition: Linking practice with theory* (2nd ed.). New York, NY: Springer.

Schmidt, N. (2010). Enrichment: A new way of looking at work/family issues. *Women in Higher Education, 19*(10), 22–23.

Schrecker, E. (1999). From green to gray: The stages of academic life. *Academe, 85*(3), 2.

Schultheiss, D.E.P. (2006). The interface of work and family life. *Professional Psychology: Research and Practice, 37,* 334–341.

Schuster, J.H., & Wheeler, D.W. (Eds.) (1990). *Enhancing faculty careers: Strategies for development and renewal.* San Francisco, CA: Jossey-Bass.

Secret, M. (2000). Identifying the family, job, and workplace characteristics of employees who use work-family benefits. *Family Relations, 49*(2), 217–225.

Sendjaya, S., Sarros, J.C., & Santora, J.C. (2008). Defining and measuring servant leadership behavior in organizations. *Journal of Management Studies, 45,* 401–424.

Shannon, M., & Grierson, D. (2004). Mandatory retirement and older worker employment. *The Canadian Journal of Economics / Revue canadienne d'economique, 37*(3), 528–551.

Sharp, V.F. (2005). When retirement equals eviction. *Academe, 91*(2), 125.

Sheaks, C., Pitt-Catsouphes, M., & Smyer, M.A. (2007). *Legal and research summary sheet: Phased retirement.* Retrieved from http://scholarship.law.georgetown.edu/cgi/viewcontent.cgi?article=1057&context=legal

Shollen, S. L., Bland, C. J., Finstad, D. A., & Taylor, A. L. (2009). Organizational climate and family life: How these factors affect the status of women faculty at one medical school. *Academic Medicine, 84*(1), 87–94.

Shore, L. M., & Tetrick, L. E. (1991). A construct validity study of the survey of perceived organizational support. *Journal of Applied Psychology, 5,* 637–643.

Shore, M. S., Barksdale, K., & Shore, T. H. (1995). Managerial perceptions of employee commitment to the organization. *Academy of Management Journal, 38*(6), 1593–1615.

Smith, D. B., & Moen, P. (1998). Spousal influence on retirement: His, her, and their perceptions. *Journal of Marriage & Family, 60*(3), 734–744.

Smith, S. P. (1991). Ending mandatory retirement in the arts and sciences. *The American Economic Review, 81*(2), 106–110.

Sonart, G., & Holton, G. (1995). *Who succeeds in science? The gender dimension.* New Brunswick, NJ: Rutgers University Press.

Sorcinelli, M. D., & Near, J. P. (1989). Relations between work and life away from work among university faculty. *The Journal of Higher Education, 60*(1), 59–81.

Sperber, M. (2007). Why I stopped teaching and don't miss it. *Chronicle of Higher Education, 53*(42), C1–C4.

Stalker, J., & Prentice, S. (1998). *The illusion of inclusion: Women in post-secondary education.* Halifax, Nova Scotia: Fernwood Publishing.

Stetz, T., Stetz, M., & Bliese, P. (2006). The importance of self-efficacy in the moderating effects of social support on stressor-strain relationships. *Work & Stress, 20*(1), 49–59.

Stevens, D. P., Minnotte, K. L., & Kiger, G. (2004). Differences in work-to-family and family-to-work spillover among professional and nonprofessional workers. *Sociological Spectrum, 24,* 535–551.

Still, M. C. (2006). *Litigating the maternal wall: U.S. lawsuits charging discrimination against workers with family responsibilities.* Retrieved from www.worklifelaw.org/pubs/FRDreport.pdf

Stites-Doe, S. (2006). Antecedents and consequences of faculty women's academic-parental role balancing. *Journal of Family and Economic Issues, 27*(3), 495–512.

Stoddard, M., & Madsen, S. R. (2007). *Toward an understanding of the link between work-family enrichment and individual health.* Retrieved from www.ibam.com/pubs/jbam/articles/vol9/no1/JBAM_9_1_1.pdf

Strazdins, L., & Broom, D. H. (2004). Acts of love (and work): Gender imbalance in emotional work and women's psychological distress. *Journal of Family Issues, 25*(3), 356–378.

Sugar, J. A. et al. (2005). Academic administrators and faculty retirement in a new era. *Educational Gerontology, 31*(5), 405–418.

Swanberg, J. E., James, J. B., Werner, M., & McKechnie, S. P. (2008). Workplace flexibility for hourly lower-wage employees: A strategic business practice within one national retail firm. *The Psychologist-Manager Journal, 11*(1), 5–29.

Swanson, D. L., & Johnston, D. D. (2003). Mothering in the Ivy Tower: Interviews with academic mothers. *Journal of the Association for Research on Mothering, 5,* 63–75.

Swiss, D. J., & Walker, J. P. (1993). *Women and the work/family dilemma.* New York, NY: Wiley.

Thompson, C. A., Beauvais, L. L., & Allen, T. D. (2006). Work and family from an industrial/organizational psychology perspective. In M. Pitt-Catsouphes, E. E. Kossek, & S. Sweet (Eds.), *The work and family handbook: Multi-disciplinary perspectives and approaches* (pp. 283–307). Mahwah, NJ: Lawrence Erlbaum Associates.

Thompson, C. A., & Prottas, D. J. (2006). Relationships among organizational family support, job autonomy, perceived control, and employee well-being. *Journal of Occupational Health Psychology, 11,* 100–118.

Thompson, C. A., Thomas, C. C., & Maier, M. (1992). Work-family conflict and the bottom line: Reassessing corporate policies and initiatives. In U. Sekaran & F. T. Leong (Eds.), *Women-power: Managing in times of demographic turbulence* (pp. 59–84). Newbury Park, CA: Sage.

Thompson, D. (2012). The 23 best countries for work-life balance (we are number 23). *The Atlantic.* Retrieved from www.theatlantic.com/business/archive/2012/01/the-23-best-countries-for-work-life-balance-we-are-number-23/250830/

Thornton, A., & Young-DeMarco, L. (2001). Four decades of trends in attitudes toward family issues in the United States: The 1960s through the 1990s. *Journal of Marriage and Family, 63*(4), 1009–1037.

Thornton, S. R. (2003). Maternity and childrearing leave policies for faculty: The legal and practical challenges of complying with Title VII. *Southern California Review of Law and Women's Studies, 12*(2), 161–2.

Toepell, A. R. (2003). Academic mothers and their experiences navigating the academy. *Journal of the Association on Mothering, 5,* 93–102.

Townsend, B. K. (1998). Female faculty: Satisfaction with employment in the community college. *Community College Journal of Research and Practice, 22,* 655–662.

Townsend, B. K., & LaPaglia, N. (2000). Are we marginalized within academe? Perceptions of two-year college faculty. *Community College Review, 28*(1), 41–48.

Trombly, S. B. (1993). What we know about women at community colleges: An examination of the literature using feminist phase theory. *Journal of Higher Education, 64*(2), 186–211.

Trombly, S. B. (2005). Values, policies and practices affecting the hiring process for full-time arts and sciences faculty in community colleges. *Journal of Higher Education, 76*(4), 423–447.

Trower, C. A. (2004). Is your campus a great place to work? *Trusteeship, 12*(4), 20–24.

Tucker, A. (1993). *Chairing the academic department* (3rd ed.). Phoenix, AZ: American Council on Education and The Oryx Press.

Turner, C.S.V., Gonzalez, J.C., & Wood, J.L. (2008). Faculty of color in academe: What 20 years of literature tells us. *Journal of Diversity in Higher Education, 1*(3), 139–168.

Tytherleigh, M.Y., Webb, C., Cooper, C.L., & Ricketts, C. (2005). Occupational stress in UK higher education institutions: A comparative study of all staff categories. *Higher Education Research & Development, 24,* 41–61.

Ugrin, J.C., Odom, M.D., & Pearson, J.M. (2008). Exploring the importance of mentoring for new scholars: A social exchange perspective. *Journal of Information Systems Education, 19*(3), 343–350.

Valcour, M., Ollier-Malaterre, A., Matz-Costa, C., Pitt-Catsouphes, M., & Brown, M. (2011). Influences on employee perceptions of organizational work-life support: Signals and resources. *Journal of Vocational Behavior, 79,* 588–595.

Van Daalen, G., Willemsen, T.M., & Sanders, K. (2006). Reducing work-family conflict through different sources of social support. *Journal of Vocational Behavior, 69,* 462–476.

Van Dierendonck, D., Haynes, C., Borrill, C., & Stride, C. (2004). Leadership behavior and subordinate well-being. *Journal of Occupational Health Psychology, 9,* 165–175.

van Steenbergen, E.F., Ellemers, N., & Mooijaart, A. (2007). How work and family can facilitate each other: Distinct types of work-family facilitation and outcomes for men and women. *Journal of Occupational Health Psychology, 12,* 279–300.

Vecchio, R.P., & Boatwright, K.J. (2002). Preferences for idealized styles of supervision. *Leadership Quarterly, 168,* 1–16.

Voydanoff, P. (2005). The effects of community demands, resources, and strategies on the nature and consequences of the work-family interface. An agenda for future research. *Family Relations, 54*(5), 583–595.

Wallace, J.E., & Young, M.C. (2009). Family responsibilities, productivity, and earnings: A study of gender differences among Canadian lawyers. *Journal of Family and Economic Issues, 30*(3), 305–319.

Waltman, J., & Hollenshead, C. (2007). *Principles for best practices: A collection of suggested procedures for improving the climate for women faculty members.* Retrieved from www.cew.umich.edu/sites/default/files/BestPractices12-07.pdf

Waltman, J., & Sullivan, B. (2007, February). Creating and supporting a flexible work-life environment for faculty and staff. *Effective Practices for Academic Leaders* (Issue 2; pp. 1–16). Sterling, VA: Stylus.

Walumbwa, F.O., & Lawler, J.J. (2003). Building effective organizations: Transformational leadership, collective orientation, work-related attitudes and withdrawal behaviors in three emerging economies. *International Journal of Human Resource Management, 14,* 1083–1101.

Ward, K., & Wolf-Wendel, L. (2004). Fear factor: How safe is it to make time for family? *Academe, 90*(6), 28–31.

Waters, M.A., & Bardoel, E.A. (2006). Work-family policies in the context of higher education: Useful or symbolic? *Asia Pacific Journal of Human Resources, 44*(1), 67–82.

Welch, L. (1990). *Women in higher education: Changes and challenges.* New York, NY: Praeger.

WFD Consulting and Alliance for Work-Life Progress. (2010). *The state of work-life 2010.* Retrieved from www.wfd.com/news/wl2010.html

Wheeler, D. L. (2008). The art and science of managing faculty retirements. *The Chronicle of Higher Education, 54*(40), A15.

Williams, J. C. (1999). *Unbending gender: Why work and family conflict and what to do about it.* New York, NY: Oxford University Press.

Williams, J. C. (2005, February 11). Are your parental-leave policies legal? *The Chronicle of Higher Education.* Retrieved from http://chronicle.com/article/Are-Your-Parental-Leave/45098

Williams, J. C., & Cooper, H. C. (2004). The public policy of motherhood. *Journal of Social Issues, 60*(4), 849–865.

Williams, J. C., & Cuddy, A. J.C. (2012). Will working mothers take your company to court? *Harvard Business Review.* Retrieved from http://hbr.org/2012/09/will-working-mothers-take-your-company-to-court/ar/1

Wilson. R. (1996, October 11). Report praises twenty-nine colleges for "family friendly" policies. *The Chronicle of Higher Education,* A13–A14.

Wilson, R. (2001, November 9). A push to help new parents prepare for tenure review. *The Chronicle of Higher Education,* A10–A12.

Wilson, R. (2004, December 3). Where the elite teach, it's still a man's world. *The Chronicle of Higher Education,* A8–A14.

Winkler, A. E. (1998, April). Earnings of husbands and wives in dual-earner families. *Monthly Labor Review,* 42–48.

Winslow, S. (2010). Gender inequality and time allocations among academic faculty. *Gender & Society, 24,* 769–793.

Wolf-Wendel, L. E. et al. (2000). Dual-career couples: Keeping them together. *The Journal of Higher Education, 71*(3), 291–321.

Wolverton, M., Gmelch, W. H., Montez, J., & Nies, C. (2001). *The changing nature of the academic deanship.* San Francisco, CA: Jossey-Bass.

Woodring, P. (1977). Viewpoint 2: The good life after sixty. *Change, 9*(9), 12–63.

Woodward, D. (2007). Work-life balancing strategies used by women managers in British "modern" universities. *Equal Opportunities International: Equality, Diversity and Inclusion, 26,* 6–17.

Workplace Flexibility. (2010). *Flexible work arrangements: A definition and examples.* Retrieved from http://workplaceflexibility2010.org/images/uploads/general_information/fwa_definitionsexamples.pdf

Yakoboski, P. (2000). *Report of the working group on phased retirement.* Retrieved from www.dol.gov/ebsa/publications/phasedr1.htm

Yakoboski, P. (2007). Are you planning and saving for retirement? *Academe, 93*(3), 31–33.

Zedeck, S., & Mosier, K.L. (1990). Work in the family and employing organization. *American Psychologist, 45,* 240–251.

Zigler, E.F., & Frank, M. (1988). *The parental leave crisis: Toward a national policy.* New Haven, CT: Yale University Press.

Index

Page numbers in italics refer to tables.